Turning the Tide

Turning the Tide

Making Life Better for Deaf and
Hard of Hearing Schoolchildren

Gina A. Oliva and
Linda Risser Lytle

Gallaudet University Press
WASHINGTON, DC

Gallaudet University Press
Washington, DC 20002
http://gupress.gallaudet.edu

Library of Congress Cataloging-in-Publication Data
Oliva, Gina A.
  Turning the tide : making life better for deaf and hard of hearing
schoolchildren / Gina A. Oliva and Linda Risser Lytle.
      pages cm
  Includes bibliographical references and index.
  ISBN 978-1-56368-599-6 (hardcover : alk. paper) —
ISBN 978-1-56368-600-9 (e-book)
  1. Deaf children—Education—United States.   2. Hearing impaired
children—Education—United States.   3. Mainstreaming in education—
United States.   4. Deaf children—United States   5. Hearing impaired
children—United States.   I. Lytle, Linda Risser.   II. Title.
  HV2430.O45 2014
  371.91'2—dc23
                                                        2013042488

Cover photograph: from l. to r., Megan Mays, AuQueche Rogers, and
Cornelius Johnson, courtesy of Camp SummerSign in Brentwood, TN,
from a film produced by STARS Nashville-Services for Students Who Are
Deaf or Hard of Hearing.

In memory of

Fausto Delgado

Born February 6, 1997
Veracruz, Mexico

Died November 12, 2013
Richmond, California

May his short life inspire us all to turn the tide.

CONTENTS

FOREWORD

Turning the Tide is a timely and much needed addition to the field of educating deaf and hard of hearing children. Personal narratives told by deaf and hard of hearing adults offer us powerful insights into the experiences of childhood, and in particular, into the nature of education. In this text, Gina Oliva and Linda Lytle have delivered a highly readable account of their research that sought to uncover the perspectives of people who have lived the experience of "inclusive" education over the past 30 years in the United States. From these narratives, readers—whether parent, educator, interpreter, or administrator— can discover the layers of meaning that adults attach to their educational experiences, and by doing so, examine what works well and what does not work well in the current approach to education for deaf and hard of hearing children.

As an educator and an interpreter, I appreciate the work conducted by Oliva and Lytle in this crucial area and believe this book makes an important contribution to our field. Their findings mirror what my own research with Deaf children has shown, highlighting the very stark realities of an education that is too often academically inadequate and most often socially isolating, leading to serious challenges that can persist throughout life. Oliva and Lytle have countered the existing educational literature and movements that tout an "inclusive" education for all, by bringing forward the voices and experiences of those who have lived it as students every day. If schools are to respond sensibly to the needs of deaf and hard of hearing children, the perspectives of those who have lived the experience must be taken into account.

I was particularly drawn to the quotes of former students whose passionate words demonstrate how school can be a very lonely experience for many deaf and hard of hearing students as they struggle to find a peer group that can accept them and with which they can learn to communicate effectively. These themes are consistent with my own studies in a Canadian context, and they are part of a common international narrative about school experiences. In other words, the experiences of Oliva and Lytle's American subjects have mirrored reports from deaf and hard of hearing individuals from all over the world.

The authors help us to see what it means to experience a mediated education via a signed language interpreter. The stories captured in these pages characterize the struggles that deaf and hard of hearing students face daily when working with interpreters who may or may not be able to represent the content and interactional demands of the classroom. Oliva and Lytle expose myths of working with an interpreter, as well as the problems of creating friendships with other children when that has to be first mediated by another adult. One might be tempted to say these reported experiences are local phenomena, or are no longer representative of the current educational system. However, at each international conference I attend on education, these themes continue to play out as current researchers share their findings. As well, organizations such as the World Federation of the Deaf (WFD) continue to lobby for legislation that supports meaningful education using signed languages, pointing to the United Nations Convention on the Rights of Persons With Disabilities (UNCRPD) as one mechanism by which countries can improve education for deaf children. This book highlights and reinforces the global movement for educational reforms that will serve deaf children effectively, while supporting their linguistic human rights.

Educators and interpreters must question the premise behind using an interpreter for children who have not yet developed language fluency, as well as question the lack of criteria for placing a student in a mainstream environment. This book illustrates the assumption made by educators and administrators about school processes that involving interpreters and deaf children may result in the child having a very isolating experience in the mainstream. One of the important issues explored in the book is social and/or relational bullying as an extension of what many of the participants describe as being made to feel invisible. This topic has had very little attention in the body of literature that centers on Deaf education, and I hope this will lead to further research and crucial conversations among students, parents, teachers, and administrators about how to create safe and nurturing learning spaces for deaf children. The theme "being in a group, but not part of a group" sums up so many of the stories that shape this book.

I also deeply appreciate learning from Oliva and Lytle of the significant ways in which parents and teachers can and do make a difference, and how frequently deaf and hard of hearing children want to be with others like them, who can relate to their struggles, celebrate their successes and share a bond that supports the development of a healthy self-concept. Oliva and Lytle provide several hopeful examples of the kinds of programs and supports that are needed if deaf and hard of hearing children are to have opportunities that mirror those of their nondeaf peers. Oliva shares research she conducted about summer and weekend programs, stressing the role that camps continue to play in the lives of deaf children, from fostering identity development to creating shared narratives and experiences, and networks of social support. Oliva and Lytle introduce the concept of working with allies who can support the life enhancement of deaf children, drawing from examples of parents, advocates, and scholars. The discussion of audism in the context of how many people need to be part of the process of helping parents understand the deaf life experience is a very good reminder of the power of multiple experiences and perspectives in shaping positive views of being deaf. Finally, the authors leave us with their recommendations for improving the education of deaf and hard of hearing students, stressing the need for collaboration and coordinated efforts that result in systemic change.

Turning the Tide ultimately both challenges and invites all involved in the education of deaf and hard of hearing students to explore ways in which each can work toward positive change by first aligning ourselves with those who have the lived experience. I thank the authors for contributing their powerful message and for continuing to act as ambassadors for the Deaf community's voice in educational policy and practice.

DEBRA RUSSELL
David Peikoff Chair of Deaf Studies
Director, Western Canadian Centre of Deaf Studies

PREFACE

THE WORK of this book has been a labor of love. Both of us spent our entire K–12 years in general education classrooms in our respective neighborhood public schools, Linda in Pennsylvania and Gina in Connecticut. Throughout our lives and careers we came to know many other deaf and hard of hearing individuals who had been "alone in the mainstream." Gina, of course, has already written a book about this experience: *Alone in the Mainstream: A Deaf Woman Remembers Public School* (Oliva, 2004). The consensus of all we met and talked to was that this experience was far from optimal. We met individuals who, despite having a high school diploma, clearly did not have the literacy skills expected of high school graduates. We met others who had a first-rate education but suffered deplorably because they were so totally alone and left out.

We have been friends for many years, having met as seniors at Gallaudet University. Gina was at that time a visiting student—after lucking into learning about Gallaudet, she had requested a year there in lieu of completing her senior year at Washington College. Linda was in awe of Gina when she met her because, after enduring 12 years in public school, Linda had decided that she could not survive another 4 years being a solitary deaf student in college. And here was Gina who had done just that.

Gina got her first hearing aid at age 5, after her kindergarten teacher noticed something amiss. With the 50-db loss she had through most of elementary school, she was able to use hearing and lipreading (a skill she naturally developed) with all her teachers, but she recalls never being able to "hear" the other kids in the school environment. By middle school it became evident that Gina had a progressive loss (like her father's) and thus it became more difficult to follow what was being said in all but the most ideal environments. In other words, if the teacher spoke very clearly and the room was quiet, she could follow. But by her college years, she essentially could hear/lipread none of her professors. She would ask to borrow notes, and she spent a lot more time reading and doing homework than her college peers.

Linda was born with a severe hearing loss that became profound over the years. She also attended public schools, using the little hearing she had and her reasonably good lipreading skills, intently focusing on her teachers during the school day and reading and studying voraciously in the evenings and weekends. She got by, mostly with the help of the director of the county hearing and speech center, who visited her weekly and provided much-needed social-emotional support during the high school years. After high school, looking for something different and hopefully better, she chose to attend Gallaudet University.

Although our hearing abilities were somewhat different, our school experiences were rather similar up until the college years. Gina had more hearing with which to "get by" in high school and college; nevertheless, attending Gallaudet and meeting other deaf and hard of hearing individuals changed both of our lives for the better. In our own ways, we have both been centered on working with deaf and hard of hearing individuals to develop their skills in learning, coping, and thriving in the world today. Much of this work has been in educational environments.

Linda is currently a professor in the Department of Counseling at Gallaudet University and director of the Summers & Online School Counseling Program within that department. She started her career by traveling up through the school ranks from teacher's aide to high school English teacher to school psychologist at a residential school for the deaf, where many of the students had first attended public schools. Mostly as a result of her growing frustration with the unmet social and emotional needs of her students and with the limited skills she had to help them, she took a detour from working in the schools to pursue advanced training and then to establish a private practice, providing individual, group, and family psychotherapy to deaf and hard of hearing individuals and their hearing family members, which she did for almost 20 years. In 2004, she returned to the educational setting, this time at the university level, and is now back full circle, this time teaching, supervising, and mentoring students who aspire to be professional counselors working with deaf and hard of hearing children and adults in schools, mental health agencies, and other settings.

The development of identity, particularly in deaf and hard of hearing individuals who have frequently internalized not-good-enough self-images has always been an area of interest for Linda. She found it exciting to see how individuals' self-concepts grow and strengthen upon meeting others like themselves. This is transformative! Meeting others like oneself when one previously had few or no peers with similar experiences can completely change the course of people's lives—no longer are they lacking something; instead, they have gained something enormously valuable: an identity as a deaf or hard of hearing person and a community of others like themselves.

In the course of writing this book, Linda came across another author, Andrew Solomon, who pointed to the need to end isolation through association with others like oneself as a universal one. Not only do deaf and hard of hearing people have this need, but all those with a disability or a defining characteristic not shared with their parents do as well (Solomon, 2012). Parents cannot give what they do not have, but that doesn't mean a child needs to go without. Blessedly, there are others in the world who are the same as us, if only we can find them.

Gina's trajectory has been a bit less linear than Linda's. She began her professional career at Gallaudet right after college and stayed there until her retirement (from Gallaudet) in 2009. While at Gallaudet she worked in various, seemingly diverse departments or settings. However, the defining thread has been her focus on "leisure" and she attributes this to the pervasive barriers she felt in her K–12 years—barriers to social and recreational involvement with her peers and with her family members as well. From the time she was very young, Gina was aware that her hearing loss prevented her from being involved at the depth and breadth to which she felt capable. A simple example might be a family dinner conversation about baseball, let's say the Yankees. Gina knew who the Yankees were, and even knew the names of some of their star players from the "trading cards" that would come with a pack of bubble gum. But because of the natural quick give-and-take at the dinner table, she could not hear/lipread the specifics of the conversation, and therefore could not participate.

At Gallaudet, Gina worked first in student activities, planning extra- and cocurricular activities. During this time, she obtained a master's degree in counseling (from Linda's future department, as it happened). Then she had a brief stint in outreach, planning workshops for the Deaf community—this quickly led to her authoring and obtaining a grant to train student-service personnel at colleges and universities about the needs of deaf and hard of hearing college students. Soon, however, she was back focused on leisure with a 20-year-long involvement leading exercise programs—training aerobics instructors and personal trainers, both deaf and hearing in the "Art of Visual Cueing." Always the focus was on creating opportunities and improving the recreational and leisure lives of deaf and hard of hearing adults. Gina received two national awards for this work, one from the IDEA Health and Fitness Association and one from the President's Council on Physical Fitness and Sports. She also completed her doctorate in recreation and leisure studies (University of Maryland) during this time period. With the doctorate, she became a faculty member in Gallaudet's Department of Physical Education and Recreation, obtaining the rank of professor.

Gina's father died on her 46th birthday, and it was this event that ignited the flame within her to write a book that would capture the great disparity between how Gina had chosen to live her life and how her father had chosen to live his. Robert M. Oliva had a hearing loss very much like Gina's, but he never chose to associate with other individuals with hearing loss. She wanted to capture the common experiences that deaf and hard of hearing children have in general education classrooms and to show how the lack of support for interaction and friendships with other deaf and hard of hearing children can exacerbate feelings of isolation and hopelessness. This flame grew and grew and eventually became *Alone in the Mainstream*.

Gina had been thinking for some time that her work focused on "solitaires" was unfinished; there was still much to say. As a result of her 2004 publication, she heard from time to time "out of the blue" from various individuals concerned with mainstream education. One email that appeared in her inbox was from a K–12 interpreter. That email was too good to not share and in sharing it with Linda, a new flame started to burn. That flame became this book.

Like *Alone in the Mainstream*, this book provides a lay person's education regarding the complex system that enfolds the great majority of deaf and hard of hearing children in their K–12 years. Here we take the reader forward to show the ongoing evolution of the impact of P.L. 94-142 on deaf and hard of hearing children. We include the voices of a new generation of deaf and hard of hearing individuals who are younger than those in *Alone in the Mainstream*. The individuals who shared their experiences for that first book are now (in 2013) between the ages of 35 and 65. The individuals whose stories and comments are included here were, at the time of our study, between 18 and 34.

Our purpose in writing this book is to make the case that adding sign language interpreters to the neighborhood public school does not and cannot create equitable access. Providing an itinerant teacher to check up on deaf or hard of hearing students once a week or maybe once a month does not create equitable access. Putting a cochlear implant in a deaf child likewise does not create equitable access: Newer technology allows more access to sound and spoken language only if the family of a child who is implanted is able to provide the training needed to activate the implant's potential, and if the child has the cognitive and emotional qualities to benefit from such. So, not all children benefit to a great extent from cochlear implants. We are additionally concerned about the needs of the whole child, including social and emotional needs. The frequently limited attention to these needs and the dispersal of children (and their families) with this low-incidence disability into far-flung areas creates a dearth of social and friendship opportunities for these children.

We wrote with several audiences in mind: parents, teachers and teachers-in-training, interpreters and interpreters-in-training, and school administrators. We know that many previously mainstreamed deaf and hard of hearing adults will enjoy reading it also, as they will see (for the umpteenth time, or perhaps for the first time) that many others share their feelings and experiences. But mostly we wrote it for the current and future generations of deaf and hard of hearing children and youth who are (or will be) mainstreamed alone. Our deepest hope for each of them is that they will find they are not alone after all and that there is a community of others that they will come to realize are "just like me," and then they will be "home."

Acknowledgments

We wish to thank the Gallaudet University Research Institute for three Priority Grants and two Small Grants awarded to us between 2000 and 2012, without which neither *Alone in the Mainstream* nor *Turning the Tide* would have come to fruition. Thank you Mike, Len, Chip, Senda, and others.

We thank Claire Ramsey and Donna Mertens for their pioneering work in qualitative methods with deaf and hard of hearing individuals, which inspired both *Alone in the Mainstream* and *Turning the Tide*.

We thank the individuals who gave their time and energy to our focus groups and online survey. You were the best, and we hope we have done justice to all you so generously shared with us.

We thank all the camp and weekend program directors who allowed Dr. Oliva and her graduate assistants to visit and observe between 2005 and 2010. We'd like to particularly spotlight Camp SummerSign (starsnashville.org) in Nashville, Tennessee, whose program in filmmaking produced two outstanding films. The first, *Alone in a Hearing World* (2011), focused on a deaf boy's daily struggles in his general education environment and ended with him feeling frustrated, angry, and sad. In 2012 the campers decided they wanted a more positive ending to their film, which resulted in *My New Life in the Mainstream* (http://youtu.be /dvilmMRwmC0). In this film, the actors convey a powerful message about how it is possible for a single person to make

xix

a difference in the school life of a deaf student. This movie represents what students wish would happen in general education settings, which perfectly mirrors our hopes as well.

We are proud to have a clip from *My New Life in the Mainstream* as our cover photograph, a clip from a film written by real deaf students, portraying real hopes about change in general education settings, all put together during a summer camp experience with deaf and hard of hearing peers. We think this is a perfect cover.

We also thank the many individuals—too numerous to mention—who helped us with technology, shared on-the-job experiences, read drafts, or simply encouraged us along the way.

We thank Ivey Wallace at Gallaudet University Press for her support, encouragement, and editing.

Finally a special thanks to the many heroes who continue to advocate for equitable educational opportunities for deaf and hard of hearing children today and tomorrow. You inspire us, and we hope our work will return the favor.

We welcome input—if you would like to contact the authors, please email gina.oliva09@gmail.com and/or lrlytle@gmail.com.

Introduction

It has been almost four decades since the original passage of P.L. 94-142, known as the Individuals With Disabilities Education Act (IDEA). Two huge differences between then and now concerning the education of deaf and hard of hearing students in general education are the greater presence of sign language interpreters and the increasing presence of itinerant teachers of the deaf in K–12 schools. We also note, that over those four decades, student enrollment in residential schools for the deaf decreased dramatically, whereas enrollment in general education settings increased.

The Government Accountability Office (U.S. Government Accountability Office, 2011) reported that there were 78,000 deaf or hard of hearing children in the United States in the 2008 count (the last count available). This is considered by numerous researchers to be an undercount. Still, we concede that deafness is considered a low-incidence disability compared to, for example, the generic category of "learning disability." Because deafness is a low-incidence disability, while the numbers of deaf and hard of hearing students enrolled in general education programs increased, the students themselves were dispersed throughout their school systems and it became increasingly common for these students to never meet another deaf or hard of hearing student.

From the mid-1970s through the 1980s, many deaf and hard of hearing children were educated in what were called at the time "self-contained classrooms." These were classes of deaf and hard of hearing children, often of varying ages, in a single class-room in a regular public school, taught by a specially trained teacher of the deaf, along with aide(s). Over the next 40 years, as slowly but surely more and more of those children were placed in regular classrooms, those teaching jobs evolved into itinerant positions. The teacher of the deaf is now responsible, not for a classroom, but for some number of children who are often the only deaf child in the classroom, in different schools.

Hand in hand with that trend, today greater numbers of deaf and hard of hearing children are in regular education classrooms with support services. The presence of interpreters in K–12 settings is sometimes referred to as a "mediated education." That is, students are getting their instructional messages not directly from teachers but from an interpreter, through sign language, cued speech, oral interpreting, or transliteration services. In a mediated education, communication between teachers and peers and the deaf or hard of hearing child is indirect.

Since that long-ago time when P.L. 94-142 was being formulated, deaf and hard of hearing adults involved in the education of deaf and hard of hearing children have been concerned about the differential impact of this law on the children, and the adults we interviewed spoke adamantly about this. Deaf and hard of hearing children, blind children, and children with developmental disabilities have totally different needs. Any adult who knows a child with a disability knows that that child's needs are unique to that disability, and within each disability group there is variation. But it seems many people either do not know this, choose to ignore it, or feel powerless to act with the knowledge they have.

Over the years our informants as well as many other individuals have individually, collectively, consistently, and frequently spoken up to say that the evolving push for *all* children with disabilities to be educated in their neighborhood public schools presents a major pitfall for deaf and hard of hearing children. Being in an environment of ongoing, ever-present spoken conversation as well as ambient noise (from air conditioners, computers, paper shuffling, etc.) places deaf and hard of hearing children and youth in a seriously limited environment.

Those who push for "inclusion" for deaf and hard of hearing children seem to either be unaware of or choose to ignore the fact that the constant informal transmissions of information that take place daily in the school are just as important as formal classroom discourse. Although it is possible for a deaf or hard of hearing child well trained in using a cochlear implant or hearing aid to sit in the front of the classroom and be able to discern all or most of what his or her teacher is saying *and* what classmates are saying, such children are the exception rather than the rule. In addition, deaf and hard of hearing children are very frequently excluded from companionship with others like themselves, and often of even knowing there are others like themselves who use cochlear implants, hearing aids, interpreters, and so on. This exclusion has dire consequences to a child's language development, cognitive development, achievement, career development, self-concept, and identity. And so the law that was designed to create access is seen instead by the deaf and hard of hearing adults as *restricting* full participation in education for deaf and hard of hearing children.

Numerous local, regional, national, and international organizations led by deaf adults and their allies continue the fight to educate and convince the powers-that-be in federal and state governments as well as in local education agencies that this is no small matter and the children have significant unmet needs. These organizations are working together to improve the lives of the increasing numbers of deaf and hard of hearing children who find themselves in their neighborhood schools and missing out on important information and socialization on a daily basis.

The Conference of Educational Administrators of Schools and Programs for the Deaf (www.ceasd.org/idea) has launched a "Child First" campaign to reverse this trend toward "one size fits all," in which school placement decisions are based on what the local school district has to offer and not on the needs of the child, and the range of options mentioned in the original IDEA law is falling by the wayside. Simultaneously, leaders in the field of sign language interpreter training are working to address the fact that large numbers of individuals who are working as "interpreters" in public schools do not have the training necessary to ensure that the school setting could even remotely become a somewhat equitable environment. Medical interpreting and legal interpreting are two areas in which the interpreting profession already supports specialized training, and now there is strong support for advanced specialty training in general education interpreting. This push in professional interpreting circles is aimed at stopping the current widespread practice among public schools of employing individuals with a two-year crash course in the recognized language of American Sign Language and paying them as little as possible.

Another positive and growing development is the increasing number of deaf professionals and hearing allies who have become active in Early Hearing Detection and Intervention (EHDI). On a national scale, EHDI is supported by the well-funded National Center for Hearing Assessment and Management (NCHAM) and serves as a resource center for all who work in infant hearing screening and in the agencies that support the families of infants and toddlers who have been identified as deaf. NCHAM sponsors an annual conference where those concerned can come together to learn and share. Individuals who work in early intervention have degrees in education, audiology, the social sciences, linguistics, and even law and medicine. However, there is no comparable national center or conference for teachers of deaf and hard of hearing children, including itinerant teachers or K–12 interpreters from across the nation to come together to learn and share. This concerns us greatly and it is a large part of our recommendations.

Despite the many recommendations—in articles, conference presentations, legislative testimonies, and so forth—that deaf and hard of hearing adults and their allies have given forth, there is great resistance to these efforts to change the existing one-size-fits-all educational environment, and there are a lot of dollars invested in this resistance. Well-funded private/ nonprofit organizations that are allied with the companies that manufacture cochlear implants are focused on convincing families that the best thing for infants identified as deaf is for them to be implanted as early as possible. These organizations, directly and/or indirectly, promote the idea that using sign language with such babies is detrimental to the development of their ability to speak. This perceived detriment to spoken language becomes confused with the overall issue of language acquisition, and the message becomes "signing with deaf babies thwarts their language development." These organizations and their allies continue to promote this idea despite the obviously erroneous message conveyed—ample recent scientific research totally refutes the idea of signs creating barriers to or lags in language acquisition.

The "baby sign" movement, using signs with all infants to give them a way of making their needs known long before they are able to speak, is becoming more and more accepted and is now supported by research. How ironic that there is a movement for sign language to be used with babies who can hear, while families with deaf infants are told that to sign with their babies is not a good idea.

At the U.S. federal level, there is no clear focused assessment on the achievement or quality of life of deaf and hard of hearing children, specifically, as a group. The focus is on *disabled children,* so actually all the government can tell us is how many disabled children are in neighborhood schools and how many are in other environments (such as separate schools). When we asked why this was so, we were told—by a federal official who adamantly warned us not to identify her—that the government "can't burden the states by requiring them to disaggregate the numbers." So what they can tell us is information like how many days these disabled kids are absent and what percentage of them graduate from high school. Big deal.

Thanks to the efforts of deaf and hard of hearing adults, some particularly assertive parents, and other allies, some states have taken it upon themselves to dig deeper to see what is happening with various groups of children with special needs. However, there remains no uniformity, and just about everyone we talked to who is aware of this situation would agree that it is a big mess. One very savvy and involved person told us, "Reading your chapter made me so mad, but the worst part is I don't know who to be mad at!" We think the buck stops with the federal and state governments, but we recognize that the challenge is so overwhelming that it behooves us, every one of us, to do something to effect change for the benefit of these children.

In this book, we explain further the above-described state of affairs by summarizing the research and advocacy efforts that we think parents and others should know about. In addition, we present the voices of adults who have been subjected to the IDEA law since the mid-1980s. Our oldest research participants entered kindergarten in 1983 and graduated from high school in 1996; our youngest entered kindergarten in 1999 and graduated in 2012. It is appalling that there is so little research on the perspective of adults who were educated in general education settings. Yet they are really the only ones who can tell it like it is. Governments, educational experts, and school systems ought to listen to people like them on a regular, ongoing basis.

WE BEGIN the book with a description of our research process and methods. Here you will meet our focus group participants—deaf and hard of hearing adults ages 18 to 34 who spent at least 5 of their K–12 years as the only deaf or hard of hearing child in their school. We set this age criteria to represent the generation following those who participated in the study that was documented in *Alone in the Mainstream* (Oliva, 2004). Intuitively and from conversations with others, we knew some things would be different and some things would be the same. We set out to document the voices of this new generation, to have them tell their own stories.

We also conducted an online survey that attracted over 200 responses. Of note, almost half of these respondents did not fit our criteria—either they were older than 34 or they had not spent at least 5 years as the only deaf or hard of hearing student in their school. All clamored to tell their stories. So suffice it to say that what we report is the tip of the iceberg. Often, deaf and hard of hearing children are not able to articulate what they are missing in their day-to-day K–12 lives. It is only as adults, particularly after they have had (hopefully) the opportunity to be in environments where they have equitable communication access, that they are able to process and explain to others what their lives were like during those years. And given the sheer numbers of deaf and hard of hearing adults who grew up alone in the mainstream, we think that most would emphatically nod their heads and say, "Me too! Me too!" upon reading what our focus group participants and survey respondents had to say.

Without our many research participants who shared freely of themselves during many hours, both writing and talking, we would not have this book. A Gallaudet freshman, upon reading *Alone in the Mainstream* in 2004, commented how nice it was to know that there were other "solitaires" in the world, even though they are separated by "miles and years." Finding others who were (or are) spending their days in general education classrooms is like finding a piece of one's self. Indeed, the push for mainstreaming is worldwide, and the issues, thus, are worldwide. Not surprisingly, our topic captured the enthusiastic interest of a wide range of formerly mainstreamed deaf and hard of hearing young adults. Chapters 2, 3, and 4 are focused on their perspectives and stories.

In Chapter 2, we look closely at the important issue of friendships and socialization—both of which posed real difficulties for our deaf and hard of hearing young adults as they were growing up. We discuss the numbing effects of having conversations swirl all about without being a part of them. In this chapter, we also describe an exciting new research study that gives rich, detailed examples of missing conversations in the school life of a mainstreamed 13-year-old deaf girl.

Chapter 3 addresses issues of identity development. Our focus group participants longed to meet others "like me" and, failing that, they often compared themselves to hearing peers. In those comparisons with their hearing classmates, too often, they fell short. We show how positive identity development is greatly enhanced by meeting other deaf peers and deaf adults. These individuals heavily influenced our participants' lives. We show how parents, teachers, interpreters, and others in the school can assist in boosting positive identity development.

As stated earlier, a major impetus to writing this book was our conversations with K–12 interpreters. In our focus groups we learned that formerly mainstreamed adults had strong feelings and much to say about their K–12 interpreters and their mediated educations. This is shared in Chapter 4. It is interesting to note that in *Alone in the Mainstream*, only 5 out of the 60 research participants had interpreters in their school day, whereas the majority of this current group had interpreters. This is a major shift in the general education scene as a result of P.L. 94-142 and its subsequent iterations as IDEA.

Chapters 5 and 6 focus on the current system for educating deaf and hard of hearing children in the United States, including key elements of

IDEA, advocacy and reform efforts, and the phenomena of itinerant teaching and K–12 interpreting. Our eyes grew wide when we learned that a Canadian counterpart of ours working on a somewhat similar book used the phrase "the illusion of inclusion." Debra Russell, a leading Canadian interpreter trainer, first used the phrase when referring to mediated education in Canadian public schools. It resonated loudly with us—it affirmed what we suspected and our voluminous reading and investigating affirmed this further. Some would say that having an interpreter makes a public education perfectly fine. We vehemently disagree.

Chapter 7 reports on Gina's investigation into the phenomenon of "Deaf camps," which took place shortly after the publication of her first book. This research was inspired by stories she heard in the fall semesters as her students returned from summer vacations. Their enthusiastic stories of being camp counselors got Gina thinking that these camps could be a kind of remedy for the issues faced by mainstreamed deaf and hard of hearing students, and prompted her to spend several summers visiting, observing, and interviewing at several of these Deaf camps. We believe that summer and weekend programs are a critical part of the short-term, here-and-now solution to the inherent dangers of being "alone in the mainstream," and thus we include this chapter.

In Chapter 8, we showcase the work of deaf and hard of hearing adults who are currently putting forth great effort in several areas, carrying on the now decades-long battle to educate hearing individuals about the needs of deaf and hard of hearing schoolchildren. Some particular individuals and efforts were selected primarily because we felt their particular projects are groundbreaking, still unfolding as we were completing this manuscript, and show promise for making significant inroads. Others were chosen to give the reader a very up-close view on how parents who are deaf themselves view and deal with issues faced by their deaf and hard of hearing children. We believe these individuals have taken very bold steps to do their part, to be part of the "us," to effect change. *Madness in the Mainstream* (Drolsbaugh, 2013) is the fitting name of a book recently published by one of these parents. The author is a professional within the schools, a father of a mainstreamed hard of hearing child, and himself a former solitaire.

Granted, the chapters in which we share stories from our research participants and also the chapters on K–12 interpreting seem to paint a rather negative picture. But, we do see much hope in the work we showcase in Chapters 5 and 9 and in the work of many other individuals and organizations. We are especially heartened by the development of early detection and intervention services because their very existence shows that in the last 10 years, people have become increasingly aware that deaf and hard of hearing children do in fact have unique needs and thus deserve special attention on both state and national levels.

Our final chapter summarizes the recommendations we make throughout the book. We align these with the recommendations and current efforts of our colleagues in the interpreting field, the deaf education field, and the early intervention field. There are many individuals and organizations working to make things better for deaf and hard of hearing children, and we applaud all of them. We regret that there is not even close to enough sharing and oversight on the national level, and we do feel that needs to change.

It is our wish that readers will come to more clearly envision the day-to-day lives of current school-aged deaf and hard of hearing children. You will come to know these lives through the voices of relatively young adults who not very long ago were in those childhood shoes. These adults, it is our staunch belief, know better than anyone what today's deaf and hard of hearing schoolchildren are experiencing. You will read the stories of sign language interpreters currently working with these children—expressing their frustration at how little they can convey from all the competing information that permeates a public school day. You also will come to know the work, guided by experience, of scholars, parents, and advocates who are all doing their part to make positive changes in the lives of deaf and hard of hearing children.

We hope our work will make a difference in the lives of deaf and hard of hearing schoolchildren, today and in years to come.

1

Our Research Process

"The I tells a story of the self, and that story becomes a part of the ME."

(McAdams, Josselson, & Lieblich, 2006)

STORYTELLING is a powerful tool, and it is a particularly Deaf-friendly one. Many Deaf people have made storytelling a fine art and most, regardless of age, enjoy telling a good story—particularly stories about themselves. We feel these life stories are vitally important to shaping successful educational policies for current and future generations of deaf and hard of hearing children.

All people create stories that help make sense of their lives and understand themselves better, and these stories include both personal perspectives and the perspectives of others who are in one's social world. Because schools are the largest social milieu of children and teens, the experience of the self in the school setting is particularly powerful and lasting (Winslade & Monk, 2007), for better or for worse. As we find for mainstreamed deaf and hard of hearing students, it is most frequently for worse.

Narrative research is especially appealing to Linda who, as a therapist, is naturally drawn to a process in which the simple telling of a personal narrative to interested, respectful, nonjudgmental others leads to positive change within individuals.

Incredible as it seems, one can change one's identity, one's self-esteem, and one's future path in the process of telling one's life story to others. We have been part of this process for others, and we have done it ourselves.

What we learned in this research is that our participants had had very few previous opportunities to share their stories with others who were like them, that is, who had also been the only deaf or hard of hearing student in their general education classrooms. This process of sharing their school stories with others who shared similar experiences was especially powerful and created both highly engaging focus groups and lasting individual changes. We had the distinct enjoyment and satisfaction of knowing that while the focus groups benefitted our research, and us, it was also highly beneficial to our participants. Their reauthored stories became healthier parts of themselves that they could take into the future and use to enrich their lives.

The Value of Retrospective Storytelling

In this volume, we give voice to deaf and hard of hearing adults who had the common experience of being the only deaf or hard of hearing child in their K–12 schools. Their stories are enlightening about the mainstream experience. We hope that in listening to their stories, readers will work to improve the school experience for current and future mainstreamed deaf and hard of hearing children. Placing deaf and hard of hearing children in the "least restrictive environment" is a primary goal of American education, and educators need to learn more about the experiences of the students they serve. They need to understand why many deaf and hard of hearing people characterize general education as the *most* restrictive environment. This is perhaps the most important message in our work. Parents and educators can learn much about the school lives of deaf and hard of hearing students if the students themselves are given more voice to say what works and what doesn't work, that is, what makes it restrictive. The experiences of deaf and hard of hearing students (both former and current) should inform educational policy, but often their voices are not sought.

We believe that the most helpful information about the mainstream experience comes from the perspective of young adults looking back. Research tells us that it is not until adolescence or later that we are able to look at our past experiences and put them into a whole story that makes sense (Habermas & Bluck, 2000). Children are at a distinct disadvantage in being able to describe their lives because they lack awareness of others' lives and critical thinking skills, and they often voice feelings and ideas they believe adults want to hear.

Telling stories from a retrospective perspective allows more fullness of description, along with a better grasp of language in which to tell them. This may be even more so for deaf and hard of hearing individuals because of language and communication delays and because growing up, they often lacked friendships—or even awareness—of others like themselves, and this colored their self-narratives. Additionally, distance from earlier experiences provides a necessary perspective for understanding them. Therefore, for our research, rather than have students report from the middle of their stories, we asked individuals to tell us about being alone in the mainstream from their current perspectives as deaf adults. We believe that story to be more honest.

Indeed, several of our research participants told us that if we had posed these same questions to them while they were in school, they might have answered differently. For one thing, at a younger age, they were invested in pleasing others, particularly their parents. And their parents did not want to hear, or could not bear to hear, how bad it really was. Additionally, they were invested in making their solitary experiences as positive as they could because they realized they were stuck in it and rarely could it be changed. As a result, they often told themselves it was not so bad, when it actually was close to intolerable. For example, one of the focus group participants was provided with a note taker for her entire K–12 career and was now asking herself how she possibly could have developed language using only a note taker and constant vigilance as she searched for visual clues in the classroom. A mystery!

These are powerful self-narratives that our deaf and hard of hearing young adults have shared about what has defined them. It is part of the fabric of their selves and has been integrated into their identities, for both better and worse.

Qualitative Research and Our Research Design

Research that involves the analysis of stories is a form of qualitative research. Qualitative research allows researchers to look at, and hopefully make sense of, things and people in their natural settings, using in-depth descriptive data. It is a particularly important method for learning about people with disabilities for it allows others to see the world as experienced by the disabled person. Peck and Furman (1992) address the benefits of using this kind of research to study issues in special education, especially because many of the issues affecting policies about inclusion are more political than technical. Stanfield (1994) discusses the benefits of qualitative research methods in studying the experiences of people of color. Mertens (1998) gives support to the importance of qualitative research in studying children in special education settings because of a multitude of factors, including small sample sizes and the wide range of diversity within any specified group of students with disabilities.

Qualitative research, which asks people to describe and give meanings to their own experiences, in fact benefits from the inclusion of the researchers' own knowledge and experiences. In qualitative studies, the researchers are not trying to be neutral participants and recorders of data. Rather, their own experiences, beliefs, and biases inform the study. Both of us were the only deaf child in our respective neighborhood schools, albeit well before PL-94-142/IDEA was implemented. We have personal experience, academic knowledge, and intense interest in the topic we are researching. We presented ourselves to our focus groups as "one of them" and asked them to tell us the most current version of our shared stories.

Our Research Questions and Process

We used several methods to collect stories and data. We conducted three focus groups and asked each focus group member to submit an essay prior to the meeting itself. We also posted a Google survey and invited respondents to submit essays. We identified potential focus group members by first exploring our own social networks for adults who fit our research criteria: currently between the ages of 18 and 34, mainstreamed alone (or as one of a very few others) for at least 5 years of their K–12 grades, and a 50 dB or greater loss in both ears since childhood. We then used a technique called "snowballing," asking these colleagues to spread the word that we were looking for focus group participants in three cities.

Once participants were identified and the group dates were set, we asked each member to complete a brief background survey and to write a two- to four-page essay describing his or her solitary experience in the mainstream. Many participants wrote significantly more than that. This was similar to the technique used for *Alone in the Mainstream* (Oliva, 2004), and Gina's participants wrote voluminously as well. We solicited the essays for the purpose of getting participants in the proper mindset prior to the focus group itself. Additionally, these essays were used as part of the data for this book. Participants who both participated in our focus groups and submitted an essay were given a $50 gift card as a small token of appreciation.

Simultaneously with the focus groups, we set up a Google survey and asked our focus group members, former and current students, and young friends to share it widely and post it on their Facebook pages. We received a total of 221 responses to that survey; however, nearly half of those did not fit in our target age group. (This is almost twice the number of initial essays Gina received in 2004, telling us yet again how anxious formerly mainstreamed deaf and hard of hearing adults are to share their stories.) Once we eliminated those who were outside of the 18-to-34 age range, we were left with 113 responses. Borg and Gall (1989), in Mertens (2005) recommend a survey sample size of 100, so we are confident that our sample size is large enough for generalizations to be made.

We must share a word of caution, however. Our approach to the research task was heavily written-English focused. Although our focus group meetings were in ASL, our Google survey used written English (we took care to phrase the questions simply), and written essays were solicited from our focus group participants and our survey respondents. One of our focus group participants requested a videophone interview instead of an essay, and we complied. This research left out potential participants who perhaps lacked sufficient English literacy to read our survey, did not have access to computers, lacked social media skills, or were simply outside of the social networks of our mostly college-educated, professional contacts in the Deaf community. Our respondents were an elite group and our results may therefore not be generalizable to the many deaf and hard of hearing individuals with less successful educational and literacy outcomes. They are also possibly not generalizable to those deaf and hard of hearing formerly mainstreamed individuals who are not identified with the Deaf community. These individuals are likely isolated still. We acknowledge that there are many individuals who fit these various groups and that their voices are important to add to this discussion. We hope other researchers can find them and give them voice.

Our respondents reported that they struggled socially, emotionally, and sometimes academically in their K–12 school years, in spite of their facility with the English language. Our hunch is that many of the deaf and hard of hearing adults who were not represented in our research struggled much more, and that as adults they likely feel less confident, are more isolated and lonely, and are less vocationally successful than our sample. Again, their stories are important and would broaden our understanding and perspectives of the mainstream experience.

The focus groups conversations were immensely enjoyable and enriching for all involved. We held groups in three cities across the United States, with six to eight members attending each group. In addition to group members and ourselves, we had a cameraperson filming each group as a record for us. All focus group members were fluent signers—although some more than others—and lively, often passionate discussion took place on a variety of topics. There was a marvelous synergy within the three groups.

As facilitators, we had questions, which are called *prompts,* for each group. The prompts we used in our focus groups were broad rather than specific, and were designed to elicit memories of a wide range of experiences. Two prompts, for example, asked simply, "What were some of your best memories of being mainstreamed" and "What were some of your worst memories of being mainstreamed?" These prompts were sufficiently unstructured so that themes of great relevance and interest to our group members surfaced. The self-narratives that resulted from these questions, because they were shared in a group format, became in some cases rich group narratives in the sense that all members of the group fully understood and shared similar experiences.

The focus group participants told us they were delighted to get to know other deaf and hard of hearing previously mainstreamed young adults, as this was a special find in their local deaf communities. These "solitaires," borrowing a term from *Alone in the Mainstream*, shared a special connection. Sharing stories with one another was both painful and enjoyable. As adults, the participants were fully cognizant of the fact that a growing majority of deaf and hard of hearing students are in general education classrooms. (Gallaudet Research Institute, April, 2011; U.S. Government Accountability Office, 2011), and they knew their experiences as solitaries in the mainstream were not unusual. However it was the first time that many of them could share their stories in depth with so many others who had the same experiences, and this was awesomely powerful. We were honored to be a part of this telling.

In another fascinating process we watched unfold, our focus group members, both in their essays and in group discussions, acknowledged and appreciated how simply telling their stories to interested others helped to put some final building blocks into their own identity processes. In reflecting on their experiences, they became aware of strengths they had and forgave themselves for perceived failures or flaws of character. In some cases they were able to make important connections between disparate life experiences and gain some welcome clarity. By applying critical reasoning skills to their life stories, they understood themselves better, gaining both self-acceptance and a sharper sense of identity.

The final prompt to our focus groups was in the form of a task: We asked participants to work in small groups (generally three members) to design a system for the education of deaf and hard of hearing children that would prevent many of the painful experiences they had discussed. We wanted to give them the opportunity to use their knowledge to help others who are now in the same situation. They relished this power to use their experiences to benefit others.

We asked our survey participants similar questions: "What one or two things made your experience in the mainstream significantly more positive?

And if it was not a positive experience, and you could have changed one or two things to make it positive, what would you have changed?" Because many of our subjects participated in our study precisely because they wanted to change things for current and future deaf and hard of hearing students, this question was given serious thought and received numerous creative responses.

Many of our informants (both focus group members and survey respondents) were adamant that no child should be educated as the only deaf or hard of hearing child in the school. Many said that this was the most restrictive educational setting possible. Nearly all acknowledged that their parents had done their best with the limited options they had; however, our informants did not so easily let schools off the hook. They clearly saw areas where systemic changes within schools could result in improved educational experiences for deaf and hard of hearing children in general education settings. Listening to their ideas was exciting for us, because it was clear our participants were passionate about improving mainstream education and they had excellent ideas for how to do so.

Their suggestions for change covered several main areas. Not surprisingly, they had suggestions for improving interpreter training and teacher training. Another area given considerable attention was direct advice to current and future deaf and hard of hearing students. They also had advice for school district administrators that covered broader systemic changes. They had advice for parents. Many of their recommendations and advice are included throughout this book, and we are hopeful that experts in education as well as parents will listen carefully to the wise words of deaf and hard of hearing children who are now grown up and experts themselves.

Demographics of Focus Group Participants

The 21 members of our three focus groups were widely diverse. They represented 18 different states and all regions of the country (although the focus groups were held in only three geographical locations). A few members were from families who were the first generation settling in America. Members of the Deaf community are clearly globally mobile, a fact that one of our participants called to our attention. In the end, we felt the three cities in which our focus groups were held were of little importance because our members represented such wide state and regional areas. To protect confidentiality, we choose not to name our research sites.

The majority of our focus group participants were white (17), two were Hispanic, and two were African American. We had 14 women and 7 men in our groups and ages ranged from 25 to 34. Fourteen members of our group had hearing parents. The seven participants who had deaf parents (either one or both) added an interesting aspect to our research, which will be discussed. Four of the focus group participants had cochlear implants. Twelve members had spent at least 8 years alone in the mainstream and seven had spent their entire 12 years in that environment. Fourteen had also attended colleges in which they were the only deaf or hard of hearing student in their classes. Looking at the number of years spent alone in the mainstream, these participants clearly should be considered experts on the topic.

Our focus group participants were highly educated, which adds a different level of expertise. All except two of our participants had college degrees, and these two were currently students. The majority had master's degrees or were working toward such, and one had a doctorate. Furthermore, the majority of these individuals currently work within educational settings. Other professions represented included informational technology, video production, photography, and sales. We had a school bus driver, American Sign Language (ASL) teachers, coordinators of various academic or professional departments, and even a Ms. Deaf America. Our focus group participants were clearly intelligent, thoughtful individuals who had the ability to reflect on their past school experiences and to make thoughtful recommendations for change for future generations of deaf and hard of hearing children.

A third of our participants did not sign while they were growing up, but by the time of our study all used ASL (some more fluently than others) in addition to written and/or spoken English. All *valued* ASL and saw it as contributing to their identity. We did not look for individuals who signed and it was never part of our research criteria; however, we weren't surprised that these were the deaf and hard of hearing adults who found us, for our professional and personal identities are with the signing Deaf community.

The Special Value of Focus Groups in Addressing the Mainstream Experience

Our focus group members spent 4 hours with us, in each group. Prior to attending the focus groups, they completed a background survey and submitted essays describing their experiences in the mainstream. They clearly wanted to participate, and some participants were particularly eloquent. One young woman, who had spent an equal number of years in solitary mainstreamed environments and in Deaf schools, wanted to emphasize to parents that her Deaf school years and her mainstream years contributed equally to making her the person she is today. She also felt she had messages for both hearing parents and the Deaf community—to parents, she wanted to convey that it's never too late to provide a child with social opportunities and support. She also wanted to show the Deaf community (and particularly Deaf educators) that there are positive experiences and benefits to being mainstreamed.

Our participants wanted to reach out to deaf and hard of hearing students in the mainstream today to assure them they are not alone. They were deeply hopeful that school administrators and educational interpreters would listen to what they had to say, for it had required for most of them a journey into adulthood to then be able to reflect and find words to describe their general education successes as well as their many wounds and battle scars.

The focus groups were lively, creative, and thoughtful. There were many more similarities among the three groups than there were differences. As facilitators, we had participants address specific questions about their experiences alone in the mainstream as well as brainstorm possible ideas for creating a better general education experience. Focus group members expressed their appreciation for the opportunity to share and process their experiences with others who shared similar educational backgrounds. What we envisioned as a way for us to learn about the experiences of young deaf and hard of hearing adults today turned into a healthy, cathartic experience for many of the participants.

Some readers may be asking how generalizable our findings are. This is a fair question. We cannot claim that our focus group participants were a representative sample of previously mainstreamed deaf and hard of hearing children and youth, but we feel they were a particularly insightful and articulate sample with much to offer. For all the reasons previously given—education, profession, ASL fluency, and clarity of identity as a deaf or hard of hearing individual—this group may not "look like" many of the deaf and hard of hearing adults who are products of mainstream education. These are adults who experienced life in both listening/speaking and signing educational settings (sometimes as students and sometimes as employees), and as such they have struggled with identity and have important stories to tell. When putting together focus groups, representativeness matters, but so do other factors such as the ability of members to think about, define, and process a research problem (Stewart & Shamdasani, 1990). Our research questions focused particularly on giving voice to formerly mainstreamed deaf and hard of hearing adults who had the perspective of both worlds.

We feel strongly that it is not possible to reflect on one's experiences until one knows what one is missing and what one has. The young adults in our focus groups, although they demonstrated awareness of having missed a great deal in their K–12 years, have successfully navigated from one life path to another. Somehow they, or their parents, found a way to avail themselves of enriching opportunities even when it required extraordinary effort. They clearly know what they missed during their elementary and secondary school years, and they have gone on to create full, rich lives for themselves. They also know how to articulate their thoughts and feelings to share them with others. Although most deaf and hard of hearing students are still educationally behind their hearing peers (Antia, Jones, Reed, & Kreimeyer, 2009; Traxler, 2000), the members of our focus groups are way ahead.

All of our focus group participants could be classified as bilingual—English and ASL—and bicultural. Several of them are also bimodal, that is they were comfortable with and skilled at using both signs and speech. They see bilingualism, and in some cases multilingualism, as being crucial to their success. Our participants value being able to connect to hearing people through English and deaf people using ASL and refuse to limit themselves to one or the other, in spite of often having been pressured to do so. Much research confirms that bilingualism and biculturalism are important to the development of high self-esteem (Jambor & Elliott, 2005), language and cognitive development (Humphries, et al., 2012; Kushalnagar et al., 2010; Schick, 2007), and to a clear sense of identity (Bat-Chava, 2000; Leigh, 2009; Skelton & Valentine, 2003). Participants in our focus groups want parents to know this research, to educate themselves about language acquisition, to stop being afraid of sign language, to support their child's ASL development, and to become bilingual or multilingual themselves.

As we share our focus group participants' insights, we use some demographic coding that may help you to know who is contributing. We first identify if the participant is male or female, then we add age, followed by region of the country. So for example, "M31W" is our code for a 31-year-old male who lives in the western region of the United States.

Demographics of Survey Respondents

As a check and supplement to data received from our focus groups, we also include stories and comments from the 113 respondents to our posted Google survey. These survey responses confirm in large part what we learned from our focus group participants.

The survey participants were born between 1978 and 1993 and attended elementary and secondary schools in 33 states. Forty-seven percent reported spending 11 to 13 years alone (or as one of a very few) in the mainstream, and 39% had also attended a school for deaf students at some point. Twenty-seven percent had a split day in which they attended both mainstreamed and deaf schools. Seventy-four percent of the respondents had hearing families, whereas 18% had one deaf or hard of hearing and one hearing parent and 10% had two deaf or hard of hearing parents. Seventy-three percent identified themselves as Deaf whereas the remainder identified as either hard of hearing (19%) or hearing impaired (5%).

We asked both open-ended questions, where we invited our respondents to share their experiences with us and to offer suggestions for improving education for deaf and hard of hearing students in today's schools, and specific questions about the participants' elementary, middle, and high school experiences. We hoped to be able to identify levels of schooling that were particularly successful or problematic. Information in this area was less helpful than we had hoped, as there was much variation of experiences and many conflicting feelings. For example, 62% of the respondents reported that they felt the mainstream experience had made them strong rather than hurting their self-esteem, but only 15% said they would most likely place a deaf child of their own in a mainstreamed setting. In the words of one of our survey respondents,

> . . . Being mainstreamed forced me how to learn to survive and adapt to a world of hearing people who have different conversational behaviors than HOH/Deaf people do. It's made me strong like nothing else ever has. I don't know what I would be like if I didn't have to try so hard as a child and teen.

The survey respondents matched in passion the focus group members in their wish to share their experiences and to advise us on what they felt needed to be improved for current and future deaf and hard of hearing students. They gave thoughtful answers to our many questions, and 15 participants wrote substantial essays in response to our invitation to do so. The 113 survey respondents join the voices of the 21 focus group members. When we include personal narratives from the survey respondents, we identify them in a general way in order to distinguish them from the focus group respondents.

2

Friendships and Social Access: Outside Looking In

Friendship is born at that moment when one person says to another: "What! You too? I thought I was the only one."
—C. S. Lewis, *The Four Loves*

THINK BACK to your school years. What comes first to mind? Is it the marvelous teacher you had in freshman lit or the thrill of learning trigonometry? We very much doubt it. More likely, your positive memories are about friendships you made or the teacher who always brought chocolate chip cookies in fourth grade. (Linda's youngest daughter has a favorite memory about her first grade teacher allowing her students to rub her feet. How strange is that?) Our point is that we believe that when policy makers and educators focus solely on academic support and accommodations for deaf and hard of hearing students, they ignore vitally important experiences and connections that happen during the school day, but perhaps not in the classroom.

Although there is some recognition on the federal level that deaf and hard of hearing students have "social, emotional, and cultural needs including opportunities for peer interactions and communication" (http://www2.ed.gov/about/offices/list/ocr/docs/hq9806.html) that should be considered in educational programming, too often policy makers, educators, and parents wrongly assume that deaf and hard of hearing students will be able to manage on their own, both inside and outside of the classroom. Perhaps they assume that nothing other than information transfer happens in the classroom or that nothing of consequence at all happens outside of the classroom. Research and our participants tell us that is not so. The result of not paying attention to essential interactions inside and outside of classroom environments is extremely impoverished social interactions for deaf and hard of hearing children. Full participation is denied to them, and developmental delays and a shocking dearth of learning result.

One way to look at this dearth of friendships and social opportunities is through a concept called *social capital*. Social capital (i.e., relationships and networks of relationships) during the K–12 years is often not appreciated or given importance. Schools seem to pay no attention at all to whether or not relationships are being formed (perhaps simply assuming that they are), yet relationships are the heart of education (Ramsey, 1997). There is research that shows that minority students in particular need relationship networks in order to succeed academically (Cohen & Steel, 2002; Stanton-Salazar, 1997, 2001).

What are relationships built on? Conversations. Placing a deaf or hard of hearing child in an environment where participating in basic conversations is a daily struggle precludes any healthy development of relationships, that is, social capital. Wilkens and Hehir (2008) say social capital is increasingly at risk for our deaf and hard of hearing students as more of them are receiving cochlear implants and attending general education classrooms, which results in vastly diminished opportunities to build relationships with other deaf and hard of hearing children and adults. For those who argue that attending mainstream schools opens doors for the development of social capital in the mainstream (or hearing world) rather than, or in addition to, deaf social capital, we have one thing to say: It is not happening. In some kind of pie-in-the-sky wish, hearing social capital sounds wonderful. Our research participants say it isn't so, and as a result many deaf and hard of hearing students are attending school and then entering adulthood without either deaf or hearing social networks.

There are researchers who specialize in the impact of leisure experiences on human development. One such researcher is Kleiber (1999), who defined a concept he calls the *fourth environment*. The fourth environment is represented by places where people go to hang out with others, away from home, work, and school. The conversations that take place in these environments are critical to our sense of social support. Today's youth go to shopping malls, coffee shops, sports centers, and so forth, to meet their needs to congregate with one another to talk, build relationships, and make sense of their lives. For adolescents in particular, an important element of these environments is the absence of adults. The school bus and the locker room certainly fall within this category. Our research participants told us they were rarely, if ever, able to access such social milieus. On the school bus and in the cafeteria, hallways, and locker room they most often felt the most invisible and excluded. However, once they found deaf and hard of hearing peers, life changed. These deaf and hard of hearing peers provided the fourth environment milieu in which social capital could develop. These peers became critical to their developing sense of selves.

In this chapter we share what our research participants told us about friendships and social interactions they had while growing up in solitary mainstream environments. We also share some important research from other scholars that addresses the impoverished social experiences of deaf and hard of hearing students in general education environments. Our goal for this chapter is to help you, the reader, to experience to some extent the lonely, powerless position that many deaf and hard of hearing students experience on a daily basis while attending general education schools. We hope that as you read, you will start wondering what schools can do to improve this situation so that the burden is less on the individual students, who certainly are the least able to handle this burden. We start on a personal level, sharing the words of our focus group participants and survey respondents.

Friendships in the Mainstream

We didn't directly approach the question of friendships in our focus group discussions; however, it always came up. In the group discussions and the essays, participants talked about how they were always on the outside looking in on the various levels of friendships in their schools. We were told:

- "Only 'nice' girls will befriend you."
- "Girls will be friends with boys."
- "Boys will generally not be your friends, unless it is for sex."
- "Rarely do we get to pick our friends; instead they pick us or ever-so-kindly allow us to hang with them."

In essence, we were told that by middle school, friendships between deaf and hard of hearing students and their hearing peers were rarely easy, of sufficient quality or quantity, or enduring. Furthermore, we were told they couldn't get past the "deaf kid" label and its accompanying communication barrier often enough to be actually known by most classmates.

Our focus group participants yearned for the free, easy companionship they saw taking place around them each and every day but rarely could grasp. They wanted to be friends with those they perceived as fun, interesting, or having similar interests. Instead, their friends were often those who, for whatever reasons, were willing to have a deaf friend. Often these individuals were on the fringes of group-belonging themselves. In other cases, they were the teacher's pet, clearly out to meet their own needs for control, recognition, or to feel important. For this reason, our participants told us their friendships changed often. From grade to grade, they often could not count on the same friendships.

Having a friend in school made such a difference! Of great importance was the fact that someone actually knew you and cared about your well-being. Our respondents told us these were generally the rare friendships that began in the neighborhood or during early elementary school days. But equally important, these were the friends who would keep them in the loop and tell them what was going on in the classroom and also in the hallways, playing fields, and lunchroom. Friendships changed tremendously between the years of elementary school and high school, with most of the changes occurring at the middle school years. In this chapter, we focus on middle and high school friendship issues. This is not to say that deaf and hard of hearing students feel accepted and included in friendship circles in elementary school, for many of our participants felt extremely lonely at this level too, but the pain of later school years, in comparison, made elementary school feel downright pleasant. What hurt the most was that it was clear to all our participants that their social rejection was not due to differences in anything other than ability to hear and communicate freely.

Twenty-five percent of our survey respondents said they had friends in school (that is hearing friends), which means an overwhelming 75% did not consider any of their classmates to be of significant importance to their school happiness and did not mention them in their responses. However, even that 25% is a stretch. *Friend* was defined very broadly. For one person it meant having a quiet girl in her classroom with whom she passed notes back and forth. Or as another person said, "I had friends . . . kinda." Others of our survey respondents noted they had one or two friends who loyally stuck by their sides, often learning ASL, and they were wonderful helps through their school days.

One of our focus group participants had this to say about friendships.

> Although I made nice friends due to my tenacious spirit, it required increased effort and concentration. This is when frustrations of being left out of conversations and loneliness sunk in. I felt like I had to pick out friends who would be willing to put up with my Deaf voice and hang out with me, and my choices were limited. It takes really kind people and open-minded people to be willing to hang out with Deaf people during middle school years and be willing to have one-on-ones and repeat what others are saying. I envied the "groupies" and their natural ability to just click together and have informal conversations. Sometimes I wanted to be part of the "cool" clique because they were into makeup, fashion, music, dance, and boys, but I often could tell that they would not be kind to me. My best friends often changed every year, depending on their patience level.   (F28W)

Not being able to choose one's friends, but rather being relegated to wait to be chosen is a powerless position. On the one hand, the deaf and hard of hearing students were extremely grateful to have a friend. On the other hand, they often felt that their friendship needs were not being met, leaving them longing for more or different friends. As they shared these stories with us, they were in hindsight able to identify a certain resentfulness they felt with certain of their friendships. They were resentful about needing to be grateful. Gratefulness in friendships implies inequality (unless perhaps both are equally grateful), and a one-down position is never a good prescription for friendships.

Hard of hearing individuals in our focus groups often had different friendship and social experiences than their deaf peers. They were more often included in friendship cliques and were more likely to have a group of friends they kept throughout their schooling. By middle school, these friends were more likely to stay by them outside of school, even if they did not stay by them *in* school. These friends, regardless of their inconsistency, were counted as true friends and they were forgiven for not always being loyal.

One of our hard of hearing participants took things into her own hands. She decided to choose her own friends, and she chose based on loudness. Her friends were the extroverts, the cut-ups, and the loud, boisterous ones. She could *hear* them, and in that circle she felt included. The downside (although in retrospect, it was probably an upside) of this is that by high school these friends had become "wild," and her parents did not allow her to hang out with them on weekends and late nights. However, during the school day, these were the perfect friends for her.

One of our focus group participants gave a short treatise of his view of the social hierarchy in schools and of how he fit into it. All the members of his group laughed uproariously, immediately understanding what he was saying and agreeing that this was their experience too. According to his three-tier theory, at the very top, there are the truly cool and popular kids who would never, ever condescend to befriend a deaf person. They probably didn't even *see* their deaf peer. Below this was the group of kids who for various reasons had been able to secure some recognition for themselves and our participant discovered he was able to move up to this tier based on his performance on the swim team. Membership in this tier is often short and fleeting as it depends on skill during a specific school-recognized event. After swim team season, he says he became a nobody again, which pushed him down to Tier 3—the nerds and the invisible. For our participant, and for many of his deaf peers who were also relegated to Tier 3 in the social hierarchy, each day as he dressed for school, he had to put on his brave face, in addition to choosing a trendy outfit. The fact that this respondent had previously attended an oral school for deaf students where he was, in his own estimation, in the top social tier, just made this whole demotion in social status more difficult, but also more clear, for him.

While this story was hilarious in its telling, it was also a powerful reminder of how lonely our participant used to be and how fortunate he now felt to have friends with whom he could share this, who totally resonated with his experiences. Yes, they all said, this is my story too.

Another of our focus group members had experiences that illustrate this same concept, albeit more harshly. The pain and bitterness of her years of social rejection appear still raw. Her experiences were also well appreciated by members of her focus group, who quickly supported her by adding their own stories of mean classmates. We wondered, is this a form of bullying? This is her story:

> I thought high school would be better because I thought they would "grow up," but they never did. I did not go to Friday night football games or dances, and I was only popular for a few months my sophomore year when I got my driver's license and a car [when no one else had one]. Girls would ask me to drive them to the mall after school but never really invited me to join them. It was an awful feeling. I was still eating my lunches in the bathroom or the car. I seriously considered deaf school because there had to be more to high school than this.   (F30NW)

This story, and others like it, made us curious about the incidence of bullying in the schools, and we made this a direct question to our focus group. Were you ever bullied? Although most denied being bullied, we learned that some of our research participants were bullied and often. Some, looking back, can't quite believe they were never bullied, because they often felt very alone and different. Others have sharp memories of being taunted, spit on, and worse, beaten. There appeared to be no gender differences. Bullies were both male and female and the victims were of both genders as well.

Many of our participants told of more subtly being rejected, excluded, or made to feel invisible. When discussing bullying, the predominant definition for most of us seems to be physical or verbal threat or harm. However, there is a third definition of bullying that is social or relational. *Social bullying* focuses on hurting someone by purposely excluding them, spreading rumors, creating public embarrassment, and by directing others to not be friends (http://www.stopbullying.gov/what-is-bullying/definition/index .html#types). Using that definition of social bullying, bullying happened quite frequently to the deaf and hard of hearing individuals in our study. As a result, attending school sometimes required considerable courage, or as one of our participants said, "putting on a brave face along with each day's school outfit."

In exploring friendships (or lack thereof) we were also interested in gender differences. We had learned there seemed to be no gender differences in terms of being bullied, but we were also curious if there was a gender difference to experiences with friendships in general. When we asked, we were told by both men and women that girls befriended them much more frequently than boys did. During adolescence, our female focus group participants told us that boys generally only wanted one of two things from them—sex or signs for dirty words. Male focus group members had even more difficulties with friendships. We learned from the men in our focus groups that they were viewed as socially deviant (a description they both perceived indirectly from peer behavior and directly by asking rare friends) and as a result were often ignored by both male and female peers. Boys did *slightly* better with female friendships; they had more friends who were girls than friends who were boys.

In trying to understand what we were being told, we looked at research into gender differences in socialization. Because boys in general are not socialized to be "nice" and girls are, it made sense to us that boys generally could (and did) ignore their deaf peers, except for the times when they had earned situational recognition (remember the story about our participant's social recognition as a swim team member?). The resulting difference was that hearing girls would sometimes befriend deaf girls and occasionally deaf boys, but rarely did hearing boys befriend deaf peers of either gender. This finding is worthy of exploration, as deaf middle and high school boys are clearly at an even more serious disadvantage in the social realm, which puts them at even greater risk.

A discussion of high school friendships cannot be complete without a discussion of dating. Again, we did not specifically inquire about dating, but we learned some things about it regardless. Not surprisingly, none of the men in our focus groups dated during high school. Girls were more likely to date and sometimes these boyfriends opened doors to social acceptance. However, even for girls, dating was rare. Only two of our survey respondents mentioned boyfriends. Because high school dating is generally a group activity, when girls did date, it gave them a small circle of "friends." These friends may not have been well known or close, but we were told it was an important and improved difference to be identified as "Tony's girlfriend," rather than "the deaf girl." Some of the women in our study unfortunately learned that it wasn't their personality that was so appealing; it was the sex. And other women said they did not date at all during high school; they were never asked. We urge you to consider how huge a disadvantage that is for deaf girls and boys as they leave high school and move into the next phrase of life development.

Being on the social fringes and being powerless to change this, knowing furthermore that they had done nothing to deserve this rejection sometimes led to depression. If our respondents had been asked at age 16 if they were depressed, they might not have been able to identify it. But looking back a few were able to reflect on their feelings and behaviors of the time and acknowledged depression. Others of our research participants told us they just closed off their social needs and focused on what they could do well—sports, academics, creative arts, or outside-of-school activities. These filled the void and also permitted them to legitimately stop trying to do something they were failing so dismally at. They could tell themselves they didn't need it. The psychologist in Linda needs to point out that while this was a highly successful strategy to use while growing up, it is not a key to successful adult relationships.

My "Deaf Fix"

By high school, a lucky few of our participants (and 12% of our survey respondents) had serendipitously found deaf and hard of hearing friends. Once found, these friendships held a sacred place in their lives. In fact, this was so important that our focus group participants had a term for it: "deaf fix." Deaf friends were most often met in summer camps or previous schools. Those from Deaf families often had deaf family friends. Regardless of what happened (or didn't happen) in school, these deaf friends were the ones who our participants felt truly knew and really understood them. There were no communication barriers. Our participants saw being able to hang out with deaf friends as affirming and strengthening to their identities and self-concepts. In *Alone in the Mainstream*, Gina defined a concept she labeled "met deaf wow," which identified the same feeling. Meeting deaf peers and having regular contact with them caused a pivotal change in self-concept and filled a need not previously met.

In fact, "hanging out with deaf friends" at times did not even mean gathering in a physical spot. We had respondents tell us that their computer was their best friend as it allowed them a social connection. Thanks to the Internet and social media, online chats fill this need for many mainstreamed students. This is a far cry from the deaf pen pal Linda had in her high school days, but carries the same power and serves the same purpose.

Those members of our research study who had deaf and hard of hearing friends put these friendships high on their priority list of high school activities, emphasizing again and again the importance of these friends in their lives. These were the relationships created by rich conversation, transpiring immediately and directly, rather than being transferred to them secondhand. In these gatherings of deaf peers, they were not passive observers or bystanders, but involved, active participants—this interaction fed their souls. All of our participants said clearly and unequivocally: All deaf children, particularly those who are mainstreamed, need deaf friends. Yet only

12% of our survey respondents said that they had had a deaf friend while in school and many of those were out-of-state, online friendships.

Those who had deaf friends, such as the following informant, couldn't imagine how others survived without these friendships.

> When I was in high school I was able to get my social fix by going to [a nearby city with many deaf college students] and meeting up with deaf friends. Most of them were mainstreamed through the program so we all formed a "deaf teen club" and got together once a month and I think that really helped me get through being alone at my school. The other deaf kids were all mainstreamed as well so we shared that common link.   (F30NE)

Tommy Horejes, a Deaf professor at Gallaudet University and the author of *Social Constructions of Deafness*, writes about his personal struggle to find himself a secure niche in his mainstream school, one he was able to achieve only once he began to value the deaf friends he had.

> In high school, I felt the most normal ever. I was content with my integrated identity: my identity with my hearing world (academically, athletically, and socially) as well as my deaf identity in my deaf world with Boy Scouts and with many deaf friends who were also mainstreamed at other high schools. There were times where I would have to drive 20–30 miles just to meet with deaf friends; we rotated locations where to meet up and were notorious for staying up during the wee hours, talking and catching up. We did not have the luxury of telephones to converse during the week, so weekends were our opportunity to catch up and to get our "deaf fix"—sign language.
>
> (Horejes, 2012, p. 37)

The stress of constantly trying to access parts of conversations and the sadness of being always on the sidelines socially took a toll on many of our informants. Even the most successfully mainstreamed students suffered. For example, one of our participants was truly immersed in the hearing world (she had good friends in school, good grades, and participated in a dance program), but she met some deaf peers while in high school, and these friends became of paramount importance to her. Her story serves as a caution to those of us who want to say, "This person is successfully mainstreamed because they have it all—friends, good grades, activities." For deaf and hard of hearing students, there may be still a large hole that only other deaf and hard of hearing peers can fill. This is what she had to say:

> I needed breaks from the hearing setting. When I went home, the first thing I did was to get on the computer and go on AOL to talk with my Deaf friends to get my Deaf fix. I would often talk with them for 3 hours until dinnertime then I would do my homework or go back on the computer to talk with my Deaf friends more.   (F28W)

The major differences between friendships with deaf peers and friendships with hearing peers were that the deaf student was able to (a) be a full and equal participant; (b) converse with ease; (c) feel respected, accepted, and valued; and (d) feel emotionally safe and supported. A major factor in successful friendships is how easy and natural they feel, and this quality was most apparent with the deaf friendships our informants described. In contrast, friendships with hearing peers required considerable effort and sustained attention, which might pay off in valuable friendships, but came at a considerable cost. A final quality that most of the deaf and hard of hearing participants noted was the depth of connection with deaf/deaf friendships versus the superficiality of many deaf/hearing friendships.

In addition to enhanced self-esteem, there is another reason deaf friendships are important. Friendships with other signing deaf children, beginning in childhood, are crucial for development of language skills (Humphries et al., 2012). It's long been known that bilingual skills are highly beneficial to developing language and cognitive skills for hearing children, and this is as true for deaf children. While language development is not the focus of this book, we feel this is important to mention because language development is always an important issue with deaf children and affects all areas of life, including friendships.

Conversations: The Building Blocks of Social Connections

However, we learned that there is a larger issue at stake than friendships. It is not only the superficiality of friendships that deaf and hard of hearing students deal with daily. It is much more profound than that. Day in and day out, there is superficiality of conversation, very often combined with an absolute inability to "overhear" conversations that are taking place—this is at the very heart of the social deprivation our informants report. This happens every single day, week after week, month after month, and year after year. It has been interesting for us to realize that deaf researchers have put "labels" on this phenomenon that we as former solitaires know intuitively, but that the larger culture truly has no words or descriptors for. This phenomenon is totally outside of "normal experience" and is perhaps most difficult for an individual with intact hearing to comprehend. But those of us who have been there, including our study participants, know it intuitively as a uniquely Deaf experience.

Case in point: Around 2005 we were approached by a colleague to write a chapter for a collection of essays on the experiences of deaf students. We completed our chapter, but the actual collection never came to fruition. The title of our chapter was "Ubiquitous Conversation," which identified a concept that we were both intimately attuned to; however, we had to wrack our brains for what to call it. We were aware that deaf people understood this concept. In fact, Deaf people have long had a sign (i.e., a word) for this phenomenon, and it looks like this: Imagine two Pac-man icons, made with your two hands facing each other, snip, clip, chomping away but not going anywhere. They just face each other and chomp. Now, take those Pac-man-facing-each-other chomping hands and move them around in a stirring-the-cauldron kind of movement. There, you have it—"people blabbing and blabbing all around and as usual I don't have a clue what they are talking about." That's ASL for "hearing-people-bantering-around-me-while-I-am-oblivious-to-what-they-are-saying." This Pac-man-hands phenomenon demonstrates that for deaf individuals, the experience of being unable to access ubiquitous conversation is universal. The fact that Deaf people have a sign for this concept powerfully illustrates the awareness of what they are missing.

Still not convinced? Perhaps this dream of Linda's will do that for you. This dream came to her regularly between the ages of 9 and 17.

> I am at a party or a gathering of people. I wander around moving through the crowd. People are laughing, smiling, talking casually with each other. A

few talk to me. I smile, nod my head, and move on. I understand nothing. I wake up. The same old familiar feelings await me: I'm frustrated, sad, and very, very angry. I feel betrayed by my own self. My real life is filled with enough scenarios such as this. I am furious that in my unconscious state, I am still unable to fill in my world with conversation and connect with those around me. I understand fully that I am the creator of my dreams and that, as this creator, I still lack words. I have no clue as to what people talk about and I have a deep yearning to know and to belong to this casual social world.

This dream completely disappeared after Linda arrived at Gallaudet University, met other deaf people, learned sign language, and found a social world that welcomed her as a full participant. Once she was no longer a mere observer in a world she often didn't understand, there was no further need for pretend understanding. The dream? Poof! Gone!

Pivotal Research on Ubiquitous Conversation in Schools

Ubiquitous conversation is a concept we both felt deserved much more attention, and we were disappointed when the editor of the proposed collection of articles told us the project was on hold indefinitely. Imagine our delight when we came across a very recent dissertation by Mindy Hopper, who had just found a way to define and study this same phenomenon. Our hats are off to her! Hopper (2011) came up with a brilliant and innovative way to document the information a mainstreamed 13-year deaf girl missed on the school bus, in the hallways, and in the lunchroom (all fourth environments). Her work allows the reader to see what this young woman did not "hear" or "see" or "receive."

Hopper began her research by identifying a main deaf subject, Jasmine (a pseudonym, as are the other names), and additionally asked her to identify one deaf friend and two hearing friends. Jasmine considered Cali and Belle to be her hearing friends and also to be sources of informal learning. They all attended the same neighborhood school and Cali rode the same school bus. A deaf friend, Marissa, was also part of the study. Marissa attended a different school, a nearby school for the deaf. As part of the research, Jasmine and Cali were directed to "freewrite," that is, to write freely about what they saw, heard, and engaged in on the bus and up until their first class began. In a 4-week period, they freewrote for 2 minutes, twice a day, twice a week, for a total of 16 freewriting entries.

The results of the freewriting were quite telling. Of Jasmine's writings, 40 journal entries she wrote involved something she saw and 26 involved a conversation. She wrote primarily about what she saw (clothing, hairstyles, the kind of handbags or backpacks they carried, students standing in groups, giving each other high-fives, laughing, etc.) and secondarily about conversations she was involved with. She initiated two thirds of these conversations (17) and one third (9) was initiated by others. In contrast, Cali's freewriting entries were virtually all about things she overheard. She wrote about students talking about things such as school traditions, current films, a contagious illness making its rounds at the school, and similar kinds of information.

When Hopper talked to the girls about what this all meant, they concluded (both Hopper and the young students) that the only way the deaf student would know any of the information that was being conversed about (e.g., what Cali wrote about) was if a hearing peer told her directly. If not directly told, she simply remained "out of the loop." Because communication from hearing peer to deaf peer was invariably done on a one-to-one basis, rather as part of a group conversation, the hearing peer literally had to "go out of her way" or "make a special point" to inform the deaf student of what was being said.

When Hopper showed Jasmine her hearing friend's freewriting, she was quite surprised to realize just how much she missed. At one point, pointing to about six lines of text, Jasmine said, "this is more than I would learn on my own in a whole day!" In addition to not receiving information, Jasmine was aware of her severely limited social contributions. "The average number of words I spoke in a single day (at the hearing school) is one or two words. I just stay quiet. I like to talk, yes, but at the hearing school, how?" (Hopper, 2011, p. 163). Hopper's research so exactly illustrates the ubiquitous conversation phenomenon that all the focus group participants and we know so well. Once again the experiences and feelings of being "alone" extend across the miles and the *years*.

Hopper had a few more highly interesting threads we wish to pull from her study to share with you. Through her various data collection methods and through discussion with her deaf subjects (Jasmine and Marissa), she concluded that these deaf students were always in a "bystander" role when with a hearing group, but that when they were with a deaf group they could take on the whole range of conversational roles. In discussing this with the two deaf girls, they surmised that their hearing peers knew them very superficially. In fact, they felt that all their hearing peers knew about them was that they would smile—because in their enforced bystander role, they were really helpless to do anything but smile.

Hopper also concluded that hearing peers and teachers were vastly over-estimating the amount of information their deaf peers were absorbing.

> When these Deaf students mingled as peripheral participants with their hearing peers, the latter students, as well as school personnel, seemed to interpret deaf students' physical presence with hearing peers as equivalent to the genuine conversations in which hearing students regularly participated. Schools did not seem to realize that [the deaf girls] have been marginalized, positioned as peripheral participants or bystanders.   (2011, pp. 103–104)

Although it was not part of the original research design, Jasmine wanted to know what Hopper was learning, and she wanted her deaf friend Marissa to be part of the discussions. During these discussions, Jasmine was able to reflect on and think about the roles her various friends played in her life, and how much she valued the friendship with Marissa. Both girls became much more aware of what was missed by deaf children on the bus, in the hallways, and in the lunchroom (fourth environments)—in terms of the *extent* and *degree* of information missed. They also became aware that their preference was for deeper conversation—topic was unimportant. It was the frequent superficiality of information received that bothered them.

Hopper learned that the deaf girls intensely disliked that they had to rely on [hearing] friends for information—what Hopper labeled "reliance." Jasmine said, "I just get used to it" (2011, p.172), illustrating the powerless-ness imposed on her with this situation. To get information, she had to take the initiative to "nudge and ask." The girls were also aware that they were being placed in a one-down position in the social hierarchy, as having and sharing information was part of status. But there was nothing they could do about it. If they wanted information, they had to ask for it. Even so, they often got the information late and were "last to know."

Deaf and hard of hearing students are bystanders only because they have no other option, as Hopper's study shows so well. It is not because they are shy or passive by nature; these roles are forced upon them. One of our focus group participants, remembering being starved for social opportunities while in middle school and shared this reminiscence:

> I think about the moments I spent observing students, teachers, and people in general. I observed, wrote in my journals, had few friends who were real friends. But I remember lunch hours where I would be at my most uncomfortable moments—holding a cafeteria tray (or my lunch box) and scanning the crowd for who to sit with, with the fear of being rejected, to eat in silence. Sometimes, I would sneak home (which was three blocks away) and eat lunch there. (F28SE)

Hopper's study provides stark evidence of the value of a deaf friend for each and every deaf child. She was able to show the paucity of information that is communicated to deaf children in the general education school setting, as well as the peripheral bystander roles they most often are relegated to. Access to information leads to full participation, neither of which her subject or our informants had. The shared experience of deaf friendships, juxtaposed with the impoverished social environment of the school, is simply priceless and, we argue, necessary for ameliorating the deleterious impact of the latter.

Classroom Discourse for Deaf and Hard of Hearing Children in Public Schools

Hopper is not the only researcher to come to these conclusions, although she is one of the more recent and her thinking is strongly along the same lines as ours. An earlier researcher, Claire Ramsey (1997), spent a full year observing three mainstreamed 7-year-old deaf boys. She noticed many ways in which the deaf boys were being left out of the classroom discourse. For example, the boys' hearing classmates had a limited sign language vocabulary and used this with their deaf peers in small ways that were perhaps helpful, but were surely not respectful or mutual:

> The children were doing seatwork and [the teachers] were roaming around the room. Janna [hearing] poked Paul [deaf] and showed him a ring she was wearing. Although Mrs. Rogers did not see Janna get Paul's attention, she did notice that Paul suspended work on his math paper to admire Janna's ring. She called out "Janna please touch Paul." (This was a method she had developed for enlisting the hearing children's help in physically managing the deaf children's attention).
>
> Janna poked Paul and brusquely signed "PAY ATTENTION," a much more explicit directive than Mrs. Rogers' tone of voice indicated.   (p. 70)

The hearing classmates would also use their limited sign vocabulary to make evaluative comments, such as "GOOD," to a deaf classmate. Interactions between these deaf children and their hearing classmates were limited to the hearing children giving commands to the deaf children, and to the hearing children answering questions about schoolwork or expectations, interactions that again were not respectful or built on any kind of mutuality within relationships. Ramsey concluded:

> For the purposes of learning and development, the interaction among deaf and hearing children in the mainstreaming classroom . . . was highly constrained and not developmentally helpful . . . few parents of hearing children would judge sufficient for their own children the personal contact and peer interaction that was available in the mainstream for deaf second graders at Aspen School [pseudonym].   (p. 74)

We concur with Ramsey's conclusion and are appalled at her findings. Her method of spending time (a full year!) observing in an actual classroom is to be commended. Her ability to comprehend conversations of both the young deaf boys and their hearing classmates, as well as her ability to hear the conversations around her (teachers, aides, interpreters, administrators) enabled her to paint what we feel is a crisply clear picture of the lives of most mainstreamed children.

Both Ramsey and Hopper fault the schools for ignoring the vast amount of information deaf and hard of hearing students are not obtaining in the classrooms and outside of the classrooms. Both say, and rightfully so, this is not acceptable. Placing an interpreter or note taker in the classroom is not enough, as we show in subsequent chapters. Access to information (regardless of whether it is academic or not) is a gateway to knowledge as well as to rich, successful relationships. Participation in class discussions has been tied to good social outcomes (Antia, Jones, Luckner, Kreimeyer, & Reed, 2011) Deaf students should not be marginalized and relegated to sketchy hand-me-down information. Ignoring the fact that deaf and hard of hearing children are at this huge disadvantage is greatly damaging. So what can be done?

Building Awareness and Change

We believe one of the first things needed is further evidence of the *extent* and *degree* of information missed. Also needed is evidence of the persistent day-after-day nature of the information missed. We suspect if evidence is not collected on an ongoing basis, people will forget how bad it really is. Remember when we were talking about the phenomenon of missing out on ubiquitous conversation? We suspect this is such an elusive concept that most people who are not deaf themselves will truly not grasp the pervasiveness of it and will need to be reminded again and again.

In our chapters herein on educational interpreting and on what our young informants had to say, a very stark message emerges: Parents and teachers do not know what children are missing on an ongoing basis; however, what they are missing has serious consequences to social-emotional development. Yoshinaga and her colleagues (Goberis et al., 2012) studied the topic of pragmatic language, that is, language used for social purposes. They found that deaf and hard of hearing children are several years behind hearing children in the development of pragmatic language. Hearing children seem to learn this kind of language through incidental learning. Deaf children learn the same concepts much more slowly, imperfectly, and often need direct instruction simply because they are not picking up peer conversations. Anything that can be done to remedy that will improve life for deaf and hard of hearing children.

We propose that the best and easiest way to learn the missing pieces is to make the educational interpreter responsible for reporting on such. She hears, and she knows what she has conveyed and what she has not. For students who do not have educational interpreters, we recommend that a variation of Hopper's research design be employed periodically in order to assess this. Young interpreter trainees or even nearby college students could provide what Hopper's "Cali" provided—ongoing records of the conversational threads that are floating around all day, each day, completely out of the reach of a deaf or hard of hearing student. This information should be used in two ways: as a report to parents and teachers so they are aware of what is missing and as information given to the child so it is *not* missed.

In closing this chapter, we ask a question (one that Hopper also asked) that is important to understanding and to fixing this gap in educational accommodations: Are deaf and hard of hearing students even aware of how much information they are missing? Hopper's subject, Jasmine, was shocked to see how much she was missing. Our focus group participants told many stories of how they lived their school lives simply accepting the status quo until at various points and in various ways, they were enlightened to all they were missing.

For example, one of our participants attended a summer conference where CART[1] was being used, and immediately a light bulb went off in her head. She realized how much information this was compared to what she was getting in her daily school life. She was getting every word! No more sketch summaries. She had no idea she had been missing so much! Convincing her school district to provide CART, however, was a whole different dilemma, and the message here is that it is not enough to identify the missing piece but that a lot of smart advocacy also needs to happen.

Another participant had a note taker and later an oral interpreter in his classrooms where he typically just shut down and didn't even try to absorb the information. Ironically, this boy knew ASL but used it only

---

1. CART stands for Communication Access Realtime Translation: captioning services provided to deaf people so they can immediately read on a small computer screen everything that is being said in the room.

with his deaf friends outside of his school. In school, he internalized his parents' need for him to be an oral success. His note taker/oral interpreter happened to be a CODA (child of deaf adults), and she knew signs. One day, certainly motivated by her own frustration as well as her concern for him, she offered to use ASL (in complete disregard of his high school IEP [Individualized Education Program]) and immediately our participant felt this enormous difference in being able to be present in the classroom as a full and equal participant. He made sure his parents changed his IEP, and he never looked back.

Many of our respondents said that meeting deaf people and learning ASL was the turning point for them. It was a paradigm shift. They finally understood what full communication access was about. In *Alone in the Mainstream* (Oliva, 2004), many of the contributors also said full access was a concept they were not intimately familiar with until they met other deaf people. It seems you truly cannot know what is being missed until you experience full conversational access, and this truly explains all the studies in which mainstreamed deaf and hard of hearing students report to researchers that everything is fine.

These are just a few of the stories we have gathered, and our wish is that they lead to creative ways to advocate within school programs for communication access for all deaf and hard of hearing students both within the classrooms and in the fourth environments within the schools. Our definition of communication access includes the small conversations that enrich our lives in a multitude of ways, in addition to class lectures and discussions. As we will learn in Chapter 4, providing interpreters is only a partial answer, and it comes with its own very unique issues and concerns.

3

The Struggle to Shape an Identity

"I had to compare myself to the hearing standard as that was all
I knew."   (Focus group participant)

IDENTITY encompasses many aspects. One of its defining
characteristics is that it includes both our past and present
experiences, and the meanings we place on those experiences,
as well as the future possibilities we see for ourselves. For example, adolescents ask themselves not only "Who am I?" but
also "How will I fit into the world?" Identity includes our culture, our understanding about ourselves in terms of abilities,
attitudes, and behaviors, and our spirituality. It includes our
understanding of race, ethnicity, disability, age, and gender.

Another important aspect of identity is that it changes over
time, and that in times of crisis and transition, we are most
challenged as to how we define ourselves. Identity is based
on two disparate concepts: how we see ourselves and how we
think others see us. If these two concepts do not match, the
process of forming a strong, healthy identity is much more
difficult. The term for this is *psychosocial mutuality* (Erikson,
1968). Psychosocial mutuality says that if my self-concept and
my knowledge of how others view me do not match, I must
somehow integrate and explain these differences to myself. I
don't have to accept the larger community's evaluation of me;
however, I cannot ignore it.

Many researchers have studied how being deaf impacts identity development (Bat-Chava, 2000; Glickman, 1996; Lytle, 1987; Maxwell-McCaw, 2001; Weinberg & Sterritt, 1986). Deaf identity has been explored in terms of a disability framework, a social identity framework, as an acculturation model, and as a racial identity model. The racial identity model is interesting in that it approaches identity as membership within a minority group and assumes shared experiences of oppression and discrimination from the majority culture. In the case of deaf individuals, the hearing culture is the majority culture. Glickman (1996) developed a model of culturally deaf identities in which he divided identities along a hearing world–deaf world spectrum where the highest level of identity development is a bicultural model. In this model, aspects of both deaf and hearing worlds are valued and appreciated and the deaf individual is comfortable in both worlds. Those who grow up in both environments have a natural head start with this development.

Sadly, growing up in environments that are equally supportive and valuing of the deaf child is a rare and precious thing. Too often, deaf children grow up in one culture—the hearing culture. They are made to feel they need to hide parts of themselves in order to be accepted by the majority (hearing) culture. They live in speech-only environments where conversational access is enormously difficult and often not possible, and this limits their language, cognitive, and social development, in addition to their identity development. This language deprivation has serious consequences (Humphries et al., 2012) to literacy, relationships, and academic and career success. As a result, too many deaf individuals are neither comfortable nor successful in either the deaf or hearing world.

Parents, Teachers, Community, and Deaf Peers in Identity Development

Parents, teachers, and deaf peers all can play important roles in supporting deaf and hard of hearing children and youth and in strengthening their self-concepts and sense of identity. Those of our research participants who felt most supported in their identities as deaf or hard of hearing individuals were considerably more comfortable in their schools, and we learned that parents, teachers, and deaf peers played a large role in this process.

Parents

Parents who knew it was important for their child to have deaf and hard of hearing peers worked hard to make sure frequent opportunities were there, either in the school or at camps and social events. Often this required creative scheduling from school districts, and extraordinary advocacy and parental involvement. This is one participant's story:

> My parents were aware of the fact that it was also important for me to be in a Deaf environment. So, the decision was made to put me at a local public school in [city]. There was another Deaf girl who would also be attending this school in my class. We would have a sign language interpreter and it was only for like one or two classes at the end of the day. So we would be at the Deaf school all day until after lunch and then get on a bus and go for one or two classes at the local elementary school. (M31NE)

Some parents set a strong example for their deaf or hard of hearing child through advocacy, their own values and behaviors, and through open communication. We believe parents are vitally important to the development of their child's healthy identity and self-concept, so we want to give examples of what our participants shared with us about their parents' efforts, in advocacy for their child that demonstrated and transmitted their values, and in communicating with their child.

PARENTS AS ADVOCATES

Many of our participants mentioned the strong lessons in advocacy they learned from watching their parents fight for their educational rights year after year, never giving up. In fact, 16% of the survey respondents mentioned parental advocacy as extremely important shapers of their educational experiences, and the vast majority of our focus group members had involved, supportive families. One woman mentioned how by middle school she was fighting her own battles—for example, telling her interpreters how she wanted them to do their job—because she had learned this at her mother's knee. It was such a huge part of their home life that it was impossible not to absorb these lessons.

Typically, it was the mothers who were most involved in their child's education. They were involved in the day-to-day communication with teachers and parents, attended IEP meetings, and made sure necessary accommodations were in place. Tutors were found, homework help was provided, and the school was kept accountable for meeting their child's needs. Moms also often took over the role of teaching others how to communicate with their child. We are sure there are many mothers of deaf or hard of hearing children who make the painful choice to put their careers on the back burner and use their skills and energy on the home front, to fight for their child. It shouldn't have to be like this. In our eyes, and the eyes of their children, these moms are truly heroes.

Dads were also powerful allies. One young woman who was fighting an uphill battle with her school district to convince them to use CART in her classes made little progress until her dad threatened a lawsuit. After a year of fighting, funding was finally provided for those services, and for the first time she felt like she was "on an equal playing field with hearing peers" in class (although not outside of class). This same woman stated quite strongly that parents who want their children mainstreamed must be dedicated and involved at *all* times in their child's education. She realized she could not possibly have won her fight for CART without her parents' backing.

Our participants felt enormously grateful to their parents, and they were keenly aware of how lucky they were to clearly have had parents in their corner, fighting complicated, time-consuming battles to assure they had the best education possible. Research has proven there is a strong connection between parental involvement and school success (Weiss, Bouffard, Bridgiall, & Gordon, 2009). Our participants recognized that the difference between their own successes and the struggles of some of their peers was deeply tied to parental involvement. Parents were viewed as crucial to their deaf child's success. Schools will not be able or willing to do all they should; therefore, parents must be a visible fighting presence as strong and perpetual advocates. And if they are not able to be, our respondents stated unequivocally, their child will be better off in a school for the deaf.

Education for deaf and hard of hearing children should not be so highly dependent on parents' involvement in the educational process. Not all parents have the education, knowledge, time, confidence, or ability to navigate the American educational system and to successfully go into battle for their child. This is especially true for parents of color, recent immigrants, and those in the lower socioeconomic classes. Without an involved parent in their corner, many deaf and hard of hearing children who are alone in the mainstream have no one to advocate for them, and they suffer greatly for it. There should be a process in place to successfully look out for the best interests of each and every school-aged deaf or hard of hearing child that is not so heavily dependent on a single parent or set of parents.

A common quandary for parents of deaf children is that they are faced with few acceptable educational choices in their local communities. Feeling strongly about wanting their child to live at home, parents often do not consider residential schools. As a result parents sometimes end up doing unbelievably difficult things for their children. One of our participants said his mother drove him back and forth to school, putting in hour-and-a-half drives each way daily. She did this because she knew he needed to be in a school with other deaf children. When his parents started looking at mainstream programs, they worked hard to find a school where there would be at least one other deaf child in the same classroom. In spite of their planning and hard work, their son went through school alone, as the other deaf child soon left the school.

This young man, looking back, recognized the sacrifices his parents made for him and appreciated the home support he received as well (his parents signed, they provided him with tutors, he had closed-captioned TV, etc.). He also recognized that as lonely and unhappy as he was, there was not a lot that could be done. This story is both sad and confirming. We are sure there were painful days for both parents and son, however they were all on the same page and nobody was being fooled into thinking this was a good situation. They openly acknowledged that this was merely the best situation they could currently manage. They had their son home. He was getting a good education. He had a supportive family who signed and was able to provide him with educational enhancements. The one thing that would have made it a better (much better) situation would have been to provide their son with a critical mass of deaf and hard of hearing peers and adults. And this, like so many other families in their situation, they could not do.

A few of our participants had deaf mentors involved with their families, and all were strongly supportive of such. Mentors were seen as a vast source of information and resources. Equally as important, if not more important, they were seen as role models for the deaf child. For parents, they were adult models of what their deaf child would become. Knowing a well-adjusted deaf adult, rather than having superficial knowledge of some stereotypical deaf adult, is enormously important in building hope, realistic expectations for the future, and language competence—all of which support a child's growing sense of self.

COMMUNICATION: DIFFICULT CONVERSATIONS

There can be no doubt that being a successful and happy mainstreamed student takes both considerable work and considerable luck. It also takes considerable communication between child and parents. Regardless of the language and communication used in the family, it is vital that the parent and child have the ability to engage in lengthy and substantive conversations about difficult topics. Our participants told us very clearly that they knew the great sacrifices their parents had made for them and thus tried to be careful not to overburden them with school troubles or to disappoint them by not meeting expectations. Hence, our informants did not always share their troubles with a parent. However, when they did, the best parents were the ones who were able to bear difficult conversations and—together—to find solutions to educational problems.

Our participants stressed the importance of parents being able to discern the words that were *not* said. For example, clearly everything is often *not* fine, even though that's what parents are told. Kids sometimes don't know how to talk about difficult issues and need their parents to guide them. All of which goes to say, when kids do share their mainstreaming issues, parents need to be able to both listen and to brainstorm solutions. For some families of our research participants, the solution to school troubles was to add interpreting services to the IEP. In other cases, a change of schools was needed and sometimes that change was to a school for the deaf. One woman in our study described life after a transfer to the state school for the deaf: "I had more relationships, had challenging classes, had extracurricular activities, had everything that a normal high school kid could have. My self-esteem soared." Another participant and his parents agreed to his skipping his senior year in high school and getting an early college start at the Rochester Institute of Technology, which has a large body of deaf students. This saved him from needing to suffer through another full year of isolation in his public school.

One woman, who gave many great examples of how she had to work double to prove herself, had parents who told her by word and example that it was not a problem to be deaf, but that the world might send her that message and therefore she would have to work harder and differently to get what she wanted in life. While her parents acknowledged the unfairness of this, they allowed no excuses for not doing the extra work. She took that message to heart and it has become a large part of her daily strategy:

> Sometimes that means, making sure I read and study all the rules from the handbook/manual while my peers can randomly learn by eavesdropping conversations. Sometimes that means I must follow up a million times with my class/staff to remind them how Deaf I really am. Sometimes that means accepting how others may think I am a snob or rude since I can't hear their "hellos." Sometimes that means I have to kick my mother under the table to let her know I am not following the group discussion. So many "sometimes that means . . ." but I have accepted it as a part of my life. (F30S)

Teachers

Instead of embracing their deaf identity and their sign languages, many deaf and hard of hearing kids in public schools do everything they can to hide these aspects of themselves, even when it is clear to all that they are not hiding anything. We learned that the difference between feeling a need to hide these deaf aspects of self and being comfortable with being seen unabashedly as deaf, was often in the behavior and attitudes of the parents and teachers.

The participants mentioned frequently that their teachers made a difference in how they felt about themselves and in how they fit into the school social environment. Some teachers were special—they took a personal interest in their deaf students and were not afraid to get to know them. Some teachers were just so much better than others at recognizing the needs of a deaf or hard of hearing child and doing something about it. Some teachers were somehow comfortable and flexible with using different communication strategies. These teachers were the ones who engaged with the deaf child and made the child feel included and valued rather than awkward, dumb, or embarrassed. They were the ones who made ASL (and by default, the deaf or hard of hearing student) seem fun and cool, such as our participant says in this excerpt.

> I used the AM/FM system so much more in the 6th grade. I remembered I avoided using it up until that point. I didn't like how it made me stand out in the classroom and brought attention to me. It's probably also because my sixth grade teacher, Mrs. B., had a ball with it. She loved wearing the mic! Mrs. B. really loved the idea of having a deaf kid in her classroom. She took ASL classes and showed me off to her friends. She wanted to be "besties" with my Mom. Anyway, Mrs. B. really had high expectations of me and told me often that I had potential to do better, grade-wise. Thanks to her, my grades improved so much that year.   (F30W)

Sometimes, our participants told us, the teachers who were most fearless and able to support them were in nonacademic departments such as shop and creative arts. One of our participants had this to say:

> I always signed up for art classes every semester because there was not much talking in the class and art teachers are always the most expressive in the body language. They were comfortable with me. I felt relaxed in the art classes. I may not be the best artist but I love the environment in the art class. I did have secret desires for taking foreign language [classes], advanced history and advanced technology classes but I did not want to deal with an interpreter so art classes were always a best choice for me.   (F25SE)

F30NE's teacher had a wonderful idea. "The one thing that made my transition into the new school much easier was having a small informal meeting with my teacher. My teacher invited a few of the students who would be in my class so we had some interaction time getting to know each other so I wasn't entering my first day blind. I think that really set a good tone for the year, and it ended up that one of the first classmates I met at that first meeting later became an interpreter."

These stories are important because they illustrate clearly what many others also said: Teachers who were not afraid to communicate with their deaf students clearly enabled student–teacher relationships to flourish. Additionally, these teachers became positive models for peers and other adults in the school. Observing an engaging interaction between a hearing teacher and a deaf or hard of hearing student, made it easier for others to try also. Hence relationships between deaf and hearing peers were also much more probable. As we saw in the above stories about the art and shop teachers, direct communication did not always mean speech. What was important was being *comfortable* and *flexible*. Teachers who always communicated with their deaf students through the interpreters, or who made the interpreter their primary relationship rather than the student, were viewed as far less effective teachers.

Respondents who did not have good experiences with teachers often recognized the difference a supportive teacher would have made. We heard such comments as

- "I wanted my teachers to be more knowledgeable, understanding, and open about having a deaf student so I didn't have to feel so much like a freak,"
- "My school had low expectations for deaf students," and
- "Teachers don't get it!"

Research shows that having strong relationships supports school achievement (Putnam, 2000). In general, our participants told us these relationships are *not* happening. Other researchers, who also used focus groups as means of gathering data, also identified teachers as being able to make a difference in the successful school experiences of oral deaf students (Eriks-Brophy et al., 2006). We need to find ways to help general education teachers feel comfortable communicating with the deaf and hard of hearing students in their classrooms. We believe changing teachers' attitudes and behaviors may very well be a key that will open doors for these students in general education settings.

Small Communities

In addition to actively supportive parents and teachers, respondents identified another factor that they perceived as making a positive difference in their self-concept: the size of their community and school. Being from a small town and attending a small school, particularly one that emphasized personal strengths (e.g., a creative arts school) both made the school experience easier. Everyone in the school, and sometimes the entire town, knew the deaf individual, so no awkward explanations of being deaf were necessary. In small classes students got more attention and communication was less stressful. In small communities deaf and hard of hearing children and youth were more able to get their needs met and to have their views of self confirmed by others. Their identity seemed more assured; however, even this did not work perfectly: On leaving for college, individuals found themselves totally unprepared for knowing how to meet new people, and it was often at that point that their identity struggle began. So while they were comfortable in their identities in mainstream K–12 schools, they had significant social and personal challenges in college.

One woman in our focus group illustrated this well. She was a rarity in that she had a solid group of hearing friends whom she had grown up with in her neighborhood. In school they were rarely in the same classes and our respondent, describing herself as a straight-D student, denied her deafness most of the time and felt marginal at best. During her senior year she watched her friends all choose colleges while she herself took a job at a local CVS, feeling college was an impossibility for her due to both grades and finances. It took a couple of years and much nagging from her friends before she had the confidence and determination to change her destiny. She applied to Gallaudet University, was accepted, and became someone to be reckoned with, obtaining a B.A. and doing a semester abroad.

She is currently working toward her master's degree while employed full-time. During those years in college, she says, she did more self-exploration and soul searching than she had ever done before in her life. In the end she was able to stand up to what she knew she wanted to do, rather than giving in to others' concepts of who she was. This woman was African American. Did that contribute to her struggle? Perhaps it did, because deaf students of color have it much harder than others, and their role models and "like-me" deaf peers are much harder to find. This makes the journey toward identity much harder as well.

Deaf Peers

By middle school, nearly all of our participants said they were increasingly lonely and a "school fog" was settling around their shoulders. They described this fog as a feeling of powerlessness and despair. Part of this fog was due to the daily experience of having conversation flow above, below, and around them each day without being a part of it. Part of it was due to the sheer boredom and frustration of being in the position of bystander, watching the same interpreter hour after hour, day after day, being powerless to change much of the situation. Part of it was the inevitability of comparing themselves with hearing peers, feeling increasingly inferior and not measuring up. Our participants said that by middle school, the pain of being the only deaf or hard of hearing kid in the school became unbearable, and they were desperate to find deaf peers.

Researchers have noted this need for middle-school students to find others like themselves. Tatum (1997) studied why African American students sit together in the cafeteria, and her descriptions of racial identity formation strike a familiar chord for those of us in the Deaf community. We can relate to her description of the natural process of craving to be in the company of others like us. Finding others like us helps us to define ourselves and to find a place of belonging. It completes the missing pieces. It makes us feel *whole*.

Hearing peers frequently had little, if any, important influence on our participants' identity development, except in negative ways. Knowing other *deaf* peers, however, made a positive difference to the self-concept and resilience of our participants. Notably, it enhanced their ability to tolerate the loneliness of the school day. Additionally, once self-esteem was supported, deaf and hard of hearing students were in a much better position to be comfortable in their own skin and to embrace their identity, rather than hide it. Our participants learned that the self-confidence that results from feeling good about one's self—embracing who you are, and not trying to be someone different—is a very attractive quality and pulls others in.

Horejes (2012) says this eloquently, describing the process by which he was (finally) able to integrate his identity in both Deaf and hearing worlds.

> I started to embrace sign language as an integral component of my academic instruction, deaf cultural identity, and perception of normalcy. Sign language not only had an emotional and educational impact on me, but also gave me more leverage as a "normal" person. I was no longer struggling to adapt to the hearing society, but rather, by using sign language, I found avenues to enable the hearing society to adapt to me. My confidence soared and sign language became my "special" weapon, as if I were somehow equal in different ways (often personally feeling superior) to those hearing students. I also could feel that they looked at me as uniquely different in a positive way rather than deviant way.   (2012, p. 34)

Many of our respondents mentioned the powerful, life-changing experience of attending deaf camps. That experience is so powerful that we have included a chapter specifically about the rich relationships and personal growth that developed from camps. Deaf camps are among the richest supports of identity development available to deaf and hard of hearing kids today, particularly those who are mainstreamed alone.

The Challenge of Forming a Healthy Identity in Mainstream Environments

Psychosocial mutuality and identity development in general are important to the understanding of the mainstreamed deaf and hard of hearing student. Many of the participants in our research were well aware that they were viewed as "the deaf kid," who was additionally often also viewed as a social reject and an outsider. Our participants said they were variably viewed (depending on person and circumstance) by their peers as "really smart" or "really dumb," and much of that appraisal was based on communication competency. Of course communication competency most often meant speech competency, skills that are notoriously difficult for deaf kids to develop, no matter the effort they put into it. Many deaf children do not produce speech at the same level of competency as their hearing peers, yet that is the personal aspect of themselves that they are most frequently judged on. Self-esteem and confidence take quite a beating.

One of our participants actually begged a good friend of his to tell him what his classmates thought of him. His friend reluctantly told him that because of his speech, he was generally viewed as "a Down's syndrome kid." This statement hurt, but it wasn't as devastating as he expected it to be, because all it really did was confirm what he had always suspected. He already knew he was an outcast. Fortunately for him, his small, semiprivate laboratory school was affiliated with a university teacher-training program and an interpreter training program (ITP); additionally, the university had 50 or so deaf undergraduate students. He started socializing with this group outside of school time. Meeting other deaf students and interpreters-in-training created opportunities for deep relationships, and these relationships carried him through the isolation of his daily school life. These deaf college students and the ITP students were able to support him and *see* him as he truly was.

Looking at this boy's experience using the concept of psychosocial mutuality, what was happening? The view his peers had of him was a terrible mismatch to his own perception of self, but although it hurt, it did not surprise. He was able to dismiss their view of him by accepting that his voice was indeed odd and that these peers did not know him. More important, he was able to find a group of deaf peers (and hearing peers who signed) who confirmed his view of self. His view of self was greatly strengthened and he was able to withstand the negative views of his school peers. Indeed, Musselman, Mootilal, and MacKay (1996) found that when mainstreamed youth had deaf peers they were able to establish satisfactory relationships with both deaf and hearing peers. Having deaf peers seemed to serve as a protective buffer to self-esteem.

Our informants told us that, by and large, hearing peers did not get close enough to know them in anything more than superficial ways and thus they primarily went on first impressions and stereotypes. Deaf and hard of hearing students in mainstream schools are socially stigmatized. Reconciling that mostly negative view held by their peers (and sometimes teachers) with a positive view of self is a real challenge for adolescents, particularly as their self-image is often not so positive either. A lack of deaf role models and peers creates a void in their self-concept that deaf and hard of hearing children do not know how to fill. Their worlds are filled with others who are "not like me," and they are hungry to meet others who are "like me."

The lack of significant relationships with other deaf and hard of hearing adults and peers creates an interesting and unfair dilemma. How is it possible to understand and accept one's self without integrating the deaf or hard of hearing aspect? How can I accept myself if I don't also accept that I am deaf (or hard of hearing)? We don't think it is possible, and we have a lot of support for this belief. Remember all those researchers mentioned previously who studied deaf identity? Irene W. Leigh, a psychologist who is deaf, wrote an entire book on identity as seen through a deaf lens. In speaking of mainstreamed youth, Leigh (2009) says, "The definition of social success becomes that of 'making it' with hearing peers." Our interviews and surveys tell us that identity itself becomes based on "making it" with hearing peers, in both the academic and social environs of school. We learned that comparing one's self to hearing peers rarely results in a positive outcome.

The "Hearing Standard"

One of our focus group members said this very clearly, "I had no positive Deaf role models. I had to compare myself to the hearing standard." All of the members of her group understood this term immediately. She further explained for our benefit that what this meant for her was that she had to constantly work hard to participate in and do well enough in a variety of hearing-based activities such as speech, dance, and music. After years of doing this, as we see from this excerpt, she was both exhausted and lost in terms of identity.

> When I was in the choir (4th grade or 5th grade), I didn't really sing—I "mimicked" the songs. I would memorize the songs, and just mimic them without using my voice. I was in the back row—so that explains it. :) I truly think the music teacher and my mom had good intentions at heart, but it

didn't benefit me, and it just perpetuated the fact that my deafness didn't exist or was locked somewhere in my treasure box never to be discovered. It also perpetuated the idea that I had to work hard to make up for something I "lacked," and that became a theme for the rest of my life. It's funny—now looking back, a lot of my upraising was auditory-based. I took piano lessons, joined the choir, played the saxophone, had a bat mitzvah (had to do an oral reading of the Torah), and played the drums.   (F28W)

Participation in auditory-based activities such as dance, music, drama, and public speaking was so frequently mentioned, in fact, that it became something of a theme with our participants. It seemed as if participation in these activities allowed everyone to deny there was anything at all wrong with their ears. Looking back, our participants wondered why they were so often in activities that required hearing. They concluded that it was as if this proved something about being as close to, or as good as, hearing. These activities required an enormous amount of effort and work on their parts, and opting out of some of these activities sometimes meant an enormous letdown and disappointment for families and for themselves. It posed a conflict for them. They either continued in these activities, which became harder each year, with subsequent loss of self-esteem, or alternatively they quit the activities, resulting in feelings of disappointment and failure.

This is not to say that deaf and hard of hearing students should never be in music, dance, or other auditory-based activities. There *are* some deaf and hard of hearing individuals who love music. For some, these activities were seen as what got them through the day—one survey participant said "I wouldn't be alive today without band. Sometimes it was the only reason to go to school." However such activities need to be chosen by the student and not by others such as parents, and they should be chosen because they are truly enjoyed, and not because of trying to match a hearing ideal the student cannot meet.

Elementary School: Planting the Seeds of Identity Development

Identity development is typically seen as a task of adolescence, but of course the development of self occurs from birth to old age. A deaf or hard of hearing child is confronted with identity issues each step of the way. Most children begin to articulate some of these issues in elementary school. One of our focus group participants, a hard of hearing woman from a deaf family, reported a strong reaction to her first year of school and to meeting her hearing classmates. She pitied them because, unlike her, they could not sign. Even at 6 years old, she defined herself as a "signing person" and felt clearly superior to people who could not sign, even in an environment where she was clearly in the minority.

Although most young children may lack this clarity of self (e.g., a strong and clear concept of who they are), they don't overly concern themselves with what other children think of them. They are simply content to be themselves. If only this clarity could last throughout one's entire educational journey! What we have learned is that whereas elementary school was generally a positive experience for many of our informants, some deaf and hard of hearing children experienced considerable confusion during these years. One of our participants said that one of her most profound experiences from early elementary school was the day she realized she would "grow up and still be deaf." She had an "aha!" moment the day an older man who often visited the school to share stories with the children showed up wearing a "huge monster of a" hearing aid.

Another participant, also hard of hearing with deaf parents, was placed in a classroom with hearing children while other deaf children were in a self-contained classroom in the same school. She remembers clearly her confusion and her envy that they had each other and she was "all alone." She appreciates having her deaf family, but insists her school day was as much alone as any other deaf student in the mainstream. She and several of the other research participants who had deaf families somehow kept their school and family lives very separate and were not able to merge these disparate identities into a cohesive whole until they were much older. This same woman shared how on a school field trip to Washington, D.C., she was embarrassingly "outed" by a random encounter with a deaf man who recognized her and started a sign conversation. Suddenly her classmates saw her in a completely different light. This random encounter somehow became a trigger for more successful integration of her dual identities (hearing at school and deaf at home). Serendipitously, her classmates were seeing a part of her that she had long kept hidden, and she found, after her initial surprise and embarrassment, that she (and they) were quite okay with it. In fact, she experienced it as a relief.

Middle School and High School Identity Challenges

Our focus group participants overwhelmingly reported feeling lost, left out, frustrated, and sometimes depressed by the time they reached middle school. Middle school is a hard time for many children, but our focus group participants described this period of schooling as overwhelmingly difficult and as the "beginning of the end" of a positive school experience. School was no longer a friendly or even safe place to be. In middle school, they suddenly had to explain themselves to a multitude of strangers and few found much acceptance. Additionally, our participants had increased awareness of self and others, which was often painful.

Middle school marks the time when children notice and care more about being "different" and not fitting in. For deaf and hard of hearing children, the conversational barriers become almost insurmountable because friendships and socialization increasingly occur in group settings rather than in play dates of one or two friends, where conversation is more easily accomplished. Again and again, our participants shared stories of dramatically increased isolation and exclusion, such as this: "In spite of my speech skill, I had a relatively normal social life until I was in seventh grade and moved to middle school. That's when everything changed. Cliques were formed and I was left out. They weren't interested in sign language or trying to communicate with me in sign language" (F29C). Participating in extracurricular activities and being smart seemed to help very little, as another informant shared:

> I went on to middle school desperate to be popular, pretty, and have a lot of friends. I was the only deaf student in a student body of about 800. Most of them knew me as "that deaf girl with the interpreter lady." I played soccer, basketball, and track. While I was on those teams, the girls were really nice and friendly with me, but after the season ended, they would barely acknowledge me in the halls (or they would ask to borrow some lunch money!). . . . By 8th grade I would spend my free periods holed up in the

library reading and eating my lunch in the bathroom or the nurse's office. I hated sitting alone because EVERYBODY knew why I was sitting alone. For group projects, either they wouldn't like being paired up with "the deaf girl and her interpreter" OR they knew I was smart/paid attention and knew I would get a good grade in our project, resulting in me doing a lot/most of the work.   (F30NW)

These vignettes illustrate the difficulties deaf and hard of hearing pre-teens and teens face in school on a daily basis. There was a clear line between social acceptance in elementary school and middle school that our focus group members, in spite of their intelligence, determination, and involved parents, simply could not cross. Instead, they became increasingly isolated and cut off from the daily social milieu, which is, as we know, actually the essence of middle and high school.

Amazingly, being involved in sports and extracurricular activities helped very little, and this is something many adults involved with deaf and hard of hearing youth do not realize. Often when researchers study deaf and hard of hearing students, the number of extracurricular activities one is involved in is said to measure the quality of their school experience and success in the mainstream. Students with more activities are viewed as more successful and happy. Our focus group participants say this is not so.

It is initially satisfying to make the varsity team or to participate in band, and it definitely fills up what would be many lonely hours, but there is a distinct downside. Our focus group members talked about the loneliness of being part of such activities while still being excluded. The rides on the bus provoked particularly poignant memories. Being *in a group*, but not *part of a group* was especially painful for many. In the years looking back, many of them even ask if they were allowed to join clubs or teams not because of their qualifications, but to "give the deaf kid a chance." Being a token, whether it is for real or not, sits badly on one's shoulders. Our participants shared with us that it often felt better to decline to be on a team, rather than to participate in the off-the-field milieu as bystanders.

Of course there were exceptions. A few individuals lived for the game and told us they did not care that they were missing out on social chat and friendships. These individuals were true athletes, dedicated to the game, and generally had the respect of their teammates (note the word *respect*, not necessarily comradeship) and supportive coaches. And for some reason, these individuals apparently had less of a need for social connections, perhaps because they had these needs met elsewhere, or perhaps because of character differences. However all of these individuals also acknowledged that if they had been able to participate in conversations, their experiences in team sports would have been significantly enhanced.

Many of our focus group participants mentioned being aware by middle school that their childhood friends were having issues of their own. The elementary friendships were often still there but they were relegated to occasional arrangements outside of the school environment. Our participants ruefully recognized and accepted their friends' struggles to fit in, to make new friends, and to "be cool." Clearly, having a deaf friend in the middle school and high school environments was not cool.

During middle school, identity issues began to surface for our focus group participants. It did not matter if their families were deaf or hearing. They all seemed to struggle with feeling confident and proud of whom they were as deaf or hard of hearing individuals and more often than not, they wanted to hide this aspect of their identity while at school. Our focus group members were variously skilled at this subterfuge, and much of that depended on their level of hearing. Hard of hearing students were more successful than profoundly deaf students; however, that is not to say the latter did not try to conceal their difference. One informant explained her feelings in this way:

> As I made my way through middle school/junior high school, the boys started to pick on me because my voice didn't sound like the others. I remember feeling so awkward and not knowing my place as I started to feel different from everyone else. I was always the last to be picked for any sport activities. I started to feel ashamed of my deafness—I wanted to be like everyone else—I would refuse to wear my hair in a ponytail for the fear that people would notice my hearing aids. (F34SE)

Another informant found both social life and the classroom intolerable. As coping strategies failed and loneliness increased, he resorted to distractions and fantasy. In the 1960s, Linda used to spend her days in school writing reams of nonsense in notebooks, counting the minutes till the day was done. It seems not much has changed in the years between. These are our informant's words:

> Life became difficult the first day of entering 7th grade when I was mainstreamed. I was the only Deaf person and I never knew how to deal with that. I tried hard to fit in. I begged my mom to buy me these expensive clothes that everyone was wearing. I joined chess but later learned that was a geek club. I cracked jokes whenever I saw an appropriate place to do so. I realized nothing could change the ignorance of my classmates overnight. I started eating more, sleeping in class more because it was boring as hell to watch the same interpreter all day long, and I most of all I started to have a new friend that was not a human being.
>
> My new friend eventually became my best friend and got me through each day throughout my years in the mainstream. Most times I felt my best friend was too slow but still managed to help me get through the day by counting the minutes before I could go home. My best friend was the clock in each class[room].   (M34C)

Closing Notes on Identity

In closing this chapter, we want to briefly discuss two other groups of deaf and hard of hearing youngsters who don't so easily fit into the descriptions of those described in the previous pages. The first group consists of those students who attend schools for the deaf. Identity and self-concept issues surface there too, and we don't want to leave the reader thinking all is rosy for students who attend those schools. For example, one of our focus group members who has taught ASL to deaf students shared this perspective:

> A lot of my students at the Deaf school categorize "mainstreamed students" as "smart." . . . I recall asking my ASL class (all Deaf students) last year to raise their hands if they thought of themselves as smart. None of them did but instead pointed at the mainstreamed students or the students with excellent English skills. It shows clearly how our obsession with trying to fit into the "hearing mold" defines how successful you will be in life—no matter how deeply they can discuss politics or the way the world works in ASL, good English determines if you're smart. This saddens me—it's evidence that

Deaf education and our attitudes/perspective on how Deaf children should be educated are terribly flawed—and those attitudes are influencing the self-fulfilling prophecy that Deaf students have with their ability to succeed academically. (F28SE)

An interesting point of our respondent's writing is how she identifies the hearing standard (which she calls the hearing "mold") as being an issue not only for mainstream students, but for all deaf students (and, we add, deaf people of all ages). Even though being deaf is a core aspect of the identity of most deaf children at residential schools, and one most will tell you they feel proud of, they are still undeniably saying those who have good English skills (and speech skills) are smarter. We need to erase this misconception, which has the power of a stigma. Development of English skills has nothing to do with intelligence; rather, it has to do with having a solid foundation of a language model at a developing age, and that language does not have to be English. It could be anything—Senegalese, Chinese, or, yes, even ASL.

On the opposite end of the spectrum from those attending schools for the deaf are those deaf individuals who never find other deaf people. They never found others "like me" and are often not fully a part of a community. We looked at our survey respondents to find individuals who had not found deaf friends to learn more about that path. One of the survey respondents shared that he wished that his school had provided some sign classes in addition to the speech lessons he had, feeling it would have made a huge difference to his life today. He says, "Today I am a deaf person who is culturally hearing and I feel more alone now than I did as a child! Lip reading gets harder with age and signing ability is nearly nonexistent. I feel I have no communication methods with the deaf or hearing world." Other respondents echoed that sobering message.

Our research participants have given us several important messages for building and maintaining a strong identity. We close this chapter by repeating the two strongest ones. The most powerful message was the need to find others like themselves. The importance of getting to meet and know other deaf and hard of hearing peers and adults was crucial and contributed to a sense of wholeness. Not only did finding others "like me" confirm their sense of being okay and stem some of the loneliness, but it also had such a positive effect on their self-esteem that it also paved the way to improved friendships with hearing peers.

A second strong message was that parents have a strong role in the identity process of their child. Parents need to be strong advocates in the educational process, making sure not only that academics are accessible, but also that access to extracurricular activities, clubs, and sports is there. Excelling in one area, not matter what that area is, is a strong boost to identity; however these activities cannot be based on some hearing ideal of the parents. Additionally, parents need to be able to bear difficult conversations with their sons and daughters. Attending school as a solitary deaf or hard of hearing student will inevitably be painful at times, and needing to hide and cover up this pain makes it much worse. Acting *as if* everything is okay is never good for self-esteem and identity. Therefore parents must be able to bear this pain with the child and try to find their way toward solutions. Almost equally important is having parents meet deaf and hard of hearing people, so that they have a concrete concept of what a deaf adult can be, and thus they can become less anxious and more confident about their child's future.

4

K–12 Interpreters and
Other Placement Issues

"Mainstreamed students, current or former, are grossly misinterpreted
(pun unintended)."   (Survey respondent)

WITH the implementation of the Education for all Handicapped Children law (P.L. 94-142) in 1975, a new position
was created: that of educational interpreter. Students with
disabilities—including deaf and hard of hearing students—
were to be educated in the "least restrictive environment
(LRE)" and provided with a "free and appropriate education (FAPE)." Appropriate supports and accommodations
for learning meant that deaf students needed to be provided
with interpreters within their classrooms and/or the services
of a teacher of the deaf, and/or a speech therapist, if it was
so stipulated in their individualized educational programs
(IEPs). Since 1975, federal policies, state policies, school districts, teachers, parents, and educational interpreters have been
trying (in various degrees) to "get it right" so that deaf and
hard of hearing students actually are benefitting from inclusive
education. We have a long way to go!

Over time, scholars in the area of deaf education came to
refer to an education provided through the services of a sign
language interpreter as an "interpreted education" and later as
a "mediated education." A *mediated education*—as opposed
to education that is received directly—refers to instruction

that was received secondhand, through a sign language, oral, or cued speech interpreter. It also can refer to instruction received through text such as CART, C-print, or Typewell. These practices, as well as the practice of *pull-out*—removing students from their regular classroom to work with audiologists, speech therapists, teachers of the deaf, or other specialists—all emerged after the passage of IDEA.[2]

In Chapter 5, we discuss current issues related to how mediated education has evolved in practice and share stories from teachers of the deaf and K–12 interpreters who serve deaf and hard of hearing students in our nation's public schools. We also share the relevant contributions of our research participants. The stories of their mediated educations will illuminate how often the policies and practices are resulting in positive outcomes for children (rarely) and where they are failing (much too often). It is only with this knowledge that we can create positive changes for the future.

As part of this discussion about mediated education, we also need to say very clearly that little is actually known about how deaf children learn. We know that young deaf children do not get adequate exposure to language (any language) during the critical language period prior to age 5 and thus enter school linguistically deprived (Humphries et al., 2012). They are then faced with the challenge of learning language, academic content and skills, and social skills, all at the same time. We know that a multitude of factors makes visual learning in general education classrooms difficult (much of this is detailed in Ramsey, 1997), and we know that literacy for deaf and hard of hearing children remains far from the ideal, stubbornly staying at the third and fourth grade level for an 18-year-old (Marschark, 2007; Morere, 2011).

Experience with Interpreters

Interpreters who work in public schools have been called both *educational interpreters* and *classroom interpreters*. However our review of recent research and publications has shown that these two terms also refer to interpreting

---

2. The Individuals with Disabilities Education Act was revised in 2004 and is now entitled the Individuals with Disabilities Education Improvement Act (IDEIA), but it is still commonly known as IDEA so we use that term.

in postsecondary settings. To distinguish these very different categories, we choose the term *K–12 interpreters*. In planning this book, we sensed that K–12 interpreters and the services they provide would be a strong theme. In fact one of the reasons we wanted to write this book was to see how well students were faring with this mediated education, a component that was almost completely missing for participants in Oliva's first study who were in school between the years of 1976 and 1995, even though P.L. 94-142 was passed in 1975. In Oliva's study, only five out of 60 of the participants ever had the services of an interpreter (Oliva, 2004). In our current study, 62% of our focus group participants and 36% of our survey respondents used an interpreter at least for part of their K–12 years. It is important to note, however, that the participants and/or their parents sometimes fought for years with their school districts to obtain interpreting services, and often it was not until the later high school years that they won these battles. Nevertheless, approximately 20% of our survey respondents said that it was their interpreter who got them through the day and "saved them."

Parents and students spent considerable time and energy fighting for their rights to have K–12 interpreters (or in some cases, for transcription services). While waiting for their requests and appeals to the schools to be heard, students mostly did without; a lucky few had their moms step into the interpreting role or families paid out of pocket for interpreting services. Obviously this was not a good situation for either the students or their families; it created enormous stress. One of our participants told a poignant story of reaching her limit in the middle of her fifth-grade school day and running home crying tears of frustration. Once there, she picked up the phone and dialed her mom's work number.

> I didn't understand sounds on the phone but when I heard her voice . . . I wailed, "Mommm . . . please come hoommeee." Ten minutes later, mom arrived home with a terrified look on her face because I sounded like I was badly harmed and I told her how much I hated school. With relief that it wasn't physical harm, my mother decided that I needed an interpreter and she set out to look for one. (F28SE)

This is one mother who solved her daughter's heartache by finding an educational interpreter for her daughter herself, and paying for it out of pocket. This was in 1994, and today it may be rare for a parent to have to do this, but as we learned from our research, it still happens. Today there are still many problems with K–12 interpreting, as will become evident in this chapter and the one that follows.

One of our participants commented that "the invention of interpreters was one of the best things to ever happen for deaf people," but at the same time, getting a mediated education through interpreters or note takers "is a bad way to go." To be clear, she was talking about K–12 schooling, not postsecondary education. Widespread interpreting services opened many doors for deaf people, including access to postsecondary programs, and many of us are deeply grateful for those higher education opportunities. But again, interpreting in K–12 settings poses vastly different and troubling issues. Deaf adults who use interpreting services are nothing like deaf children who use interpreting services. Many of our respondents shared issues they had with interpreters in the elementary and secondary school years. Not all of our participants had interpreters, or it would have been the most frequently mentioned issue.

Many of our respondents voiced opinions on issues that we ourselves were concerned about. They had conflicted feelings about the fact that their closest friend in school (e.g., the constantly present interpreter) was an adult. They recognized that an adult is privy to far more information and power than students, because of age, role, and, of course, hearing status, and that this has the potential to create problems. Given this power differential between the deaf or hard of hearing student and the interpreter, it did not surprise us that our respondents characterized interpreters as either saviors or enemies, or sometimes both. In fact, their stories reminded us of Longfellow's poem—"when she was good, she was very good indeed, but when she was bad she was horrid."

My Interpreter: My Friend and Savior

Most commonly we heard that "my interpreter was my best friend" or that the interpreter "made school tolerable." Interpreters gave advice, were motherly, "protected me," and "comforted me." Good K–12 interpreters helped children to believe in and have confidence in themselves. They opened doors to communication and sometimes to relationships between student and coach or student and teacher. However, the friendships most often nourished were between interpreter and deaf student. Several respondents said they were still in touch with their interpreters in their current lives. The following two excerpts illustrate that close friendship between interpreter and student.

> During my years from 6th grade to 12th I had two permanent interpreters, one from 6th to 8th and the second from 9th to 12th. I was close with the interpreters due to the communication barrier with everyone else. I chatted with the interpreters often during the down time in class or after school while waiting for sports practices to start as well as during practice if I was not busy. As the only deaf student, fully accessible conversations were limited to those I had with my interpreter. I thought of my interpreters as more of an older adult friend. (F30NE)

There is a human need to connect. Surely if the only person available who uses the same language as the deaf child is the K–12 interpreter, the interpreter will be a primary connection. In these next quotes we can see clearly this need to connect as the students cherish their friendships with their interpreters.

> I often finished my assignments quickly so while everybody else was focused, I would chat with my interpreters—they were often very funny and always had good stories to share. I really looked at interpreters as my friends, perhaps more so than my classmates. (F30NW)

> I had interpreters. Really, they became my closest friends. They understood me and went above and beyond the line of duty in their advocacy and protection of my rights. They were generally older and stronger, more capable of flexing influence than I was when a teacher or a student was being difficult. (Survey participant)

One of our survey respondents mentioned appreciation of her interpreters as both friend and advocate:

> I had a very excellent interpreter in high school that was more like a mother to me—even though she behaved properly as an interpreter, she was still there for me if I wanted to talk.

Well, interpreters are the ones that got me through the day. I always had at least one favorite interpreter and talked to her all the time during the day.

K–12 interpreters were often major influences in our participants' lives. Their roles often veered from the act of interpreting, as they became tutors, assistant teachers, and therapists, as well as friends. The following excerpt sharply illustrates the richness of the interpreter/student relationship.

When I think of my experiences being alone in the mainstream, I think of my interpreter. She, helped me tremendously! I am amazed at how she put up with me because I know I frustrated her a lot. I frustrated my parents because I was a BRAT! But to my teachers I was a sweet and cooperative child. Yes, I was a brat to my interpreter too. I became close with her and we were together almost 8 hours a day, so we became comfortable with each other, making jokes, making fun of what people say or do. She tutored me in reading and writing, as well as other subjects that I struggled with, MATH— ugh. She got me interested in reading R. L. Stine's thriller/mystery/horror youth book series like Goosebumps, and then I "graduated" to his young adult series. I'm thankful because I HATED to read, but she explained that most people find authors that they like and then read their books because it's easy to read when you are interested in their writings/work.   (F29NE)

Here we see the K–12 interpreter playing three different roles in the child's life: friend, teacher, and mentor/parent. The relationship between the interpreter and the deaf student was clearly a friendship. We see them joking and laughing together, sometimes at the expense of other children in the classroom. In her story, there was an us-versus-them feeling to the relationship—interpreter and deaf child being on one side while the hearing children and possibly the teacher were on the other side. The deaf child had a friend who, as she said, was there 8 hours a day and she was comfortable with, and while this fed some important socialization needs, we have to wonder if this was the kind of friendship we would ideally want for our children. And furthermore, did this friendship possibly close off more appropriate peer-to-peer friendships for the student? We are not sure. Given what we know about the dearth of peer friendships our respondents had, it is highly likely this deaf child would have been friendless without the interpreter filling this role. Even so, it seems to be an important question to ask.

In the previous excerpt, we also see the interpreter's role as a teacher. It seems she was not simply "mediating" education, but rather actively tutoring and very likely teaching. It was the interpreter who got this reluctant reader hooked on reading, and we can imagine the kinds of rich conversations the interpreter and student had about books. She also tutored in reading, writing, and math. What we do not learn is where the teachers were in all of this. Were the teachers even aware of the kinds of educational influences the interpreter was imparting? Did the educational interpreter and teacher talk and possibly plan together for maximum educational impact? Were they using a team teaching concept? The interpreter in this particular example actually had dual certification as an interpreter and as a teacher, according to our respondent, so we are hopeful this kind of collaboration happened, however it is likely that it did not, as we know how very little time teachers have in their day to give to this kind of teaming.

We also see this interpreter equated in the child's mind to a parent. Our focus group member reported that she felt free to be herself, both sweetness and prickles, with both her parents and her interpreter, whereas her teachers rarely, if ever, got to see this full aspect of her. It also seems safe to say that the interpreter took on a parental role in shaping her young charge's path, for example, steering her to a certain kind of novel. There was so much going on in this particular K–12 interpreter–deaf student relationship! It should not be surprising to learn that this friendship is one that has endured to today and that our participant credits her interpreter with making her solitary mainstream experience bearable.

When we asked our participants about their interpreters, some of them felt luckier than others. Some shared that their interpreters were CODAs or married to deaf individuals, and these interpreters would introduce them to deaf family members and to the Deaf community, making them feel truly fortunate. Some of our respondents felt their interpreters had put their jobs at risk by sharing their knowledge of ASL and the Deaf community. These interpreters gave their young clients a window into a different, richer world. They offered unexpected—and much appreciated—benefits to their deaf or hard of hearing charges. These benefits were far outside what parents, teachers, administrators, or policy makers probably expected or perceived or would have allowed or supported if they had known. The impact of CODA interpreters was significant, as one survey respondent illustrates:

> My interpreter was [a] CODA. Her Deaf parents came from another city and visited us sometimes, and they supported and encouraged me to finish school then explore the Deaf community. I took their words [and] now I'm currently a college student and learning a lot about Deaf education. I wish my school had provided better accommodation and services for me.
>
> (Survey respondent)

Sometimes students who had oral or cued speech interpreters inadvertently discovered that their interpreters also knew ASL. Two of our male participants independently described how their interpreters, sensing their depression and frustration with the oral interpreting process, offered to sign. At first resistant, slowly these students came around. After all, they reported, they were feeling so desperately lost and bored that adding signing to the lesson could surely not make things much worse. The sign interpreting, once accepted, brought mind-altering experiences. Both men said that watching lessons interpreted in sign was easy (particularly compared to lipreading) and they found themselves less stressed and actually learning.

For these students, accepting sign language was the beginning of accepting their own identity as deaf individuals. Hence the process of accepting these interpreters in the classroom became hugely important to their identity and self-esteem. They found that sign language did not narrow their worlds, as they had been so often told it would, but rather it broadened and enriched their worlds.

This example cannot be fully understood without the knowledge that both of these students actually had some fluency in ASL and used it with their families and/or with deaf friends outside of the school. However, their IEP specified oral or cued-speech interpreters. In the school setting, these students defined themselves as oral students, and it took a major paradigm shift for them to allow themselves the privilege of signing. A few other respondents in our study described similar experiences. For example, one deaf and one hard of hearing participant, each with deaf parents, described completely compartmentalizing their lives; at home they were deaf signers and at school they never signed or even thought to sign, regardless of how much they sometimes struggled in the classroom.

Research on bilingual language development probably holds the answers to why such separation of two languages happens. Bilingualism does not mean equal fluency in each language at the same time, so it is normal for children to sometimes use one language for home and another for school (Mitchener, 2012). Having role models for each language in both home and school settings makes a difference in being able to develop greater fluency in each setting.

My Interpreter: My Nemesis

In a later chapter, we will discuss the dire need for more and better interpreter training for K–12 settings, and our respondents' narratives bear this out. In particular, our participants were unanimous in noticing (and feeling greatly frustrated by) their K–12 interpreters' great weaknesses with sign-to-spoken-English interpreting. The participants recalled numerous frustrating and embarrassing moments when they were called on, or raised their hands to give answers, or perhaps made a classroom presentation and their interpreters could not understand their signs well enough to accurately communicate their ideas to the class. As a result, many said they quickly learned to not trust their interpreters to interpret their signing correctly and thus became quiet students, rarely participating in class. If they had to respond to a question, they kept their answers brief and easily interpreted. Our respondents learned from experience that they would have been fools to have trusted their interpreters to represent their ideas correctly. This was said even about the "good" interpreters. In a classroom in which correct, intelligent, well-thought-out answers are everything (grades, respect, liking, image), this is a strong statement about the interpreters' need for more and specific training.

The issue of poor-quality interpreting is complicated and affects everyone in the classroom. We were told that when interpreters interpreted incompetently, deaf students looked stupid in others' eyes, leaving the students feeling frustrated, unheard, and helpless to change the situation. Our participants said it forced them, even with interpreters present, to become passive participants rather than full participants in the learning process. This illustrates quite clearly the lack of full access students had, even with interpreters present. Research confirms that social acceptance can be predicted by classroom participation because it influences and shapes both teacher and peer attitudes (Antia et al., 2011).

Additionally, the focus group participants noted that teachers mostly had no understanding of how hard it was for deaf students to participate in classroom discussions, assuming incorrectly that the interpreter equalized this process. Our participants told us that their teachers often misunderstood their lack of involvement. They said their teachers thought they did not know the answers or were unprepared for class, disinterested, or shy. Further, and additionally disheartening, they were so often quiet, nonparticipating students that they were unknown to their classmates. And finally, some of the interpreters our participants remembered were defensive about their skills and rarely admitted to making any mistakes. It was the deaf student who looked dumb and who lost the most in this process.

Again and again, our participants told stories of teachers who had no idea how to work with deaf and hard of hearing students and as a result made serious mistakes. However, teachers who truly got to know their students and embraced the challenge of accommodating learning needs made a huge difference in the lives of our focus group members. They fondly remembered the rare teachers who learned signs and/or who "saw" them. Our participants want teachers to have open minds and hearts. They believe that with training, there will be more such teachers, and that the failures they experienced were largely because their teachers simply did not know what to do so they relied on interpreters to do their jobs.

In addition to many K–12 interpreters' profound lack of skill in sign to English interpreting, we were told that these interpreters often did not have the skills necessary to interpret academic content. A story told by one of our focus group participants illustrates this. The class was learning time concepts and the teacher wanted students to understand what "quarter to" meant on the clock—for example, "it's a quarter to three." The interpreter signed "quarter" using the sign for a coin, a quarter, a 25-cent piece. This is an incorrect sign for the time concept, and it thus completely threw off the student's comprehension. As a fourth grader, our participant knew the sign the interpreter was using was related to money and she recalled asking again and again, "What do you mean?" and saying, "That doesn't make sense." The teacher became frustrated with the student and rather than trying to understand the child's confusion with the concept, the teacher ordered her to go off to the side of the room to have her interpreter explain the concept. At no time did the interpreter speak up and say, "It was my mistake," even though by this time in the lesson, our respondent felt it was quite clear that the interpreter was aware of her error.

Whereas the first part of this story speaks to lack of skills, the second part speaks to lack of professionalism. Our participant recalls this situation as one of many where she felt stupid and useless at school, and many of her focus group peers said that this was a common experience for them as well. They felt that they needed more protection from the adults in their school lives at that time, because they were frequently misunderstood and, as children and teens, they lacked the skills to advocate for themselves.

In addition to being incompetent, some K–12 interpreters were perceived as mean, bad tempered, having poor boundaries, or on a power trip. These were the interpreters our participants labeled "horrific." One participant, who at age 6 or 7 constantly struggled with understanding what he was supposed to do at any given classroom moment, told of frequently being yelled at, first by his teacher and then by his interpreter. Not surprisingly, he ended up hating school. Another participant told a story of an interpreter who also taught in an ITP and brought her students in to "practice" in the classroom. Examples of a misuse of power in the interpreting role are too often evident.

Our informants remembered simple actions reflecting a clear lack of professionalism. One story shared was of an interpreter who was going through a divorce and would arrive late and use each break to talk on her phone about her many problems. The interpreter's behavior was a clear memory for our respondent, one that colored her entire school year, made her feel she was getting second-rate services, and left her feeling more isolated than ever.

Another participant described sixth and seventh grade as "hell," due to a hot-tempered "dictator of an interpreter." "She would yell at me for being sleepy in the class, asked me about my grade on tests or quizzes and punished other students when teachers left her in charge of the class. She made other students hate me for being in their classes." Then to top this all off, the interpreter became the teacher's best friend. Feeling totally stuck, this participant described that year as the loneliest and most depressed of her life. We heard other stories of interpreters who took it upon themselves to criticize and scold both their student and other students in the classroom. We were told that students had classmates avoid them so as not to deal with their interpreters and that the interpreter's actions reflected badly on them.

Another issue expressed by our informants concerns K–12 interpreters being the sole language model for young deaf students. If the interpreter is the only other person in the school who is using sign language (which is often the case), the children they serve are exposed to only one language model. All conversation is communicated through this one individual rather than coming from myriad sources: teachers, aides, classmates, movies, even the public address system. The general feeling of our focus group members is that this is a very poor and inappropriate model. Not only do our participants' stories tell us that many K–12 interpreters are frequently not highly skilled, research shows that in addition to adults, children need other children as language models (Humphries et al., 2012).

When educated as the only deaf child in a mainstream school, with few or no outside school supports in place (such as family contact with signing community members and deaf friendships), a deaf or hard of hearing child is not exposed to the rich language models needed in order to sufficiently develop either language or reasoning skills. Many deaf and hard of hearing children, including those with cochlear implants, are still struggling with learning language during the school years, having minimal language competence in either English or ASL (Humphries et al., 2012; Morere, 2011). They are in a terrifically challenging position to learn anything.

Administering and Managing the School Day

As we listened to the experiences shared in the focus groups, we felt that what was frequently being described was a clear lack of appropriate oversight and management of interpreting services within the school. Most often the person responsible for such management seemed to know little about deaf students and their language and communication needs or about educational interpreters and their skills and their job. Neither student nor interpreter had sufficient advocates within the school, and thus both felt extremely isolated. This isolation and helplessness are illustrated in the following stories.

Some of what our participants reported was illustrative of a school system or particular teachers taking advantage of having an extra adult body in the schools. One informant's experience at her school was particularly stark. She reported that teachers often used her educational interpreters as personal assistants—they would do things such as grade papers, get the movie projector out, do prep work for projects, and be asked to keep an eye on the class if teachers needed to step outside the room. Of course, while the interpreters were performing these random tasks, their responsibility to interpret fell by the wayside.

Another issue, experienced by the same respondent, had even worse consequences for her. When any of the school team of three interpreters was indisposed, she, as the "smart one" of the group of deaf students in the school, was generally left without, as the interpreters would consider her needs to be less significant. They told her she would get by and the other deaf students needed the interpreter more than she did.

Other respondents said absent interpreters were a common problem and one that was rarely addressed appropriately. Many of these issues were administrative ones, and it became clear that those responsible for overseeing the school's interpreting services often did so inadequately, possibly having little understanding of the needs of deaf and hard of hearing students. We learned that when interpreters were absent, teachers often asked classmates who could sign or fingerspell to interpret. This was not a 5-minute kind of chore, but an all-day task, which was totally unfair to both hearing and deaf students. One of our survey respondents said friends interpreted for him for a full year! We are left wondering if the school district was even trying to find an interpreter. We also wonder what the parents of these students knew and thought and how they could have left this situation continue so long. A full year!

Surely other possibilities existed. Teacher aides, for example, could have pitched in and taken notes. It sets up a completely inaccessible school day when there is no good system in place for days interpreters are unavailable. We feel strongly the burden for this should fall on adult shoulders and not on children, who really have no choice in the matter. They must do as they are told.

In addition to telling us stories about absent interpreters, many of our respondents said they did not have sufficient interpreting services. Sometimes they had none. Sometimes interpreters were not provided for the entire school day, but rather for only a partial day. The students were aware that they needed interpreters for social conversations, even as they felt awkward in having interpreters at these times. The broad message from our research participants was that they lacked full access in their school day—they needed much more than was provided.

Another issue our participants discussed was the practice of placing the same interpreter with a student for a period of years. Regardless of the abilities or personality of a particular interpreter, having someone shadow you all day is tough. Having the same person be your shadow for years on end (our respondents said 10 years is not uncommon) is stifling! In general, our participants felt this was a poor practice. As part of the natural course of development, we try on different roles and identities, particularly during adolescence. This personal exploration becomes close to impossible when you have an adult shadow that has known you since you were a cute little first grader. We had respondents tell us they were very well behaved in school because if they misbehaved, their interpreter would know it and then their parents likely would too. Misbehaving lost its attraction quickly.

Protecting Deaf and Hard of Hearing Students

The K–12 interpreters our informants remembered sometimes lacked both basic professionalism and skills in interpreting. Adults who work with children need to be more careful, not less careful; our informants remembered even simple actions that reflected a clear lack of professionalism.

Most students share the experience of having a truly horrid teacher. Having a horrid interpreter is different in several important ways. When there is a mean teacher, there is a high likelihood that every student in the class knows and suffers, and they band together to survive that class. The teacher's meanness is known by all. In contrast, an interpreter can be mean and unjust right out in the open and nobody truly knows it (although they may sense it), except the deaf student. Moreover, this deaf student often has nobody to report to within the school and no voice with which to report it—her interpreter is her voice. The best she can do is complain to her parents, who may or may not be able to do anything to help.

This is not to imply that all or even most interpreters are "horrid"; there are bad apples in every profession. However, school systems must be aware of the possibility and prepare. Deaf and hard of hearing students are vulnerable to many kinds of mistreatment and/or incompetence. Schools must be watchdogs and protectors. There is rarely anyone in the school who is knowledgeable about the sign language interpreter's role or skill level, which means those who are unethical can do serious damage. (We talk more specifically about this in the following chapter.)

It is critical that there be people and places within the school where deaf and hard of hearing students can go for help without their regular interpreter, or a parent, or a signing peer going along. None of these individuals are appropriate interpreters for highly personal conversations, although they are possibly good advocates. Schools must step up in meeting their responsibilities to their deaf and hard of hearing students so the students are not placed in such vulnerable positions. In this volume's concluding chapter, we offer some recommendations for how schools and parents can create ways to circumvent such happenings and create better, more effective, avenues for deaf and hard of hearing students to get the support they need.

The IEP meeting is a case in point. All the focus group participants (and the authors) strongly agree that the IEP meeting is no place for the classroom interpreter. Instead, the interpreter attending the IEP should be someone who is both certified and completely out of the school district. Otherwise, how could issues possibly be discussed with any frankness and transparency? This is crucial. Input from the classroom interpreter may be important, but it can be shared before the meeting. Moreover, the classroom interpreter also has no business being in the counselor's office. That place, too, must be a safe environment in which to discuss everything and anything, including issues with one's interpreter.

Taking the Interpreter and Interpreting Out of the Middle

Almost all our focus group participants said that while their interpreters bridged communication between them and their peers and teachers, they simultaneously became barriers to direct relationships with their peers and teachers. As we talked so much about in the previous chapters, relationships that should have been present often were not. Teachers too frequently depended on the interpreter for all communication, so their primary relationship was with the interpreter, rather than the student. This lack of relationship between the teacher and deaf student is detrimental to the learning process because it is often the relationship itself that inspires learning. Additionally, if the teacher is not comfortable interacting directly with her deaf student, this discomfort is transmitted to every student in the classroom to quite possibly disastrous effect.

Many of our respondents described their best educational experiences as those in classrooms in which either no interpreter was present or when the need for an interpreter was not great. In fact, this became a common theme for best experiences. For example, one participant loved art classes, because she found her art teachers were the ones who communicated directly with her and truly knew her. Another participant had the same experience to share about his shop classes, where he said both teachers and students somehow loosened up and communicated with him directly. These stories are important to share as they reflect the difference it makes in students' lives when they are seen and known by others. Sadly, these stories also reflect how infrequently this happened.

We can't emphasize enough the harm done when teachers do not establish direct relationships with their deaf and hard of hearing students. Teachers are models of behavior. They must reach out and relate to the deaf and hard of hearing students; such behavior will in turn inspire students to expand their comfort zones and reach out to all members of the classroom community. Hearing and deaf peers inhabit the same classroom, and when they simply ignore each other and do not converse, they miss out on getting to know and benefit from each other. This lack of connection teaches and reinforces the idea that it is okay to ignore someone who is different. This message hurts everyone, deaf and hearing alike. It is not okay to inhabit an environment with others and ignore their very existence. In our increasingly multicultural society, we cannot afford to do that. Teachers hold the key to making their classrooms truly inclusive.

Given the paucity of conversation between deaf students and their teachers and hearing peers, our participants focused their social needs on their interpreters. They recognized and acknowledged, however, that the interpreter is an easy social connection, but not the best social connection. One young woman said she had a "love/hate relationship" with her interpreters. Other informants, using different terminology, described the same conflicting feelings. They deeply appreciated that their interpreter was there and often truly enjoyed their company. At the same time, all recognized there is something inherently wrong with a 12-year-old's deepest school friendship being centered around, for example, a 27-year-old woman. Interpreters are supposed to make connections happen between deaf and hearing people. They are not supposed to *be* the primary connection.

Transcription Services

A few of our research participants had transcription services (such as CART or Typewell) in middle school and high school; however, these were much more commonly mentioned as college-level accommodations. We recently learned that Alternative Communication Services (ACS), a company that provides live text transcript for deaf and hard of hearing professionals attending conferences, provides remote classroom captioning for approximately 400 deaf and hard of hearing students across the United States. When asked how the remote captioner conveys student comments made within the classroom to the student, the reply was "we just put *male student* or *female student*." This technology opens up a whole arena of possibilities for both academic learning and incidental learning.

We are glad to see transcription services being more widely available today than they were for most of our participants. We also wish to emphasize that growing requests in the K–12 arena for transcription services is a whole other area of mediated education that needs research. We need to learn from deaf and hard of hearing students about how well these services are working for them.

The Resource Room

Participants in our study told us about the resource room, one place in the school in which interpreters were generally not needed. A teacher of the deaf (TOD) would staff this room—sometimes this TOD would be at one school full time, and sometimes she was an "itinerant teacher," serving students in more than one school. For many of our participants, contact time with a TOD was part of their IEP. (We talk more about the work of TODs, including itinerant teachers, from a systematic perspective, in Chapter 6.)

We were surprised to learn that the majority of our respondents felt that by middle school, time in the resource room was not helpful academically. They felt that pull-out time (as it was and still is known) actually hurt their academics. We were told it was a "waste of time," and that a large part of the problem was that the resource room concept itself lacked flexibility and individualization (qualities that, ironically, the IEP is supposed to provide).

In our focus groups, the resource room came up as one of those commonly shared and equally loathed experiences, especially in the high school years. Resource rooms seemed to have odd rules and structures. Some participants said all they did in the resource room was homework. Others said they were forbidden to do homework and instead given mindless memorization to do. The worse part of pull-out was that it was required, and our respondents did not see this time as needed or helpful. They would much rather have been in their general education classrooms.

We should interject here that our investigation into the state of affairs with TODs (both full time and itinerant) and the related resource rooms conveys to us that the problem lies not with the teachers but with the system. Where the resource rooms are located, how much time the student has with the TOD (often less than an hour at a time), and other factors clearly complicate this entire situation. (Again, we talk about this in Chapter 6, and much more research is needed.)

However one fascinating—and although initially confusing, ultimately helpful—situation resulted for some students in the resource room. A few of our focus group participants shared that they had attended schools where there were other deaf or hard of hearing students, but whom they saw only in the resource room. Their schools followed the practice of keeping total communication, signing, oral, and cued speech students separate from one another. (This is a clear example of competing philosophies held by both parents and schools that hurt students.) Occasionally it happened that all of these deaf and hard of hearing students (total communication, signing, oral, cued speech) were placed in the same resource room (our informants believed this was connected to budget issues). Although the students were initially wary and distrustful of each other, strong friendship bonds often developed. Our focus group participants think schools are missing an opportunity to structure resource rooms into a helpful resource: a language-rich environment focusing on social interaction, self-advocacy skills, deaf culture, and other student needs. That would be a true resource room.

The IEP Process and Student Support Services

Half of our participants not only were products of mainstream education, but currently are educational professionals themselves. We should thus not be surprised at their lengthy list of ideas for change. They had much to say about many educational aspects, starting with the IEP. As K–12 students, many of them were excluded from the IEP development process and the IEP meetings. As adults, knowing how important IEPs are, they have a list of ideas they wish to share.

Those of our informants who were not excluded from the IEP process experienced the IEP meeting as negative, or even punitive. The IEP is a powerful tool, but only if one knows how to use it, and our informants felt both they and their parents lacked this knowledge. Our informants felt that both students and parents must be educated about the IEP process. Students should be involved in the process—in fact, when they reach age 14, the law requires them to be involved. We believe that in many cases students should plan and lead the meeting, even earlier than age 14, for they are the experts on what works and does not work for them. Additionally, students who plan and lead their IEP meetings benefit tremendously, learning self-advocacy, self-determination skills, problem solving, leadership, communication, and social skills as they work with adults in this process (Mitchell, Moening, & Panter, 2009). We believe that, with support, many school-age children are capable of pulling this off.

One of our survey participants was fortunate to have such an experience:

> Nowadays, when I meet other deaf adults that were mainstreamed for most, or all of their lives like I was, we always tend to go down the path discussing education, and compare ours and how they were similar and different growing up. I find that oftentimes, many of the reasons why their mainstream education wasn't as good as mine was due to adults telling them "No, you can't do this" or "You can't do that." I think that was one of the major factors in my education. Another thing I noticed is that I was allowed the freedom to choose my own classes and start going to the ARD meetings [part of the IEP process] at the end of the school years to discuss what I wanted to do for the next school year, and that gave me a greater sense of independence in figuring out what I wanted to do. I think those two factors really helped a lot, and I think they would help other deaf students as well.

As mentioned previously, the focus group participants unanimously insisted—and this is important, which is why it bears repeating—that if an interpreter is used in the IEP meeting it should never be the day-to-day interpreter assigned to be with the student. Instead an interpreter who is unaffiliated with the student should be used, so that it is safe to discuss all and any issues, including interpreter issues.

Student support services are another important part of today's schools, and our informants told us these professionals had typically not met their needs. This is a glaring omission. School counselors are responsible for supporting the academic, personal, social, and career development of all students, including those with disabilities (see www.schoolcounselor.org), yet none of our focus group members reported a significant relationship with a school counselor—at the same time, many felt the need for such a meeting.

We heard stories about the multitude of information our informants wished their school counselor had shared with them. This included in-

formation on summer camps and weekend programs, postsecondary opportunities that included deaf schools and programs, and availability of
vocational rehabilitation services. Our subjects told us that their high school
counselors were notoriously lacking in such information and resources. Students were not aware, for example, of financial opportunities available to
them, because their counselors did not know or share this information; or
they were misled because the information shared was incorrect. For some
of our participants, this missing or incorrect information resulted in serious
delays in their attending college.

It may be unrealistic to expect generalist school counselors, who generally have enormous caseloads, to know information about postsecondary
options and rehabilitation services for deaf students. (The American School
Counselor Association [ASCA] recommends a school counselor to student
ratio of 1:250, but many schools exceed that; Erford, 2007). However, there
is such a great need for generalist school counselors to be aware of the issues deaf and hard of hearing students face in the educational system that
a position paper on "Working with Deaf and Hard of Hearing Students"
was recently placed in front of the ASCA board. (Linda is one of the co-
authors of that document.) Unfortunately, the ASCA board decided not
to include this position paper because they felt the needs of deaf and hard
of hearing students were sufficiently met in the broader position paper on
students with disabilities. We disagree. School counselors who specialize in
services to deaf and hard of hearing students and/or deaf education experts
from outside the school could make a real difference and assure that gaps
in information and services are filled.

School psychologists are another group of professionals who have a major role in education of children with disabilities; however, rarely do school
psychologists have training in evaluating deaf and hard of hearing children.
Children with disabilities are required by law to participate in triennial
evaluations, and we are sure that parents who are reading this book are very
familiar with this process, which requires a review of previous evaluations,
current academic information, and the current IEP. Often schools require
a complete psychological evaluation every 3 years, and our focus group participants had participated in numerous such evaluations—but these were

mostly performed by professionals who were not qualified to evaluate deaf children. Our informants thus had no confidence in these assessments. They felt strongly that only school psychologists who were trained to assess deaf children should be performing this job, which would then result in data that could be trusted. School psychologists who work with deaf and hard of hearing children are concerned about the same issues and are making it a part of their mission; in fact a group of specialist school psychologists did succeed in convincing its board to include a position statement on needs of deaf and hard of hearing students (National Association of School Psychologists, 2012).

Successful Mediated Education

A few of our research participants told us they had excellent K–12 experiences. Factors contributing to these experiences invariably included support from various professionals within the school. For some, one person made the difference, but those who had a group of skilled and caring professionals and (we assume) some systemic support reported that they were much more involved in their own educational and developmental processes. These participants wanted to give credit to those who were there for them and truly made a difference.

> I had an amazing hearing itinerant teacher in high school, Ms. McO. She was hearing and went to Gallaudet for her master's. We met for 1 hour, once a week during my lunch period for all four years of high school. She was the person who convinced me to wear my hearing aid, to tell friends I had hearing loss, to face my disability, and to never let it stop me from reaching my goals. Without her, I honestly think I would've still been in denial of my hearing loss to this day.   (Survey respondent)

Another respondent shared the many wonderful supports she had in elementary school:

> I had an amazing interpreter who also taught me sign language, and also an amazing DHH teacher. I had such a huge support system—interpreter, DHH teacher, Speech Therapist, and awesome parents! I also had great friends in Elementary; my interpreter would help provide sign language class

after school for my friends to come and learn too; helped me build friendship, and communicate with them. She truly was wonderful.

                                                                   (Survey respondent)

This last individual spoke of the value of having his opinions heard by
those who provided services:

It was definitely most helpful when the CART, note takers, or ASL interpreters listened to what was working for me . . . or what was not working!
Sometimes, the information received from an interpreter or captioning that
was most helpful was knowing the comments from my peers, not feeling as
though I was left out of classroom conversations.   (Survey respondent)

Closing Comments on a Mediated Education

Some of our participants had attended both schools for the deaf and
mainstream programs. They generally loved the social opportunities at the
schools for the deaf and deplored the general level and scope of academics offered. They recognized and appreciated the academic advantages of
attending mainstream programs and hated the inability to be full participants and the long-lasting consequences of this social poverty. A good bit
of discussion took place on this topic in the focus groups, as well as much
wishing it could be different.

Additionally, our focus group participants were highly cognizant of the
fact that they are the mainstream success stories. They do not represent the
majority of deaf adults in their age group. Illiteracy is a huge problem for
deaf people. Fifty percent of all 18-year-old deaf and hard of hearing individuals are reading below the fourth-grade level—and this is true no matter
the form of schooling (Marschark, 2007). Our focus group participants
represent a very small percentage of deaf individuals in terms of academic
success and career achievement.

The mediated education they experienced left scars, and they want to
help the current and future generations of deaf and hard of hearing children
avoid similar scars. Our informants had many ideas for how schools can
(and should) improve social opportunities for deaf and hard of hearing
students. These ideas are included in our recommendations chapter.

Our informants expressed great compassion for the job of the interpreter; they were well aware this job lasts long hours and is thankless. After all, how many young kids think to thank their interpreter? Participants were deeply appreciative of the complicated situations their interpreters faced each day. They now understood how much their interpreters had sacrificed for them. Giving up evenings and/or weekends with their own families to ride the school bus with rambunctious kids for away games could not have been a pleasant part of their jobs. They also understood the heartache some of their interpreters must surely have felt watching their young charges being left out and ignored day after day.

The profession of K–12 interpreting services and the many management and administrative issues surrounding the interpreters within the schools impacted heavily on our informants. It is important that the educational interpreter profession and school systems pay attention to and learn from the experiences of those who were the beneficiaries of these services. The young deaf and hard of hearing children of yesterday are now grown up, and it greatly behooves the interpreting and educational experts to include them as full partners as they shape the K–12 interpreting profession of today and tomorrow.

5

A System in Need of Reform

"The only thing that interferes with my learning is my education."
(attributed to Albert Einstein)

In the last three chapters, we have shared the comments and perceptions of 134 individuals between the ages of 18 and 34 who participated in focus groups and/or wrote essays for our online survey. Our participants reported numerous detrimental issues that were common to many if not most of them, and it is dismaying that the current American public education system for deaf and hard of hearing K–12 students contributes to, if not actively causes, these negative experiences. This system is entrenched at the federal level and it has resulted in state-level policies and practices that have been evolving over the last 40 years. Several key professional organizations have issued calls for reform, and we will focus on these to illustrate the unison of these voices, to add our voice to theirs.

We believe that the Individuals With Disabilities Education Act (IDEA), originally passed in 1975 as P.L. 94-142 and called the "Education of All Handicapped Children Act," has resulted in a trade-off from one set of disadvantages to another set of disadvantages. The historic disadvantage was that deaf and hard of hearing children were usually educated in schools far from where their families lived. The current disadvantage is that these children are usually socially isolated, some to a great extent, in addition to suffering unnecessary achievement gaps and delays because of their lack of full access to the information passed along during each and every school day. We have yet to see evidence that this new practice of dispersing deaf and hard of hearing children into their home district schools results in greater achievement.

In the past, most states supported only one statewide school for the deaf, which was most often residential. Although these schools were often far from their families, deaf and hard of hearing children were provided with a strong dose of social capital from being part of their school community. Recall from Chapter 2 that social capital is built on relationships, and relationships are built from conversations. At the residential schools, adults and many peers surrounded children and conversation was most often direct. (Ladd, 2003; Lane, Hoffmeister, & Bahan, 1996). One of the perhaps more endearing points made in the groundbreaking 2007 PBS documentary *Through Deaf Eyes* (Hott & Garrey, 2007) is that the sentiment of fondness and love for one's deaf school alma mater is shared regardless of whether the primary mode of communication in the classroom was sign or speech. As alumni of Clarke School in Northampton, Massachusetts, and other oral schools attest, they still benefit greatly from an environment geared toward visual as well as aural access to language and by camaraderie with numerous other individuals "like me," with the same needs and communication styles. People have a natural need to be with like-peers; a common language builds bonds, deep friendships, and a strong sense of community. These shared life experiences support a sense of "I'm ok."

The residential schools organized sporting events, and many young people were able to play on full-fledged teams with their deaf and hard of hearing peers. Regional and national competitions were organized. In addition to sports opportunities, this critical mass of students easily communicating with each other also engendered other common extra- and cocurricular activities such as student government, debating clubs, drama, and other special interest activities. These activities built leadership, self-advocacy, self-determination, communication skills, and social skills. Still today, there are national and international opportunities such as the Deaflympics, the World Federation of the Deaf, Deaf History International,

The National Theatre of the Deaf, and other organizations built around common interests and/or concerns. Deaf people had a global community before the rest of the world had such, and they organized it themselves with skills and experiences gained at their beloved deaf schools. Gannon (2012), Van Cleve (1993), and Van Cleve and Crouch (1989) are full of historic evidence of this.

Today, it is very different: No longer are the deaf schools thriving and no longer are deaf and hard of hearing children availed of this rich social capital. The net result of the IDEA has been that a large majority of children with disabilities, including deaf and hard of hearing children, spend their K–12 days in their neighborhood schools. And this has come to be regardless of each individual child's special needs. There is ample evidence that decisions on the location of a deaf or hard of hearing child's schooling are made based on the home district's financial situation and/or misguided beliefs, and not on the child's real needs. The misguided belief is an idealistic philosophy—that it is far better for every child with a disability, regardless of educational needs, to attend the neighborhood school in the neighborhood in which the family resides. This philosophy grew especially in the 1990s, and today, with the great dispersal of deaf and hard of hearing children, we see the results.

Key IDEA Requirements

The IDEA includes two key concepts that work together: the *individualized education program (IEP)* and the *least restrictive environment (LRE)*. Each child who is identified as having a disability that affects learning must have an IEP that is developed by school personnel and then reviewed annually. The IEP, by law, describes the child's special needs and lists any accommodations that must be provided. This concept sounds good in theory; if only it were applied as (we presume) originally intended. What has come to pass is that often the school personnel's interpretation of the LRE is at cross-purposes with the child's actual needs.

It is instructive to look at what the IDEA actually says in requiring that IEP teams consider the LRE when determining where the student will attend school:

(i) To the maximum extent appropriate, children with disabilities, including children in public or private institutions or other care facilities, are educated with children who are nondisabled; and

(ii) Special classes, separate schooling, or other removal of children with disabilities from the regular educational environment occurs only if the nature or severity of the disability is such that education in regular classes with the use of supplementary aids and services cannot be achieved satisfactorily. (34 C.F.R. § 300.114)

It also provides for what is called a "continuum of alternative placements":

(a) Each public agency must ensure that a continuum of alternative placements is available to meet the needs of children with disabilities for special education and related services.

And further, that the continuum "must include . . . instruction in regular classes, special classes, special schools, home instruction, and instruction in hospitals and institutions" (34 U.S.C. §300.115).

Most people, upon hearing or reading *least restrictive environment,* would think of it as something schoolchildren should have, that it means something like "that environment which is most likely to result in optimal education for that child." For a deaf child, that is almost intuitively an environment with a heavy emphasis on the visual, but that also supports for the development of listening and speaking skills, and it should be an environment where the child can easily "talk to everyone" just like any other child. However, the definition of LRE has evolved to become "with nondisabled peers above all other considerations," and that has thus become "the neighborhood school, or the school the child would ordinarily attend if not disabled."

As Ramsey stated in 1997, "Since the LRE requirement is most often taken as a statement about physical placement rather than an assertion about learning and teaching, decision makers [may] overlook or underestimate the many specific needs of students with different disabilities." (Ramsey, 1997, p. 28). The emphasis is not on how the students are educated—with consideration for their special learning needs—but *where* they are educated.

Indicators of Compliance With IDEA

To go along with the IDEA, the federal government developed "indicators" that are used to judge whether individual states of the union are in compliance with IDEA. States report annually to the federal government on each indicator. These reports from the states provide the government with a yardstick on how well the country is doing with regard to children with disabilities. These indicators are not well known; in fact, so little known that the Web site of the National Dissemination Center for Children with Disabilities (http://nichcy.org/laws/idea/partb/indicators-partb) greets readers as follows: "So you're interested in Part B indicators, are you? Impressive. Most people have never heard of them, let alone why they are important. NICHCY is pleased to serve as a gateway to this essential information."

We contend that these indicators are the deepest root of the system that is hurting deaf and hard of hearing children, and probably children with other disabilities as well. There are 20 indicators all together, and most disheartening and damaging is that all of them require only aggregated data, meaning that numbers for all children with IEPs are lumped together in the reports—no reporting by specific disability type is required. The actual federal citation for all the indicators is 20 U.S.C. 1416(a)(3)(A), although they may be more easily accessed at the NICHCY Web site. We call your attention to those we feel are most egregious.

Indicator 5: Participation/Time in General Education Settings (LRE)
Percent of children with IEPs aged 6 through 21:
A. Removed from regular class less than 21% of the day;
B. Removed from regular class greater than 60% of the day; or
C. Served in public or private separate schools, residential placements, or homebound or hospital placements.

Indicator 6: Preschool Children in General Education Settings
(Preschool LRE)
Percent of preschool children with IEPs who received special education and related services in settings with typically developing peers (e.g., early childhood settings, home, and part-time early childhood/part-time early childhood special education settings).

With these two indicators, it is clear that the goal is related to where the children are being educated as opposed to how well they are being educated. Of the 20 indicators only two relate to achievement:

Indicator 3: Participation and Performance on Statewide Assessments
Participation and performance of children with disabilities on statewide assessments.

Indicator 7: Preschool Children with Improved Outcomes
Percent of preschool children with IEPs who demonstrate improved:
A. Positive social-emotional skills (including social relationships);
B. Acquisition and use of knowledge and skills (including early language/ communication and early literacy); and
C. Use of appropriate behaviors to meet their needs.

The other 16 indicators cover data such as graduation, drop-out, and suspension and expulsion rates; transition information; and other important information. Because this information covers *all* children with IEPs, it is of limited help to those who want to know how well (or poorly) the deaf and hard of hearing kids are faring in their state. (Some states collect disability-specific data, but they are not required to do so.) So if a parent or any interested adult wants to know how well the deaf children, or the blind children, or the children with dyslexia are performing in their particular district or even their particular state, in many if not most states, the answer may be "Sorry, we don't collect those data."

As of this writing in early 2013, the last reauthorization of IDEA was in 2004. Reauthorizations provide a time frame and format for concerned parties to make recommendations. This delay from the federal government is simply an added impetus to advocates working at the state level, which we expand upon later in this chapter.

The Government Accountability Office Report

The U.S. Government Accountability Office (GAO) released a report in 2011 that focused on the education specifically of deaf and hard of hearing children: "Deaf and Hard of Hearing Children: Federal Support for Developing Language and Literacy" (U.S. GAO, 2011), "based on documents and interviews collected from numerous sources." It states that in 2008 there were 78,000 deaf and hard of hearing students receiving IDEA Part B services (e.g., individual education services backed with federal subsidies). Of these students, 52% were being educated using speech only, 11% with sign only, and 35% with both speech and sign. The GAO also reported that of children aged 6–21, 54% were spending more than 80% of the day in a regular classroom.

The report says nothing about how well the children are doing, absolutely nothing about achievement. It does mention the shortage of qualified interpreters and teachers who have specific training in the education of deaf and hard of hearing children, and it mentions financial issues:

> Parents, educators, and advocates agree that while decisions about a child's education should be based on his or her unique needs as required by IDEA, the cost or availability of services often determines what a child receives. Some of these stakeholders said that schools might be hesitant to provide particular special services because the costs incurred are prohibitive. For example, a school district may have to pay tuition for a child if the child attends a program outside the school district in order to have his or her needs met. Also, educators and advocacy groups said schools might prefer to place children in a program the school already offers in order to keep down costs. (U.S. GAO, 2011, p. 18)

The report then reminded readers that IDEA "requires schools to provide an individualized education to children and . . . requires school districts and states to provide recourse for parents who do not agree with individualized education program decisions for their child, including the ability to seek a due process hearing." However, the GAO report said nothing about why there is a discrepancy between what the law requires and what was reported to them.

Child First and the National Summit

One of the key groups of educators who provided input to the GAO report was the Conference of Educational Administrators of Schools and Programs for the Deaf (CEASD). This group is made up of individuals from both state schools and large urban programs, most of whom have spent most of their entire careers working with deaf and hard of hearing children. Approximately 75 schools and programs send representatives to annual meetings. CEASD has launched an initiative called Child First, whose goal is to bring the IEP back to the center of what drives states, districts, schools, and teachers in decisions concerning deaf and hard of hearing students. It has been developed in preparation for the next IDEA reauthorization, and work continues to get the ducks in a row for that long-awaited possibility.

In 2010, in an effort spearheaded by Louis Abbate, CEO of the Willie Ross School for the Deaf in Massachusetts, CEASD sent a letter to Assistant Secretary of the Office of Special Education and Rehabilitation Alexa Posny. In this letter, CEASD called for a "clarification of the definition of the *least restrictive environment* to ensure that it is not being considered to be a generic, convenient place, but rather a diagnostic determination that meets the needs of individual children." The letter further suggested replacing the least restrictive environment terminology with "most enabling environment." This modification would help to steer the focus to the individual child's needs rather than on the location of the school. The letter called for attention to the indicators particularly to "the extent to which [they are] affecting school districts' practices" of giving the LRE concept—that is, one interpretation of it—much more importance than the IEP concept—that is, the child's unique and specific needs (www.ceasd.org). A response to this letter can be found at http://www2.ed.gov/policy/speced/guid/idea/letters/2011-3/stern093011lre3q2011.pdf . Readers can draw their own conclusions.

The federal government has not established any date for a reauthorization, and CEASD has decided that deaf and hard of hearing can ill afford to wait for such an action. Thus the Child First initiative is moving forward with a proposed amendment to the IDEA that could be accepted by Congress without a full-fledged reauthorization. This ambitious, and yet so appropriate and absolutely necessary, bill is called the Alice Cogswell Act of 2013. We have been privileged to receive a copy of this bill (draft date November 2012) from the executive director of CEASD (J. Finnegan, personal communication, January 24, 2013). For starters, it mentions a significant underidentification of the number of schoolchildren who need to have their hearing levels addressed.

> The widespread use [by individual states] of IDEA's disability categories has led to a sizable undercount of deaf and hard of hearing students and, consequently, [extremely inadequate services]. Indeed, while the U.S. Census Bureau supports the contention that more than 350,000 students nationally have "hearing difficulties," the Department of Education routinely reports serving under IDEA a population of approximately 73,000. This occurs . . . because students who are deaf or hard of hearing who also have additional disabilities [are frequently identified only as] having multiple disabilities. Consequently, such students' hearing disabilities are not fully acknowledged either in terms of educational agency recognized need for personnel trained to serve such students, or in terms of an individual student's need for the services of such personnel.   (proposed Alice Cogswell Act of 2013, § 2.a.7)

Of particular importance and merit in this act is its focus on state plans—it specifies that every state must develop and report (to the U.S. Department of Education) on a plan to specifically ensure that all children who are deaf or hard of hearing "are evaluated by qualified professionals, using valid and reliable assessments, for such children's need for instruction and services meeting their unique language and communication, literacy, academic, social and related learning needs" (proposed Alice Cogswell Act of 2013, § 102). Further, the state plan (required of all states) must also show how the state will support

> ongoing progress in language development, including American Sign Language and spoken language with or without visual supports, and including the provision of school-related opportunities for direct communications with peers and professional personnel in the child's language and opportunities for direct instruction in the child's language, as well as instruction in audiology, age appropriate career education, communication and language, social skills, functional skills for academic success, self-determination and advocacy (including preparation for transition to work or higher education), social emotional skills, technology, and support for the student through family education.   (§ 102)

As we read this proposed act, we can only be amazed that public education in the United States does not already ensure such basic educational needs for deaf and hard of hearing children. We are dismayed that the voices of so many people who have known what these children have needed for decades have been largely ignored or dismissed.

CEASD is not the only organization working to usher in systematic change for deaf and hard of hearing schoolchildren. Other organizations/ events filled with knowledgeable people include the National Summit on Deaf Education, the Conference of American Instructors of the Deaf (CAID), the National Association of the Deaf (NAD), and the Registry of Interpreters for the Deaf (RID). These organizations plan conferences, produce position statements, send letters to legislators, and otherwise work toward systemic reform. Their efforts are very largely in line with CEASD's Child First initiative as reflected in the letter to the assistant secretary and other of their numerous documents.

Whereas CEASD, founded in 1868, has a long history, the National Summit on Deaf Education is a much more recent phenomenon and includes individuals from a range of front-line professionals as well as the administrators who direct their work and do battle with legislators. This summit has been held annually since 2005, and reports can be found on the Web site of the National Deaf Education Project (http://www.ndepnow .org). The "summit" was born as an "agenda," and now the words National Summit and National Agenda are almost interchangeable.

In 2005, a concerned group of individuals put out a flagship document, "The National Agenda: Moving Forward on Achieving Educational Equality for Deaf and Hard of Hearing Students" (National Deaf Education Project, 2005). This document was reviewed by key individuals from CEASD, the Alexander Graham Bell Association of the Deaf, the Association of College Educators–Deaf and Hard of Hearing, the American Society for Deaf Children, the Convention of American Instructors of the Deaf, the Council on Exceptional Children, the National Association of the Deaf, and several state departments of education and local education agencies. It was posted on the Internet for comments from any interested parties. An excerpt from the preamble of this document shows alignment with the Child First Initiative:

A deaf or hard of hearing child's unique learning style, cognitive requirements, and individual communication and language needs must determine
programmatic, fiscal, and educational decisions—and not the other way
around. We have come together to work for a program that builds collectively on the knowledge, devotion, and expertise of families, educators, and
consumers in the deaf and hard of hearing communities.
(National Deaf Education Project, 2005, http://www.ndepnow.org/agenda
/agenda.htm)

The individuals and groups involved in the development of the National Agenda decided further to attempt an annual national meeting, a
National Summit on Deaf Education, and they were quite successful. The
first summit was held in 2005, bringing together several people from each
state represented, so that statewide networks within each state could be
unified and strengthened. At that first summit, 125 individuals attended,
representing 20 states. At the 2012 summit 25 states were represented by 143
individuals. Not only did these individuals represent different states, but
they also represented different workplaces and philosophical persuasions.
Nevertheless, they shared a common goal:

We recognize that until we achieve the 1:1 rule, minimally one year's growth
in one year's time, we—the education system—are failing these children. No
matter what [has been] tried in the last thirty years of special education, we
have not been able to significantly raise the overall academic performance of
DHH students. We must persist. We need systemic and systematic change.
We need accountability to assure no DHH child is left behind. We need to
maximize our resources as teacher and interpreter shortages increase. We
need to recognize the changing needs of DHH students. We need to maximize the benefits of early identification and intervention. . . . And we need
to accept that we are about all DHH children—all communication modes,
all placements, all languages, and those with additional disabilities. . . . It
is time that we channel [our passion] in a unified way towards the same
purpose and without prejudice.
(National Deaf Education Project, 2005, http://www.ndepnow.org/agenda
/agenda.htm)

The numerous papers and presentations that have been made at the
National Summit meetings are eye-opening to anyone wanting to learn

what is really happening for deaf and hard of hearing children today. Today, various state teams are focusing on different ways and means to effect reform in their respective states, aligned with the eight goals that are outlined in detail in the National Agenda document. All have that ultimate goal of seeing deaf and hard of hearing children show a year's progress in a year's time—something we all expect for all children. The individual state efforts can be viewed on the Web site as well.

The Illusion of Inclusion Impact: Other Perspectives

To connect the Summit's work with issues our focus group and survey participants brought up, we hone in on two areas: itinerant teachers of the deaf and K–12 interpreters. One could say, actually, that these professions were born out of IDEA and the philosophical push toward LRE as a location. Because our informants had so much to say about their interpreters, we have a full chapter about this issue, which follows this one. Although one could argue that issues faced by and among today's teachers of the deaf (often referred to as TODs) are certainly also worthy of a full chapter, not nearly enough has been written about the TOD of the 21st century, particularly as more and more of them function as itinerants. And thus, we have only a smattering of research upon which to report.

Teacher of the Deaf

Truthfully, the profession "teacher of the deaf" is historic. We need only remember the early influential teachers such as Laurent Clerc, Thomas Hopkins Gallaudet, and the many who came after them. However, the philosophy of inclusion as a civil rights issue leading to the definition of LRE as a location has caused a possibly unforeseen and definitely unplanned-for consequence: the erosion of the profession "teacher of the deaf." It may be merely an evolution, but considering how a majority of TODs spend their time today—as itinerant teachers or "resource room" teachers spending often 60 minutes or even 30 minutes once a week or once a month with their assigned students—there clearly has been a significant reduction in TODs' ability to impact the deaf or hard of hearing child.

In the heyday of the residential schools, TODs worked in classrooms just as all teachers do. Their students were deaf. Special techniques or methods for meeting the students' special needs were applied day in and day out, all day, with all students. During early years of IDEA (1975 to the early 1990s), numerous mainstream programs were developed in which deaf and hard of hearing students were placed in "self-contained classrooms," that is, in regular public schools, the deaf and hard of hearing children would be taught in a separate classroom. Some of these programs in urban areas had as many as 50 children. With the push for inclusion, these programs began to shrink in size, as the children first were moved into regular classrooms in the school which the deaf and hard of hearing program was located for part of the day, and in later years were either kept at or returned to their "home school," meaning the same school that their siblings and neighbors attended.

A word here about the term *inclusion.* In professional and personal circles within the Deaf community, the word inclusion is always signed or spelled out with quotation marks. The strong implication or definition of the term when used this way is that it is a huge irony. Inclusion, as the dictionary defines it, is "the act of being included or the state of being included." Further, *include* is defined as "to have as a part or member; to consider as part of or allow into a group or class" (*American Heritage Dictionary of the English Language,* ahdictionary.com). Because there is so much evidence, however, that deaf and hard of hearing students are in reality not full participants in general education classrooms, the term is seen as ironic, and thus always spelled or signed with the quotation marks to indicate this irony.

Today, there remains a slowly but surely decreasing number of "DHH programs" (also called site-based or center-based programs or self-contained classrooms) in which a TOD is employed full time and students spend part of the day in classes or in one-to-one instruction with these highly and specifically trained individuals. The rest of their day students attend regular classes with or without an interpreter, depending on the individual child. These TODs have front-row seats as the march toward the LRE as the neighborhood school continues. We interviewed several site-based TODs in various states, and asked them to share their stories. They needed to be assured anonymity in order to feel safe to share these.

> A boy from a neighboring town/county high school was sent to our program [a high school with a "deaf program," that is, a full-time TOD and 2–3 full-time interpreters]. During his first year at our school, he was in my self-contained English class with some other deaf kids. He is from a family where English is not their first language. At the end of his sophomore year he felt he could probably succeed in a regular English class and he wanted to try it with an interpreter for his junior year. I agreed that he had a good chance of success so I approved this.
>
> Once his home district realized that he was going to be in a regular English class, they wanted him back. They have to pay approximately $50,000/year in order for this boy to attend our HS with the Deaf program. The boy did not want to go back to his neighborhood HS, which actually is less than 15 miles away from our HS. He also plays sports with both hearing and deaf kids on our teams. There are generally 8–15 other deaf kids in this high school and the program has been here for more than 10 years so the hearing teachers and other kids are "used to it." The home district was fighting to bring him back, saying that if he is fully mainstreamed he does not need to attend a school outside his district. But, at this home district he would be "alone in the mainstream."

We heard variations of this story over and over again. Notice the interesting choice of words: "they wanted him back." Clearly this was a case of the boy's home district wanting their money back or at minimum not understanding his needs. This interviewee told us that the home district was sure they could hire an educational interpreter for half of that $50,000 and therefore save money. They clearly were not aware of how being deaf impacted the child's overall school experience, even at the high-school level when peer relationships are so important, or they may have felt this was unimportant. Incidental learning is also completely ignored. Recall from Chapter 2 how very important this is; if people are not well schooled in deaf education issues, they do not consider incidental learning when they think about the needs of a deaf child. They focus instead on one-to-one communication.

Fortunately for this young man, this particular TOD managed to make contact with a state-level child advocate who happened to have a deaf family member and was willing to enter the fray because of her firsthand knowledge of related issues. With this support the district came to a better understanding (or relented); the child "won" and was able to stay where he was and did not have to go back to his neighborhood school. But, apparently this is more the exception than the rule in such cases.

Often children are enrolled in center-based schools only after they have "failed" in their neighborhood schools. Too often the neighborhood school is perceived as the preferred location, and is at the top of the placement continuum. Consideration of the residential school comes only when the local district is not able to meet the student's needs—or when the parents make a fuss. Waiting until students are significantly behind in their education before making a placement decision to a residential school is seriously detrimental to learning.

> Often, the kids are put in our classes in a state of extreme need and either academic, psychological, or linguistic (or often all three) crises. Then, in the DHH program they experience a rebirth of sorts. They learn language, academics, become happy and fulfilled. So, when the [home district] administration raises the issue of return to the home school (even with interpreters) the parents are stunned. The [better educated ones] speak up. But [minority families] are very respectful of the administration, and do not want to make waves.

This situation reflects that same issue—the district "wants him back," suggesting that the administrators believe that the better educational placement is in the general education environment. This belief may be due to their lack of understanding of the complexities of language and social-emotional development for these students—they may not realize at all the importance of incidental learning and they may underestimate the value of peers/classmates. Or they may simply be looking at the bottom budget line. In this case, even after the child had minimal, if any, success in the home district and subsequently blossomed and thrived in the center program, the home district still "wanted him back." Indeed, most of our focus group participants ended up changing schools much more often than their hearing peers, as they and their parents searched for something better.

The TODs we talked to spoke amply about how unsupported they felt. Their immediate supervisors tended to be general directors of special education, and therefore the TODs in general knew more about the special needs of deaf and hard of hearing children than their superiors. For example, many TODs have some fluency in sign language, but they are rarely, if ever, involved in the evaluation of the student's interpreter(s). The voices we heard from these TODs was that generally their expertise is unrecognized, unappreciated, and underutilized.

> There is a tremendous amount of damage done to the quality of a DHH program when it is [controlled] by inadequate, unskilled, old-language, uncooperative interpreters. . . . They are often [awarded permanent positions] by a principal who neither knows signs nor even consults the DHH teacher to see how their job performance is. Therefore [this interpreter] becomes the bane of the DHH student's (and the DHH teacher's) existence for often 30 years to come.

Here is one more example, reflecting the TOD's efforts to create a more engaged and welcoming social environment for the deaf and hard of hearing children within the mainstream school:

> I taught an ASL class at night for parents for some time. There was no support from the Admin. for this even though I did it voluntarily, for no pay. In fact, I stopped teaching [these] classes because I was tired of [constantly] getting flak for entering the building at night (even though it was all prearranged). Also, I suggested to the principal, how about I teach you all (kids and teachers) a basic, 40-word or so vocabulary, and you can communicate yourselves [at recess and lunch time]. She has insisted no, for two years now.

The preceding comments were made by TODs who work in site-based deaf programs. As we have said repeatedly, however, movement is toward the LRE as the school the child would normally attend if not for the hearing difficulties—the site-based program is less and less frequently where the deaf and hard of hearing children are located. These children are now literally "all over the map," and this has resulted in a drastic change in how TODs work. A majority are now employed as "itinerant teachers."

The Itinerant Teacher

Let's take a moment here to introduce the role and function of an *itinerant teacher* of students who are deaf or hard of hearing. Deaf and hard of hearing students are attending schools in the classrooms they would be in if they did not have a disability, and they are in schools throughout their states. The itinerant teacher is assigned a caseload of students in a geographic area that varies in size depending in large part by just how geographically dispersed the children are. Children who are in general education classrooms are receiving mostly piecemeal services rather than benefitting from the highly specialized training TODs receive. Many TODs have postbaccalaureate degrees or certificates and could provide much better services if they had appropriate classrooms, time, and support. The itinerants tend to focus instead more on short-term needs such as checking the student's listening technology, doing some auditory skill development, working with the student on self-advocacy, reviewing homework, and communicating with the general education teachers. Depending on the particular caseload of the itinerant teacher, in more rural areas particularly, she may spend a good part of the day in her car.

Reporting on surveys and focus groups involving 210 itinerant TODs from around the United States, Foster and Cue (2009) shared important findings. First, their participants reported spending only 33% of their in-school time (i.e., of their time not spent commuting) with students. The other 67% was spent supporting teachers and other personnel in various ways, including working directly with classroom teachers and other support personnel (17%); planning, assessment, and record-keeping (14%); coordinating and scheduling meetings with various other professionals (13%); meeting with parents (8%); attending to technical equipment, such as FM systems, hearing aids, and cochlear implants (7%); and other miscellaneous tasks.

As a testament to how unprepared everyone has been for meeting the needs of deaf and hard of hearing children when they are dispersed throughout a region or state, adding insult to the fact that they spend only 33% of their time (apart from commuting) with students, itinerants also felt that their graduate programs did not adequately prepare them for the job. For example, for tasks related to working with students, only 27% of the respondents said they had learned the tasks in their graduate programs. For working with general education teachers and other school personnel, a dismal 13% said they had learned about this in their graduate programs. For the remaining task categories, the highest percent indicated for learning in graduate school was 20%, for "planning," and one could see that as a rather generic skill or task one learns merely by going to graduate school.

In an editorial in the *American Annals of the Deaf*, Moores (2008) noted that from various studies we know something about how itinerant teachers work—how much time they spend in their cars covering who knows how many miles, how big their caseloads are, and how much time they spend with individual students. We also know (Foster & Cue, 2009) that of the three main itinerant roles (coteaching, consulting with the regular education teacher, and working in pull-out settings), a majority of the itinerant teacher's time (beyond the commuting time) involves pull-out, which our focus group participants talked about considerably in Chapter 4.

In reference to the pull-outs, Moores (2008) commented on a qualitative study:

> Clifford (2008) observed itinerant teachers in 30-minute and 60-minute sessions, common time periods for itinerant services. Activities such as equipment maintenance and social interactions left only about 15 minutes for direct instruction. This resulted in fewer opportunities for [important pre-teaching and review tasks] or any intensive academic activities related to content areas such as math, science, or social studies. . . . In most cases the environment was less than ideal, with no real privacy. Interruptions were common, and they disrupted the flow of the lesson and projected an attitude that the work was not considered important by others.   (p. 274)

The picture we have is of these itinerant teachers running themselves ragged, spending much of the day in their cars, and having precious little time with students. And, because the job responsibilities have changed so drastically over the last 10+ years, teacher training programs have not been able to keep pace. They need to play catch-up, and fast. The children being served can't wait.

The Wisconsin Study

Carol Schweitzer, education consultant for deaf and hard of hearing programs in Wisconsin, oversaw a statewide study of itinerant teachers. She presented her findings at the 2011 National Summit on Deaf Education (Schweitzer, 2011), and we share some of them here. We hope that other states will replicate Schweitzer's efforts, because they are so very important to understanding the experiences of today's deaf and hard of hearing children.

Let's start with the numbers. Schweitzer reports that in 2011, itinerant teachers served 70% of identified deaf and hard of hearing children in Wisconsin. This means approximately 1,500 children out of 2,200 identified deaf and hard of hearing students are served by itinerants. Of these 1,500, 1,000 are the only such child in their school, essentially "alone in the mainstream." In Wisconsin, as in quite a few other states, many areas are considered rural. The itinerant teachers reported serving as few as three (those in urban areas) and as many as 49 separate schools, and the range of miles driven weekly was 158–850 miles. The amount of time they estimated spent commuting was 12% to 50% of the time. Doing a little math would tell us that the least number of hours driving, for an urban itinerant, would be almost 5 hours a week; and that an itinerant with 49 schools (and most likely at least 49 students) is in her car 20 hours a week! The Wisconsin study (Schweitzer, 2011) asked some vital questions based on these data: Does this level/design of specialized services meet the educational needs of these students? Is it enough? Does it support student success? To us it seems like such a waste of human resources. Neither highly trained teachers nor deaf and hard of hearing students are being served well by this system. There must be a better solution.

The fact-finding mission in Wisconsin was multilayered. The first step was doing a survey of itinerants to gather a broad level of data. From there, four focus groups were hosted around the state, each lasting a full day. These groups were made up of both itinerant teachers and special education directors (to whom the itinerant teachers often report). They were asked to identify benefits as well as challenges to the concept of itinerant services, and also to come up with possible solutions for those challenges. Interestingly but not surprisingly, we feel that the identified benefits and challenges reflect the entire concept of LRE as a convenient location rather than as the "most enabling environment" concept.

The benefits were focused on the deaf or hard of hearing student being able to be in his own neighborhood, as this promoted acceptance of the student in his home community. This reminds of us another of Ramsey's (1997) conclusions—that most of the regular school staff at the school where she did her year-long observation would wax eloquent, "it's so good for the normal children" (Ramsey, 1997, p. 40). We tend to think this is more a benefit to others than actually to the deaf or hard of hearing student, still, people name this as a "benefit"—a benefit to whom?

Of the challenges reported by the Wisconsin participants, some could be considered a reflection of all that driving time—lack of time with students, lack of time consulting with the students teacher(s) and interpreter(s), excessive expense, and extreme fatigue. Other challenges we see as a deeper reflection of systemic failure: "student services determined by cost to district and teacher availability" (e.g., the huge caseloads), "role of the itinerant teacher not clearly understood or valued," and "often overlooked by case-managers." Finally, isolation was a consistent message; the itinerants rarely if ever have a chance to consult or network with other itinerants. So basically everyone is "alone in the mainstream"—not only is the student isolated, but so is the itinerant teacher, and so is the student's family.

After the focus groups met, people from throughout the state gathered to review and design effective itinerant services. The participants in this work group included deaf and hard of hearing teachers and special education directors, and also outreach staff and parents. This work group met for 3 years, identifying student needs and director expectations and resulting in a model of redesign. The redesign includes organizing the state into geographical areas, creating effective DHH program teams to work with the students, identifying staff and families in the various areas, supporting educational program options (called *cluster programs*) within each area, and supporting student academic and social-emotional needs. Because this process included special education directors throughout as well as DHH program teachers, it was readily welcomed by other special education directors around the state.

At present, the process in Wisconsin continues. Change does not come quickly, but here is one state that has begun the process and moved slowly and carefully to include all stakeholders. The activity of the work group was referred back to the local areas, and the challenge now is to stir local-level support and buy-in.

Way to go! If you live in Wisconsin, ask Carol Schweitzer what you can do. If you live in other states, see if your state has begun a similar effort and join in. We know other states are working on similar issues, and by sharing the Wisconsin efforts we hope to spur more advocates to work for statewide reform initiatives.

Mobilizing Educational Efforts

TODs (both on-site and itinerant) whom we ourselves interviewed mentioned isolation as a huge issue of concern. There was a time when an organization called Convention of American Instructors of the Deaf (CAID) met annually, and TODs who worked at the Deaf schools attended for continuing education and networking opportunities. Today, however, CAID is struggling to survive, another fallout situation of IDEA. Most TODs are simply not granted state funds to attend these national conventions. Some states have responded by organizing their own conferences for TODs in their respective (and/or very nearby) states to reduce travel costs while still providing a place for the exchange of ideas. Leaders in the field estimate that fewer than one third of states provide such continuing education and networking opportunities for TODs (J. Finnegan, personal communication, January 24, 2013).

While we lament the demise of CAID, we applaud the efforts of leaders in that organization to revitalize, and we also appreciate the efforts of people involved with CEASD and the National Agenda/Summit. Because of the widespread and all-encompassing isolation of deaf and hard of hearing children, their families, and even the professionals who serve them, opportunities to share problems and solutions across the country are priceless. This brings us to the last section of this chapter, focused on one element where national support *is* available, where a venue for sharing nationwide about issues related to deaf and hard of hearing children *does* exist and is even thriving: the Early Hearing Detection and Intervention (EHDI) annual conference.

Early Hearing Detection and Intervention (EHDI)

The GAO report (U.S. GAO, 2011) mentioned earlier in this chapter concludes with a single recommendation:

> The newly reauthorized [Early Hearing Detection and Intervention] EHDI law acknowledges the importance of early access to services for children with hearing loss, in part, by encouraging states to increase follow-up rates for newborns and infants who fail a hearing screening. Meeting the needs of deaf and hard of hearing children requires an approach that begins early and is tailored to each child's needs. Given the impact that early intervention can have on a child's development and future self-sufficiency, and the level of federal funding devoted to it, the evaluation of the effectiveness of early intervention is crucial. The federally funded effort to facilitate these state evaluations is an important step and may, over time, help inform the effectiveness of early interventions for deaf and hard of hearing children. (p. 19)

So on the one hand, federal legislation dating back to 1975 has spawned a widespread, misguided, and erroneous assumption that the education of deaf and hard of hearing children can, in general, always be better provided in a neighborhood school with nondisabled children. On the other hand, in 1999 things took a long overdue turn for the better in one important regard. A bill was passed that clearly demonstrates recognition, finally, that deaf and hard of hearing children do, in fact, have very unique needs that require unique remedies.

This recognition began to show itself actually in the early 1990s as several states, prompted by increasing awareness that undetected hearing loss in infants and toddlers invariably led to language delays, began to pass legislation requiring hospitals to screen newborns for hearing loss. This concept moved to the federal level with the passing of the Newborn and Infant Hearing Screening and Intervention Act of 1999, also known as the "Walsh

Bill" after its sponsor, Representative James Walsh (R, NY). Today almost all states require universal newborn hearing screening.

Walsh was the leader and founder of the Congressional Hearing Health Caucus and worked tirelessly for the passing of the bill that bears his name. The purpose of this bill was to promote infant hearing screening in all states and to promote appropriate treatment and intervention for children found to be deaf or hard of hearing. Walsh and his aide, Martha Carmen, worked closely with CEASD and another long-standing organization filled with educators and advocates for deaf and hard of hearing individuals: the National Association of the Deaf (NAD), founded in the late 1800s. With Walsh's support, CEASD, NAD, and the American Society for Deaf Children (ASDC) were actively involved and, along with other key leaders from the Centers for Disease Control (CDC), the National Institutes of Health (NIH), and other organizations representing various medical, audiology, education, and advocacy organizations, offered their suggestions and ideas.

Kelby Brick, one of the first deaf individuals to obtain a law degree, was at that time the director of the Law and Advocacy Center at the NAD. Between 1998 and 2005 Brick gave numerous presentations and wrote articles advocating for Deaf professionals' involvement in the early intervention system. He coordinated the development of recommendations from the NAD and we call your attention to some key segments:

> The system should support the development of the whole child and of language and literacy. . . . Families need information about the lives . . . of deaf and hard of hearing individuals who have achieved optimal adjustments in all phases of life . . . and have attained self-actualizing levels of functioning, all with or without the benefits of hearing aids, cochlear implants, and other assistive devices.
>
> Medical professionals have historically been the first point of contact for parents of deaf children. Their expertise is valuable but is primarily limited only to their medical areas of expertise. They should not be viewed as, nor should they function as, experts with regard to larger issues such as the educational, psychological, social, and linguistic needs of the deaf child.
>
> Physicians, audiologists, and allied professionals should refer parents to qualified experts in deafness and to other appropriate resources so that

parents can make fully informed decisions—that is, decisions that incorporate far more than just the medical-surgical. Such decisions involve language preferences and usage, educational placement and training opportunities, psychological and social development.

(K. Brick, personal communication, February 2013)

Unfortunately, Brick, by his own reckoning became a voice in the wilderness when Walsh's aide Martha Carmen died unexpectedly in 2003, leaving the members of the NAD and like-minded organizations without their steadfast ally. By the time the actual bill came about, and the meetings were dwindling, Brick found himself "alone in the EHDI organization."

> Obviously, [a few other Deaf advocates] and I were not enough back then— it was like trying to stop a tsunami with a mitt. I remember trying to get more people involved but they immediately noted the folly of a few people with mitts trying to stop the tsumani and ran for shelter. They saw that a few very powerful people (without Walsh as a powerful counterbalance) wanted the medical model to prevail, who were very focused on "fixing ears." They didn't care and/or did not respect the knowledge and experience that Deaf adult professionals brought to the table. They did not recognize the unique and not-to-be-found-elsewhere value of the knowledge, experience, and perspective of adults who had once been the very children this bill was to assist.   (K. Brick, personal communication, February 6, 2013)

Since the enactment of the Walsh Bill, a very great majority of all newborns are screened, and thus a great majority of deaf and hard of hearing children in the United States are identified as such in infancy. The bill also led to the multimillion-dollar (federal dollars) establishment of the National Center for Hearing Assessment and Management (NCHAM), which is housed at Utah State University. NCHAM "serves as the National Resource Center for the implementation and improvement of comprehensive and effective Early Hearing Detection and Intervention (EHDI) systems," which are basically state-managed systems. The Web site continues: "As a multidisciplinary center, our goal is to ensure that all infants and toddlers with hearing loss are identified as early as possible and provided with timely and appropriate audiological, educational, and medical inter vention" (NCHAM, 2013). Since 2002, NCHAM has sponsored an Annual Hearing Detection and Intervention Meeting.

Stemming from Brick's work and the resourceful network that is the Deaf community, a few Deaf professionals and their few hearing allies began to attend the conference regularly. For the first five years, they were collectively "alone at EHDI." Among themselves they often discussed the NAD recommendations, and how they saw that salient points from those recommendations were falling by the wayside. From their own experiences as well as their professional knowledge, they knew that children and their families needed early and regular contact with deaf and hard of hearing adults, and that access to both signed and spoken language, especially sign language from birth, would do a great deal to ward off the "linguistic deprivation" that has been the bane of deaf people's lives since time began. They knew from their own experiences that family members using visual communication would better and more easily allow the child access to conversation and to incidental learning within the family, and thereby facilitate normal cognitive and social development. They were not and are not opposed to spoken language—they simply know that a bilingual approach will serve the child better.

In 2008, one of the plenary sessions at the annual EHDI conference was focused on the then-recently-released PBS documentary *Through Deaf Eyes* (Hott & Garrey, 2007). The plenary included several Deaf professionals who had been featured in that documentary. Because of this milestone and also from the groundswell of awareness that had been spreading from the efforts of Brick and the few others, there were approximately 15–20 Deaf professionals in attendance at that conference. Attendance at the conference by deaf and hard of hearing professionals grew each year thereafter, and by 2012, there were at least 60–70 Deaf professionals at the conference. (We know this based on the number of requests for interpreting and/or CART services at various sessions.) EHDI conference attendance in general has grown from approximately 600 individuals in 2008 to almost 950 in 2012 (K. White, personal communication, April 5, 2013).

Why the groundswell? Deaf and hard of hearing adults care about deaf and hard of hearing children. These 60–70 professionals don't all work in early intervention per se. Many, if not most, have to convince employers that their attendance at this conference is critical. Quite a few attend with their own personal funds. They do it because they feel their knowledge and experience, both personal and professional, can add to parents' understanding of their deaf children from infancy through adulthood.

We absolutely agree that Deaf adults must be listened to and involved at all levels. The retrospective views we shared in earlier chapters attests to this, not to mention other previous works by Deaf professionals and more we will mention in coming chapters. We need more Deaf professionals in the EHDI system. Deaf individuals must be working as EHDI specialists/administrators, educators, and other support services providers. They must be in partnership with the overall EHDI system so that families of deaf and hard of hearing children will receive a more balanced plate of information and support. Families deserve a broad and positive vision of what their children can achieve as they grow. They deserve a vision that includes community with other deaf and hard of hearing children and their families—neither the children nor their families should ever feel "alone in the mainstream." This is a vision that allows the whole self to develop, blossom, and soar. The involvement of Deaf individuals who have grown up in the system, along with other EHDI professionals, will give the families such a broad and positive vision.

The NAD has continued to advocate for this involvement; its members have been attempting to obtain federal funds to develop a program of Deaf mentors. Movement in this direction on a national scale has been very slow, but certain states are at various stages of development and/or refinement of statewide programs to bring Deaf mentors/role models to families. (We talk more about this in Chapter 8.)

The EHDI system continues to grow. In 2010, the Walsh Bill requirements were expanded to emphasize services that states must make available to families once a child has been identified through the newborn screening. The Early Hearing Detection and Intervention Act of 2010 requires the Department of Health and Human Services to provide means for "developing and monitoring the efficacy of statewide programs and systems for hearing screening of newborns and infants, prompt evaluation and diagnosis of children referred from screening programs, and appropriate education, audiological, and medical interventions for children identified with hearing loss" (HR. 1246, S. 3199).

We cannot overstate the importance of the EHDI bills, nor of the federal funding of NCHAM and EHDI. They send a strong message that deaf and hard of hearing children have unique needs that are different from the needs of children with other disabilities and need to be appropriately and effectively addressed. However, while we applaud the federal attention to and funding for deaf and hard of hearing children from 0–5 years old, we remain concerned about bias.

It is abundantly clear from any perusal of the NCHAM Web site and the literature it puts out that the efforts of educators who are focused on the whole child and particularly on language acquisition and socioemotional health (e.g., CEASD and those involved in the National Agenda) are counteracted by organizations that push a fairly uniform focus on the ears, the mechanism of hearing, and the development of speech. In a global sense (both literally and figuratively), this push works hand in hand with the inclusion philosophy we talked about earlier. One could say it is only natural for people in general, who by and large have never themselves been deaf, to think these ideas are best for deaf people—they "should" learn to speak verbally, and hear, and they "should be 'in the mainstream'" 24/7. But deaf people, and their allies, have been saying "but, but, but . . ."—speaking against both of these ideas for centuries. Not that speech and hearing and inclusion are not important, but they miss another very important part of deaf and hard of hearing individuals' needs: early language acquisition and social capital. For early language acquisition, they need daily exposure to a visual language from the moment of birth, and for social capital, they need deaf and hard of hearing friends as well as hearing friends.

Current research in neuroscience is clear in its findings that visual language clearly supports cognitive, social, emotional, and language development. We are far past the time when anyone can say that exposing a deaf or hard of hearing child to a visual language (ASL) is in any way harmful to the development of a spoken language (Kovelman et al., 2009; Kushalnagar et al., 2010; Petitto, 2013; Petitto et al., 2001; Petitto & Kovelman, 2003).

Not long ago, people just took sides—you were either for ASL or for speech development—without much more than strong philosophical feelings to support their statements. Today, neuroscience tells us clearly that visual language greatly benefits children and that if we expose deaf children to a visual language as well as a spoken language during their critical language periods, we can give them skills that will change their trajectory in life, giving them a much higher chance for success. Early visual language development even *helps* spoken language development. And that includes children with cochlear implants (Preisler, Tvingstedt, & Ahlstrom, 2005; Seal, Nussbaum, Belzner, Scott, & Waddy-Smith, 2011). Early language development, visual language learning, and bilingual language development are all proven to facilitate language development in both deaf and hearing children. We can't say strongly enough that visual language (ASL), English, and speech can all work together beautifully and that is what deaf and hard of hearing children deserve.

Kelby Brick summarized his comments about EHDI's evolution from the early days of his involvement in the NAD's Law and Advocacy Center:

> The success [of EHDI] must be paired with the recognition that EHDI still does not do enough to make sure the families of the newly identified DHH children are directed to necessary language resources and making sure that those resources are available for those families. Too many deaf children are still growing up deprived of language during the very critical 0–3 years as a result of professionals and multimillion dollar nonprofits perpetuating bigotry or ignorance by directing families away from sign language.
>
> (K. Brick, personal communication, September 3, 2012)

In addition, too many deaf and hard of hearing children and too many families of these children spend years not realizing the vast and rich resource that is the Deaf community. Because of the push toward inclusion, fewer and fewer deaf and hard of hearing children and their families will learn about this rich resource, or at least not soon enough.

Nevertheless, we have learned from NCHAM and EHDI that these national systems provide a vehicle for input, and thus for hope. More and more, at EHDI there are presentations about bilingualism and the brain research that supports it. More and more, there are presentations about the value of Deaf mentors and how the various statewide EHDI systems can be sure that families have opportunities to meet other families with deaf or hard of hearing children as well as deaf or hard of hearing adults. More and more, individuals on the front lines of EHDI see the value of a national conference where these ideas are shared.

Now if only there were something similar for K–12, or at least K–5. That will be one of our major recommendations.

6

K–12 Interpreters and Mediated Education: More and Better Is Not Enough

"I have been a K–12 interpreter for over 8 years. One thing remains the same for each child I have worked with. I feel inadequate."

(K–12 interpreter, 2012)

To start our discussion on interpreting in the general education setting, we must begin by asking some basic questions about how deaf children learn. Given the linguistic deprivation deaf and hard of hearing children often experience, how can deaf and hard of hearing students who are not fluent language users use interpreters? Educators lack knowledge about *how* deaf children learn. How do they learn to read? And how do they learn indirectly through interpreters? There is so little research available to answer these important questions (although studies now being reported on visual language development give us hope). Yet deaf and hard of hearing children are placed in classrooms with the expectation that they will learn just the same way as every other child in that classroom. There is a dangerous assumption being made that placing interpreters in classrooms suddenly equalizes classroom discourse for deaf and hard of hearing students, which we know is not true. Those best in position to really know what is happening *today* in mainstream settings are the classroom interpreters. They see and hear on a daily basis the lives of deaf and hard of hearing children.

As Deaf adults, we, Gina and Linda, have both been in more situations than we can count in which we received information through sign language interpreters. Working at Gallaudet University and living in the Washington, D.C., area, we have been blessed with many excellent interpreters. We also have had our share of less-skilled interpreters, and we know firsthand how that can cripple our learning and our ability to participate in discussions and conversations.

Neither of us had the benefit of interpreters during our elementary and secondary schooling, so we can't say from personal experience what it is like to work with interpreters in K–12 settings. However our participants in this research study were wonderful, and often passionate, informants about the topic. We also met K–12 interpreters who were deeply concerned about how the students they worked with were faring in their general education settings and they shared their stories with us too. In Chapter 4, we shared the experiences of our research participants. In this chapter, we share some stories from K–12 interpreters.

Much thought went into decisions about which information to include in this chapter. From the numerous books, articles, and Web sites on educational interpreting and classroom interpreting specific to K–12, we gleaned what we think parents, teachers, administrators, and others concerned with deaf and hard of hearing children should know. Despite the fact that we are not experts in the field of interpreting, we are passing on what struck us, as Deaf professionals from our own academic fields, as important. We encourage interested readers to see our reference list and learn more about this very important topic.

Does Jenny Need an Interpreter?

Parents and general education teachers have great difficulty assessing how much conversational information a deaf or hard of hearing child is able to receive and process. Parents have difficulty figuring this out in their homes, and it is much harder in the neighborhood school. Students have hearing aids, cochlear implants, FM systems, note takers, and/or sign, oral, or cue interpreters, all of which make it easy to wildly overestimate what the child is hearing and/or receiving and processing. Both formal and informal assessment will give some idea as to how much a child has learned; however, there are few means by which to assess how much conversational content the child is receiving—and, as a corollary, what information she or he is *missing*. In addition, there is a tendency to overestimate how much a child with a cochlear implant is receiving and processing. How much the child benefits from the implant depends on numerous variables, the most important of which is probably how much training the child received postimplant. Many people are under the misconception that an implant automatically provides normal or near-normal hearing. However, a child born deaf must be trained to use the implant through many hours of auditory-verbal therapy and other kinds of practice. During the toddler and preschool years, while other children have been playing and developing other skills, the child with an implant has been spending hours being trained to use her implant.

The indications are that more and more children will have cochlear implants, and more and more parents will expect miracles from them. This will result in an increasing number of children alone in the mainstream with few, if any, adults who have experience with such children. From interviews with various professionals in various states (teachers of the deaf, state-level consultants, social workers), we have concluded that a great majority of deaf and hard of hearing children currently mainstreamed have only minimal contact with a deaf education professional on a day-to-day basis. In many schools, a child might be in touch with someone who thoroughly understands the issues he faces once a month or even once a year.

One of the consequences of this lack of oversight on the child's progress, and also of just the natural progression of education, is that at some point, the adults (parents and teachers) realize that the child is not progressing normally and needs assistance beyond the implant/hearing aid and the FM system. From our interviews, it seems that this often happens when the child reaches middle school where there are now numerous teachers and classrooms to contend with. The child's parents or school personnel decide a sign language interpreter or cued language transliterator is needed. It is unfortunate that the middle school educational crisis for deaf and hard of hearing students is merely conventional wisdom. Colleagues and deaf adults all over the United States have shared with both of us that it is in middle school that students show sufficient struggle that interpreters are requested. There is no national data on how often this happens, and it is unlikely that many states are tracking this either.

Our hypothetical child—let's call her Jenny—may not know any cued speech or sign language. But still, her parents and other adults know that something must be done or Jenny will simply fall behind even more. That an interpreter is being sought for a deaf child who knows no sign language or cues is an irony in itself and makes little sense. However, it is done. Often the people in the public school system have no idea where to find an interpreter, much less how to judge the skills of an interpreter. If Jenny lives in an urban area, the adults will have better luck finding a skilled and experienced interpreter because there will be agencies that specialize in placing skilled and experienced interpreters in various settings. If she lives in a less-urban area, chances of the adults finding such a person are reduced. But often the adults will find a not-so-skilled and/or not-so-experienced interpreter to place in front of Jenny and think that will take care of things as well as possible. Maybe as well as possible, but certainly not as well as any child deserves.

Let's suppose an interpreter is found and engaged, and let's assume that the interpreter *is* expertly skilled and has 5 years of experience in elementary and middle school settings. You should know, however, that this is not the norm: The norm is minimally skilled and minimally experienced, and we will explain more about this. Humor us for a few pages and imagine that Jenny has one of the best situations available for a child like her in a public school.

So now there is an additional adult in the classroom (and possibly in the hallways, cafeteria, etc.) who from everyone's perspective is there solely to assist the child in question. Parents, teachers, aides, and classmates all receive an implicit message and possibly explicit message: "This person relays information to Jenny who can't hear very well." For most individuals in Jenny's environs, this is as far as it goes, meaning that this becomes the entirety of their comprehension of why the interpreter is in the classroom and what she does there—she is there to tell Jenny what everyone says. Little do they know that this adult holds more information about Jenny's day-to-day life than anyone else in the world. The interpreter has an enormous responsibility, which is rarely understood by anyone, often including the interpreter.

Stories from K–12 Interpreters

The first person who really opened our eyes to the need to engage K–12 interpreters in discussions about deaf and hard of hearing children in general education settings speaks with a strong voice in the coming pages. We know she is not alone in her perceptions because of responses we have seen to Gina's article on the Web site StreetLeverage.com (Oliva, 2012). She is merely perhaps one of the more bothered and conflicted by what she sees, young enough to be idealistic about possible remedies, and brave enough to step up to the plate. We hope that her comments and those of several others we will present in the rest of this chapter will not only educate parents, teachers, and administrators about really critical facts, but also spur other interpreters to come forward and join efforts to push for optimal nationwide standards in the K–12 classroom interpreting arena.

It all started with an email received in May 2011:

Dear Gina,

Hello! My name is _____ and I am a Sign Language Interpreter. I do some freelance work but mainly I have been a K–12 interpreter for eight years. I attended your book presentation several years ago and am finally getting around to reading your book *Alone in the Mainstream.* So far I am only on Chapter 6 but am already greatly impacted by what I have read. I have worked with all ages from Kindergarten up to high school. In all those settings with all different students I have used ASL, PSE, Cued Speech. Some of the kids I have worked with have had mild hearing losses, some profound. These children come from hearing families who sign, hearing families who cue, hearing families who do neither, and a couple of families where the parents are deaf themselves. One thing remains the same with each child I have worked with. I feel inadequate.

Even though I am a highly skilled interpreter, I wonder if the mainstream setting is ever a social success, even with an interpreter, and every day that I see the kids struggling I feel just awful. It is very hard to watch day in and day out.

True, I have witnessed a few hard of hearing students who can speak clearly for themselves and are able to follow conversations quite successfully using their hearing alone. I have seen them flourish, feel included, and have high self-esteem. What is much more common however, and is so heart-breaking, is witnessing my students having the "dinner table syndrome" (as you put it), where they fake interest in some task to avoid looking lost. I see a lot of "superficial participation" where onlookers think the DHH student is "just fine" (as you also put it) but really they need to look deeper. My point is, this stuff still happens even with an interpreter present!

More often than not, the Deaf student only wants to chat WITH the interpreter; not with their peers through the interpreter. For years I've heard educational interpreters talk about trying to encourage their students to ask the other kids in class what their weekend plans are, or what good movies they've seen lately, but then the DHH student either says "no that's fine" and looks crushed as if no one wants to be their friend, not even the inter-preter, or they go and ask their classmates a few engaging questions, but the conversation quickly fizzles and nothing comes of it. I think an entire book could be written on the subject of Interpreter/deaf student relationships and how complicated it can get.

Today I am not satisfied. I want to do something about this. I think people will read your book and then pause and be reflective, but then resume life thinking "nowadays schools provide more and better services than ever before." Well, I firmly believe more and better is not enough! We need to push forward to ensure a better quality of life for tomorrow's DHH students. We need to ask the right questions, find the right people to share their stories, and make suggestions for making things better.

Receiving this letter was at once exciting and scary. Would we be able to share these voices that have been largely kept silent? Is there hope that K–12 interpreting as a whole can be improved, that the status of the profession can be elevated, that the experience of mainstreamed deaf and hard of hearing kids could be significantly enhanced by the repercussions of these voices being let loose? We believe so strongly that classroom interpreters hold much valuable information about the daily experiences of deaf and hard of hearing children that we asked this new friend if we could publish her letter. With her whole-hearted "sure!" we posted her letter online at StreetLeverage.com, a blog for interpreters. The article "Sign Language Interpreters in Mainstream Classrooms: Heartbroken and Gagged" was very well received, and several other interpreters came forward to offer their stories anonymously as well. We are truly grateful for their willingness and the time they spent reflecting and writing about what they have witnessed. These classroom interpreters are not perfect. They make mistakes, but they also share a deep concern for deaf and hard of hearing students in general education classes, and they very much want to be able to provide the best possible services. What is *best,* however, is often elusive.

Brenda Schick developed "Guidelines of Professional Conduct for Educational Interpreters" with input from numerous people particularly in the state of Colorado. We reviewed the August 2007 pdf version, but it can be found on the Web site ClassroomInterpreting.org. We applaud Schick and her colleagues for taking it upon themselves to produce this document. At the same time, we think it needs to be widely reviewed periodically and even expanded with real-life situations and suggested responses. And we would want to be sure that several Deaf scholars who themselves used interpreters in their own K–12 years are involved and that such is indicated on the credits.

We present some of these real-life situations to you directly from classroom interpreters, interspersed by our comments and food for thought. The first vignette is from a day in the life of a deaf middle school student:

> 8:00 Math class: I enter the door in the back of the room, and see nothing out of the ordinary: a few clusters of kids chatting—a group of girls, standing and laughing, a small circle of boys—some sitting in chairs, others sitting on table tops talking about who made the A and B squad for basketball. Most of the chairs are still up on the tables from the night before. . . . In the front of the room among the chair-topped tables sits one boy, by himself—my

student. He sits slumped in his chair, facing the front of the room where no one and nothing is.

I walk through the clusters of chatty students and take my seat at the front of the room—a few feet away from my student and right next to the Smart Board. We make eye contact, I smile, and he looks away and quickly glances to the side and lowers his chin as if to hide. I think he is very much aware of how having the interpreter makes him a social outcast—he seems to resent what I represent to him . . . a dependency he loathes . . . I can't say I blame him. As the bell rings, a loud, zesty girl passes me to take her seat and says, "Oh my God, I love your boots!" "Thanks." I sign and say with a smile. My student slinks further into his seat.

This reminder of the typical social environment in a school helps us to picture in our minds the day-to-day life of middle school students. Chatting with each other before, between, and after classes is an integral part of school life. Being involved in this chatter is what makes a youngster a part of the school life, the social circle, and the group. This deaf boy is clearly not part of the group in this setting.

One could argue that this boy may be more isolated than the average solitary student. We know there are individual differences, and parents might want to say their outgoing child won't be like this one. Granted. However, we remember the words of one of our focus group participants, a young man who is certainly a young leader in an urban Deaf community today: "I went from being the most popular kid to the least popular kid when I went from [oral day school] to my neighborhood school."

Math Class begins. The teacher has projected this statement onto the board: "Find two consecutive even integers such that twice the lesser of the two integers is four less than two times the greater integer." She reads the problem aloud to the class and my "interpretation" is to point to the sentence so my student can read it to himself. The students are given time to work on this problem independently as the teacher walks around looking at what kids are doing, and calling out general hints to the class as he moves around. Whenever he calls out a hint, I "flag" [wave my hand at] the Deaf student to get his attention so I can interpret the hint. "Ohhh," his face says, and he returns to his work. Before he even has a chance to locate the part of the problem that the teacher just referred to, erase something and give it another crack, the teacher verbalizes yet another hint. So I hold that bit of information in my head waiting for my student to finish writing down whatever from the previous hint, but then the teacher gives still another hint. So now I have two hints to convey, which I do, but as the exercise proceeds, my student gets further behind. Meanwhile, the hearing kids are finishing up the problem, because they have been able to have their eyes on their work, pencils to the paper, while simultaneously listening to the teacher's instruction. They can absorb the teacher's hints without looking away from their work. The teacher sees that most of the class is finished, so he draws their attention back up to the board, quickly recaps and then changes the slide to the next word problem, which is equally complicated. My student has not finished the first and is obviously frustrated.

Our informant goes on to surmise what she could have done differently, and she reflects on the fact that although all the regular classroom teachers have received in-service training, which includes instructions about a deaf or hard of hearing child's disadvantage in this kind of teaching style, they rarely, if ever, change their methods. She wonders if it is too much to expect a teacher of a class of 30 students to abandon a method that works just fine for 29 of them. However, for a teacher to speak to her class while they are looking at some visual (their book, their work, a PowerPoint, slide, a computer screen) sets up an impossible situation for a deaf or hard of hearing child. Teachers talking to students while the students' eyes are trained on related material happens day in and day out. The child using an interpreter only has two eyes. Teachers are told this. But that does not mean teachers change their methods, slow down, and allow time for the deaf child to look at both the visual material and the interpreter. This takes time and effort, often more than teachers have or are willing to give.

We know how hard this is and how much else teachers have to do. We also know this is not a problem unique to teachers. Family members and friends of deaf individuals also have difficulty remembering that their deaf and hard of hearing family members' eyes can only be at one place at a time. However, try to imagine a child's having this disadvantage on a daily, regular basis, probably several times each day. A child who cannot cope with classroom discourse is obviously not learning.

The next vignette is a scenario from a home economics class, in which the students work in small groups throughout the class setting. This is a stark illustration of not only missed academic opportunities but, more germane to our focus, an impoverished social environment for the deaf or hard of hearing student.

It's cooking lab time. The kids are at separate mini kitchens with one group of four boys, one group of four girls and my student is in a group with three girls. When the kids group themselves, I have noticed that girls are more welcoming and wave him over when he's (usually) standing alone, as everyone has grouped off. They hover around each other saying little things, like, "Which drawer does this whisk go in?" and "You may want to turn the heat down on that a bit." I feel that getting in the middle of them it is far too intrusive for kids at this age, so I stand a bit off to the side watching and waiting. Out of the blue the girls will ask my student to do something, then wait for me to intercede and interpret, and by the time my student looks back from me to give his answer, they're already off doing whatever it is they just asked him to do muttering, "Never mind, it's okay," under their breath. They seem to have no patience or are feeling anxious to keep moving forward. Over and over again they assign him tasks, and then step in to "help out," and as they are doing so, they flash me a little smile. I imagine them thinking, "See? I'm so nice. I like to help out special needs kids too." Mostly my student just shrugs and says, "Okay." The bell rings. Time to move on.

As we saw in earlier chapters, our focus group participants all had experiences similar to this. In this example, this activity could be helped greatly by classmates knowing some sign language, perhaps even activity-specific signs. Or at the very least, they could learn how to include the deaf student in the group experience (get his visual attention, take turns talking and each time make sure he is looking at the speaker, speak clearly, have a note pad for jotting things down). These are easily learned behaviors and skills, even if just used in some classes or in group work, and would go a very long way in shifting the responsibility for inclusion from the deaf or hard of hearing child and his interpreter to the rest of the folks in the general education classroom, that is, the teacher and classmates. After all, if this is to be education for life and a way for the deaf child to learn how to get along in the hearing world, should not the hearing children also learn some basic skills, courtesies, and techniques for including deaf and hard of hearing people in group situations? The desire for direct communication with one's peers is universal. We elaborate on these suggestions in our final chapter.

The next vignette describes a situation in which the interpreter walked into an English class, just a few moments before class was to begin, to find the students sitting in groups that were different than their normal seating. She heard them talking animatedly about something far removed from English class—their favorite foods. Her student is seated in his usual place. Then she noticed that the teacher had written some pre-class instructions on the board—telling the students to get in groups based on a certain characteristic they had in common, a typical icebreaker activity. The minute the bell rang, the teacher started walking around asking students which food they had selected and why. She asked the deaf student, and he just shrugged. At that point the teacher began to verbally explain the whole activity to him:

> "Do you see where I wrote that on the board? It's supposed to be an ice breaker to get you kids to start sitting by new people and making friends." Obviously my student is thoroughly embarrassed and again just shrugs. I, of course, know what this means ("Leave me alone, don't talk to me like I'm an idiot in front of everyone, of course I understood what was going on, but what the heck can I do?! I can't hear them!") I wait to see if my student will advocate for himself or if the teacher will figure it out, but she doesn't.

We think this student's teacher was insensitive and condescending. Even if it was the first day of school and the teacher had no idea about the deaf student's skills, this way of addressing a student simply has no place in a classroom. Didn't the teacher have any sense of providing the child with some dignity? Think about how the other students would come to view this child. How teachers perceive and interact with students packs a wallop. Their behavior can make or break a child's entire school year. Deaf and hard of hearing students must deal with an enormous social stigma, whether we like it or not. They really need teachers to be on their side and by their daily behavior to work toward the reduction and eradication of this stigma.

Let's look at another vignette, this one from an elementary school. We include this for two reasons. First, it illustrates the profound (albeit unintended) oppressive consequences of a widespread general education practice, pull-out time, which our focus group informants detested. Secondly, it provides an example of the lack of consensus among professionals in the school system regarding the flexibility of the interpreter's role and perhaps even the role of education. In this story, a second-grade student has just returned to her regular classroom seat after her pull-out time. She could have been pulled out for speech therapy or extra math help—it does not matter.

> The teacher explains the task that the other students are already working on. They are to cut out different animal pictures from a set of papers and paste them onto other papers with categories such as "mammal," "bird," "insect," etc. When done, they will have "free time" to play games until the next period. I interpret this and my student gets to work. Within minutes the other students start bringing their completed work to the teacher's desk and then heading to play Connect 4, Guess Who, and other games in another part of the classroom. Soon my student is the only one left and still has lots of cutting to do—the other kids were working on this for an hour before my student got back from his pull-out time!!
>
> I notice that tears are welling up in my student's eyes and her hurried cutting is getting frantic and sloppy, I quickly consider my options. I could (a) do nothing, (b) encourage the student to advocate for herself and say something to the teacher, (c) say something to the teacher myself, (d) help her quickly get the work done.
>
> I decide that this situation is happening NOW and I need to act NOW. The child is too young to advocate for herself. She can't articulate how this is oppressive and an accommodation needs to be made. I look over to the teacher who is clearly in the depths of working on who knows what—she has her reading glasses on, is occasionally on the phone, typing, writing, going through papers. In retrospect, I perhaps should have interrupted her, but I decided not to. Instead, I say to my little one, "Want me to cut them out and you just paste them? Then you can get this done quickly and go play. Sound good?" I get a grateful head nod, and I go to work. Crisis defused.

This was a challenging dilemma for this interpreter and for the student as well. They both ended up seemingly feeling good about how they handled this; however, our informant reported that the classroom teacher later reprimanded the interpreter for her actions. All she really had attempted to do was to equalize classroom opportunities. We don't know the whole story; we only know our classroom interpreter informant's perspective. Her heart went out to this child who wanted to play like the other children. She obviously believed it was more important cognitively that the child be able to categorize the creatures appropriately as mammals, reptiles, insects, etc. The cutting task, she believed, was secondary. We do know that this child, because of pull-out, was missing an important part of her school day—playing with classmates.

Before we go further in this overview of the issues surrounding K–12 interpreting, we want to emphasize an important fact: The burden of communication should never fall only on the interpreter and by association, the deaf or hard of hearing child being served by that interpreter. We propose that all teachers and classmates learn to communicate directly with deaf and hard of hearing students. With monitored and respectful turn taking, clear articulation if the child has aural/lipreading skills, use of sign language and/or visual cues specific to the subject matter and/or group tasks, and through the written word, direct communication can take place at least some of the time. Classmates can be taught how to do these things—teachers need to model this true inclusiveness. These are the things families do when they have a deaf member. They are normal things a hearing person tends to do whenever a deaf and hearing person engage in a friendship. These behaviors undertaken by teachers and hearing peers would make the vignettes relayed here less likely to happen, and they would make a true difference in improving the school lives of deaf and hard of hearing children. And they could be used not only in the classroom, but also outside the formal classroom. From our focus group participants and from Mindy Hopper's research, we know how important that is as well.

K–12 Interpreter Education, Certification, and Practice Issues

To give you a broader picture of the many issues involved with the profession of educational interpreting, we now shift to take a look at interpreter education, professional certification, and practice issues. At the same time, we want to call attention to what we consider a jump, albeit a logical one, to a proposed and presumed solution that is floating around among the leaders in this arena: changing the role and training of K–12 interpreters. In general, this presumed solution would give the educational interpreter more knowledge and skills, making him a "co-teacher" (an oversimplification). We wish to state at the outset that we think a better solution is to understand what interpreting *is* and train these individuals to be effective, professional, *better interpreters*. Then we need to evolve a new and separate profession, "deaf educational specialists," who are preferably themselves Deaf, to provide the other support that children need that goes beyond mere interpreting. At the risk of getting ahead of ourselves, we wish to state this at the outset.

The majority of currently available certificate and degree programs in interpreter education are preparing individuals to interpret spoken information into sign language, but this relaying of information barely scratches the surface in the realm of making a deaf or hard of hearing child's educational experience comparable to that of a child with intact hearing. When an individual graduates from a 2-year interpreter training program, he is usually barely ready to start interpreting—imagine taking 2 years of French or Spanish and then calling oneself an interpreter. Sad to say, the first jobs many of these individuals find are in educational settings—because both the pay and the standards are low. While the official (i.e., written) standards may be higher, these are the individuals the schools are hiring. At any rate, these training programs do not, and actually cannot, in the short time the students are with them, provide the knowledge and perspective that would enable them to be effective interpreters, much less co-teachers in the K–12 setting.

There is no official or unified stance—not in the interpreting profession, nor in the deaf education profession, nor in government oversight—regarding what skills and knowledge would maximally improve the overall experience of the deaf child's experience in general education settings. Effective direct communication, which would be the ideal, is definitely not happening frequently in this setting. We feel this oversight is desperately needed. It is our hope that this chapter, along with the preceding one, will drive home the point that this state of affairs is an example of gross systematic failure, with government intervention warranted.

The activity of sign language interpreting began when Deaf people and hearing people needed to communicate with each other. Deaf adults needed access to doctors, lawyers, and postsecondary education. Over time, a professional organization was born and nurtured, and today the Registry of Interpreters for the Deaf (RID) addresses all manner of issues related to sign language interpreting. There is a certification process, and in the United States there are numerous highly skilled individuals who work as interpreters, primarily with Deaf adults—we mentioned at the beginning of this chapter that we have had experience with such highly skilled interpreters, as well as with those less skilled. The profession as a whole, however, has truly arisen to meet the needs of adults, and later in this chapter we describe how the RID communicated its views on K–12 interpreting for the GAO report mentioned in Chapter 5.

As we detailed in Chapter 5, the phenomenon of sign language interpreters for children in K–12 settings grew as a natural extension from the legislation passed in 1975, P.L. 94-142. Deaf children previously educated directly in schools with deaf and hearing teachers who signed were removed from those deaf-friendly environments and placed into public schools. These schools, ignorant of the needs of deaf children, of language acquisition, and of interpreting processes, began to seek and hire interpreters when they found themselves with deaf and hard of hearing children who required them. Frequently the individuals they hired did not have and had difficulty obtaining RID certification; their skills were simply not strong enough to be considered minimally qualified to interpret. Yet, schools needed them (deaf kids were in the schools) and sometimes (often, at least in the beginning) were hiring people with maybe one sign language class under their belt. It remains the case today that many interpreters without sufficient training and skills are hired for the K–12 setting.

Because so many of the working K–12 interpreters were having a hard time passing the standard RID certification test, some academics decided that a different test was needed for interpreters working in public schools. The Educational Interpreter Performance Assessment (EIPA) was developed, with leadership provided by Boys Town National Research Hospital, and Brenda Schick of the University of Colorado–Boulder.

Two thousand one hundred individuals took the EIPA when it was first developed, between 2002 and 2004. The test yields results on a five-point scale. Level 2 is considered *advanced beginner:* "An individual at this level is not recommended for classroom interpreting." Level 3, *intermediate:* "An interpreter at this level needs continued supervision and should be required to participate in continuing education in interpreting." Level 4, *advanced intermediate:* "An individual at this level would be able to convey much of the classroom content but may have difficulty with complex topics or rapid turn taking." Level 5, *advanced:* "An individual at this level is capable of clearly and accurately conveying the majority of interactions within the classroom" (see http://www.classroominterpreting.org/EIPA/performance /rating.asp).

The developers of EIPA consulted with various state departments of education to assist them in determining what minimum EIPA score should be required for K–12 interpreters. Some of these departments of education called in numerous experts and stakeholders to help with this determination, and some did not. Schick conveyed to us that when EIPA developers were involved, they informed state administrators that every child deserved a highly qualified interpreter, and this meant a score of 4.5 or 5 on the test. However, administrators needed to consider that most EIPA test takers simply were not scoring at this level and thus were concerned about requiring a score and then having the schools be unable to find individuals with those scores to work with their deaf and hard of hearing children. This is all wrapped up with the issue of so many interpreter training programs across the United States using just 2 years to both teach a language (ASL) and train in interpreting skills. So while the EIPA developers and others are well aware that a child deserves an interpreter with a 4.5 or 5 on the EIPA, the reality is that there are few individuals with these scores who would work in schools, at least not at the wages schools are paying, which is another major issue (B. Schick, personal communication, August 31, 2012).

ClassroomInterpreting.org recommends a minimum score of 4 for working K–12 interpreters. Marsha Gunderson, an educational consultant with the Iowa Department of Education, took it upon herself to survey states to see what EIPA score they required. As of March 2012, 10 states required a 4.0, 20 required a 3.5, and 6 required a 3.0 (M. Gunderson, personal communication, June 13, 2012). The states are spread all across the nation—there do not appear to be any regional leanings. In this total of 36 states mentioning and requiring a specific EIPA level, Northeastern, Southern, Midwestern, and Western states are included in each of these categories.

Of the 2002–2004 test takers, only 17% received a score of 4.0 or better. Another 21% received a score of 3.5. So fully 62% received a score of 3 or less (Schick, Williams, & Kupermintz, 2006). As of this writing, approximately 16,000 EIPA assessments have been completed. Some of these are repeat test-takers—those who take it again to try to improve their score, or those from the few states that require retesting after some period of time, or those who might earn more money with a higher score. The test administrators estimate that at least 10% are retakes. We were informed (B. Schick, personal communication, August 2 and August 30, 2012) that this larger group is showing essentially the same spread of scores as shown by the initial test-takers.

It is critical to note that a great majority of the individuals taking the EIPA have *already* been working in schools, for 6.5 years on average, when they take the EIPA. And, as a note of comparison, from this and other studies it is known that individuals with full RID certification will score at an average of 4.2 on the EIPA (Schick et al., 2006). So, the picture is that many, if not most, interpreters working in K–12 settings are far less skilled than those working with adults, and far less skilled than is considered standard, appropriate, and to be expected.

In their analysis of the EIPA results, the researchers honed in on a number of specific skills that are especially important in the educational setting. Included here are (a) the ability to provide a dynamically equivalent message that includes meaning contained in the prosodic elements of the teacher's utterances, (b) the ability to indicate who is speaking, and (c) the ability to use spatial mapping to convey an accurate message. For the 2,100 interpreters who took the EIPA in 2002–2004, the average score for these three skills was even lower than their overall score, with a majority scoring an average of 2.5. This means that for these key elements of the teachers' utterances, a majority of these interpreters would be "not recommended for classroom interpreting."

Of these three skills, we think parents and teachers especially need to understand the first skill, ability to convey prosody. *Prosody* is easiest to describe as the *way* that something is said—the tone, the style, the manner of communication. Prosody adds critical meaning in communication, conveying information indirectly through tone of voice, emphasis on certain words, tempo, and other elements. In one study of the use of prosody, Nicodemus (2009) observed certified and highly skilled as they interpreted a message from English into ASL. Building on the work of earlier researchers, Nicodemus had ASL-fluent Deaf adults identify phrase and sentence boundaries in these ASL interpretations and found that the highly experienced interpreters used, on average, seven prosodic markers at these boundaries. An oversimplified example might be this: When we speak with our voices, we "chunk words" together. We say, for example "theboy isgoing tothestore." We do not say: "the. boy. is. going. to. the. store." When speaking to children, teachers and other adults often exaggerate the verbal prosodic elements (tone, emphasis, etc.) in order to highlight new information, to create interest, and to emphasize grammatical structure. Highly skilled interpreters use the "prosodic markers," (head nods, eye blinks, and other subtle actions/movements) to effectively provide a sense-making translation and not "the. boy. is." If a child's interpreter does not have this skill and does not include functionally equivalent prosodic structures in his signing, a deaf child may very easily misunderstand story structure, questions versus statements, and even the mood or tone of a simple story.

A look at a few examples of prosody will help us to see exactly the kind of information the EIPA exam takers would have difficulty conveying. Concrete examples like these will really help parents and regular classroom teachers understand these subtleties, so we asked our interpreter-informants to share.

> Suppose the teacher says, "It's almost time for lunch." This could have a variety of meanings depending on how it's said. The prosody (tone, emphasis, rhythm) of that short phrase could mean several things, including: (a) You've

been working so hard I bet you hardly noticed time flew by—you've earned this break! (b) You better hurry up—you've been wasting a lot of time and your time's almost up—get a move on! (c) You need to wrap up your work and clean up.

An even simpler example might be one familiar to most of us. Suppose you asked a teenager how her day was and she responded with a simple one-word answer, "Fine." You know she's really not fine; maybe she yelled it and slammed the door, or perhaps her facial expression showed utter disgust and annoyance by even being spoken to by someone as uncool as you. But all she *uttered* was "fine." This is an example we can all relate to.

An interpreter needs to convey the actual message, including intent, implications, and unspoken but inferred conclusions from the teacher's words. Individuals who score 3.0 on the EIPA typically do not possess the ability to interpret spoken prosody into signed prosody (Schick, et al., 2006). Being able to make a facial expression to match the prosody of the teenager saying "fine" is relatively easy. However, conveying more complex prosody like that included in the "it's time for lunch" example requires much more knowledge of the language and skill in processing and conveying. In a related example, suppose a teacher said, "Clean up your tables *now*." The prosody, highlighting a certain word (*now*) through vocal emphasis, conveys that the children need to act immediately and rapidly. A highly skilled interpreter will be able to convey this emphasis by using ASL prosody such as "holding" a sign, or signing it with more tension or speed or size. If this is not accurately conveyed, a deaf student might not realize this and get punished or mocked for a slow response.

Knowledgeable parents made aware of these general shortcomings of K–12 interpreting would likely want an expert observer to regularly evaluate their child's interpreter. How well is the interpreter communicating the teacher's direct as well as indirect message? The parents might want, and might rightfully expect, this evaluation to happen at relatively frequent intervals—certainly more than once a year. They would likely want to know that their child is receiving meaningful language rather than language that looks like one big ongoing stream of information with no indication as to what is important.

The previously referenced Web site, ClassroomInterpreting.org, developed and maintained by the developers of the EIPA, is a wonderful resource on the topic of educational interpreting. Although a few other books and articles have been recently published (see the reference list), this Web site seems to be a comprehensive resource designed to easily address the questions and concerns of parents, teacher, and administrators. As we were finishing this chapter, another Web site emerged, based on the work in Canada done by the Minerva Deaf Research Lab—with which Debra Russell and her colleagues are affiliated—that we recommend as well: www .mdrltoolkit.ualberta.ca.

The authors of ClassroomInterpreting.org speak directly to the perceptions conveyed by our interpreter-informant. In addition to emphasizing that relaying the implicit messages conveyed through teacher prosody is difficult for most educational interpreters, they state that it is unrealistic to expect children to understand that they are missing something and to subsequently themselves request clarification. Parents know this from experience—they often have to probe and ask questions to ensure their children understand what they mean. It is only with experience that children learn to recognize when they do not understand something that has been said. (See http://www.classroominterpreting.org/Interpreters/children /Interpreting/monitoring.asp.)

Research on educational interpreting is continuing. One very promising study is a dissertation by Elizabeth Langer (2007). This study breaks down even further the kinds of utterances made by elementary school teachers, such as those related to beliefs, relevance (relatedness to the students' lives), explicit directions, and several others. She then analyzes how well these kinds of utterances are interpreted by interpreters with varying EIPA scores. This seems to be groundbreaking and much needed. We hope it will stimulate more of the same.

The Schick et al. (2006) study also compared scores obtained by interpreters working at the elementary level with those of interpreters working at the secondary level. The researchers found that the elementary interpreters were significantly less skilled. "This means that the interpreters with the least adequate skills may be assigned to work with younger children, with the mistaken assumption that interpreting at that level is easier or that younger children have 'less language' so that it is acceptable if the interpreter has less language" (p. 13). Any text on early language development in elementary children, especially those in K–3, will drive home that this is simply untrue. If anything, deaf children of this age need even more skilled educational interpreters as well as more skilled language models.

The RID conducted a survey of educational interpreters in 2007–2009 that supplements these findings. The results of this study are reported as "The Educational Interpreter's Niche in RID From the Practitioner's Perspective: Survey Results Submitted by the Educational Interpreter Committee" on the RID Web site (rid.org). Only 6% of the respondents indicated that they were working in elementary settings. Virtually all the respondents were working in high schools (60%) and postsecondary settings (27%). So not only do we know that elementary students' needs are great and their language and other learning is so very critical to success in subsequent grades, we also know that their interpreters are even less skilled and less likely to take the EIPA or participate in professional organizations and research.

Students Served by Educational Interpreters

Unfortunately, there is limited information about how many deaf and hard of hearing K–12 students are using interpreters. Federal laws require states to serve all students with special needs, and certain general requirements are spelled out; but individual states have ample leeway as to how they provide services and how they keep track of the number of students receiving this or that service. As such, we do not have a clear picture—rather, we have information with which to make somewhat educated guesses.

The Gallaudet Research Institute has long conducted the Annual Survey of Deaf and Hard of Hearing Children and Youth. The 2009–2011 survey reports on 37,828 children. Of these 13%, or 2,599 students, are reported to use interpreting services. Of the 78,000 deaf and hard of hearing students covered by the 2011 GAO report "Deaf and Hard of Hearing Children: Federal Support for Developing Language and Literacy" (see Chapter 5 for further discussion of the report), 11% were being educated with sign only, and 35% with both speech and sign. Although the fact that many children are using sign language interpreters is mentioned, virtually no further detail is provided. The fact that the report is titled "Language and Literacy" and yet says next to nothing about interpreting issues speaks volumes about the lack of understanding the officials at GAO have for the pitfalls of a mediated education.

Fortunately, some states do have these numbers, and we were able to get this information from a handful. For example, the Ohio Education Management Information System includes 2,546 deaf and hard of hearing students and approximately 500 K–12 interpreters (Peterson & Monikowski, 2011). From Wisconsin we have an estimate of 300 of approximately 2,200 deaf and hard of hearing students using interpreters (C. Schweitzer, personal communication, February 18, 2013) and from North Carolina approximately 400 out of 2,219 using interpreters (R. Ragin, personal communication, February 20, 2013). It seems safe to assume that there are probably upwards of 10,000 children in the United States using interpreters. No matter how we count, this is a lot of children, and a lot of interpreters to know so little about.

Interpreter Education Programs: Not Ready for Prime Time

The National Consortium of Interpreter Education Centers, (NCIEC), funded by the Rehabilitation Services Administration (RSA) of the U.S. Department of Education, is probably the best source of information about where the graduates of interpreter education programs are working, overall. Federal funds enable the National Interpreter Education Center (NIEC) and five Regional Interpreter Education Centers (RIECs) to develop and manage programs geared toward increasing the number of qualified interpreters nationwide.

As part of its grant responsibilities, NCIEC conducted general surveys in early 2007 and later in 2009. Approximately 4,000 of approximately 8,000[3]

---

3. At the time of this book's publication, RID reports 13,000 members.

members of RID responded to the 2007 survey, and approximately 3,000 responded to the 2009 survey. Results from both surveys are reported in *Interpreter Practitioner Needs Assessment Trends Analysis* (Cokely & Winston, 2010).

Approximately 23% of the individuals who responded to these surveys indicated that they spent more than 50% of their working hours in K–12 settings. This lends credence to our assertion that many working interpreters are in fact in schools, and thus deaf and hard of hearing children are receiving an interpreted education.

It is common knowledge among interpreters and also among other professionals concerned with the education of deaf and hard of hearing children that, very frequently, interpreter preparation program (IPP) graduates work in educational settings for only the first few years after completing their training. Even while they are still in school, these interpreters learn that educational settings are kind of an open door—it is relatively easy to obtain employment as a K–12 interpreter. If you want to work in that area, or simply get practice interpreting in an *easy* setting, there are plenty of opportunities. While this picture may be *slowly* changing, it is still possible; it is far too common for interpreters to be employed with minimal skill and/or in positions where no one fluent in the language is available for support, mentoring, and evaluating.

It is important to note that although EIPA requirements are an improvement over the earlier state of affairs, districts can and will say that they cannot find an interpreter meeting a minimum score level willing to work for the pay offered, and thus they hire individuals with lower scores. A colleague of ours was offered minimum wage ($7.31 an hour in 2011) to interpret for an elementary-school-age child in the state of Florida. We know schools are hurting for money, but, if they receive funds from the federal government, they should use those funds for the children listed as needing the services. And, once again, the worst part of this is that the information available is piecemeal and dependent upon the concern and passion of a few individuals and organizations. Federal and/or state governments need to do more—much more.

Looking to the Future: Information Needed!

In a letter from the RID to Alana Miller of the GAO (in response to the GAO's request for information for their previously mentioned report from the perspective of the educational interpreting profession), RID recommends "a federally commissioned study of the demographics of the nation's [deaf and hard of hearing] students and their educational support team." It recommends further, "This survey should look at the specific linguistic and cultural needs of the children and how they relate to the specific skills, experience, and credentials of the educational personnel serving them" (Bailey, 2010).

The Canadian government has already funded such a large-scale study in that nation. Debra Russell of the University of Alberta was awarded a federally funded research grant for a 3-year nationwide project involving online surveys and interviews with teachers, interpreters, parents, and students. Her study examined the effectiveness of classroom interpretation in meeting the needs of deaf and hard of hearing students from various viewpoints and stakeholders. Findings point to some disturbing patterns that suggest that interpreter-mediated education is not serving deaf and hard of hearing children well for curricula and social access (Russell & Winston, 2013). The study is showing through the analysis of actual samples that interpreters are not recognizing the ways in which teachers use language to create engagement and promote critical thinking (D. Russell, personal communication, March 20 2012).

Debra Russell, by the way, is one of Canada's leading scholars in the field of sign language interpreter training. She is one of the founding members of the World Association of Sign Language Interpreters and is the 2011–2015 president. Individuals like her all over the world lead efforts to ensure that sign language interpreters optimally serve the needs of deaf and hard of hearing consumers, including children. In both the United States and Canada, most interpreter educators have long held that K–12 interpreters must first be educated and prepared in the general field of interpretation and then be trained as specialists (Witter-Merithew & Nicodemus, 2012).

This makes sense to us. Teachers specialize—in pre-K, elementary, and secondary education—with their concomitant subject areas. Doctors and lawyers specialize. Many professions and trades offer specialties, and always the professional or craftsman or technician in question must have general skills before specializing. Why should the individuals to whom we entrust our deaf and hard of hearing children's mediated education be any different? And why should schools and governments allow them to be paid so little, in comparison?

As we close this chapter, we would like to share a summary excerpt from ClassroomInterpreting.org:

> It may come as a surprise to many professionals that not much is known about how children learn through an interpreter. The practice is still new. . . . In some sense, each student is an experiment, with the educational team responsible for monitoring success. The skills of an interpreter are certainly an important factor, but there are many other issues that are important to consider as well. (See http://www.classroominterpreting.org//Interpreters /children/index.asp.)

So, the child's education is "an experiment"—conducted by untrained "scientists"—and authorized by funders and policy makers who often, too often, know very little about deaf and hard of hearing children in general. This Web site, excellent and chock full of information as it is, offers little to help schools improve the situation or to inform readers what can be done to minimize the damage, other than that K–12 interpreters need to be better trained so they can achieve a score of 4.0 or better on the EIPA. Similar suggestions are offered on the aforementioned Minerva Deaf Research Lab Web site and in the handful of scholarly texts that focus on educational interpreting listed in our references and resources. The bottom line is that we need what Brown and Schick (2011) suggest, which echoes the recommendations that RID spelled out to the GAO in its 2010 letter:

> We need a national and international discussion about educational interpreting, but it is imperative that these discussions include all the major stakeholders in the education of DHH students: teachers, speech pathologists, parents, and consumers as well as the people doing the job—educational interpreters.   (www.rid.org/content/index.cfm/AID/225)

The category of "consumers" must include a significant number of deaf and hard of hearing adults who have been "experiments" and who are now currently working as educators, counselors, state-level consultants, and in other professional capacities. These individuals have important perspectives to share on the many professional issues interpreters struggle with on a daily basis—there is no substitute for actual experience.

We have presented data from participants in three focus groups (which included 21 individuals from 18 states), as well as from 100+ survey participants, about their K–12 experience with interpreters. We have also presented information from the literature about EIPA test-taker results, K–12 interpreters' stories, and research done by various scholars. There is more—plenty, actually—to justify this statement: Deaf and hard of hearing children who are using interpreters in general education settings are effectively denied adequate access to education and are getting short shrift. Parents and other interested parties ought to deeply educate themselves about all the issues we have presented—visit the Web sites, read the books and articles, and investigate the workings of their respective states and districts. To not do so is tantamount to turning a blind eye to reality.

7

Summer and Weekend Programs:
If You Build It, They Will Come

"I wanted to take my camp friends home with me."
(Deaf adult looking back on her days at a Deaf camp)

IN THE preceding chapters, we have shared stories, facts, and ideas we have gleaned from focus groups, an online survey, conversations with various professionals (interpreters, interpreter trainers, teachers, consultants, government officials), and the latest relevant research, articles, books, and Web sites from those same professional groups. At this point, we turn attention to a piece of our vision for a better world for deaf and hard of hearing children.

Our vision includes an element that provides respite for the children from any isolation they may feel. We hope people will get moving on this element while simultaneously working for systemic change in K–12 school systems. In our view it will be comparatively easier to add to and improve summer and weekend programs than it will be to revamp K–12 systems or improve interpreting education. We are not saying that the latter does not need revamping—we are simply saying that the children cannot wait for that to happen.

Gina spent several summers (2005–2010) investigating summer and weekend programs designed specifically for deaf and hard of hearing children around the United States. She conducted this study as a result of conversations with her college students returning from their summer vacations, in which invariably at least half of them would talk about working at summer camps for deaf and hard of hearing children. At the time of her study there were approximately 70–80 such summer camps in operation, according to a list maintained by the Clerc Center (the K–12 program located on the campus of Gallaudet University). From hearing these stories, she became convinced that summer programs hold the promise of alleviating some of the socially detrimental effects of mainstreaming, and thus she embarked on that study, visiting over 15 summer and weekend programs over the course of several years. The various summer and weekend camps and programs were diverse in the kinds of activities offered, the background of the staff hired, the geographic distribution of campers, the language skills of campers, and so on. Yet, all had something of value to offer the campers or participants: an opportunity to meet others like themselves.

Children in school today need these programs *now*. Children in school today cannot wait for nationwide or even statewide change to provide the experiences and social capital that they need to be gaining and developing *now*. Our focus group participants told us loudly and clearly, "We needed to have friends who were like us." Our focus group participants, now young adults, told us they needed their "deaf fix." This is the same phenomenon the now older participants of Gina's first study echoed again and again: "met deaf wow." Parents, teachers, other school personnel, scholars, and advocates can do much to provide opportunities for a "deaf fix" in summer and weekend programs. These programs, along with technology for staying in touch with these friends, will do much to alleviate the issues raised by our informants.

Let us turn to Gina's study, a first-person account.

Conception of a New Research Project

Around the time when *Alone in the Mainstream* was just hitting the shelves, one of my students sent me an email from her personal address, "IBgirl@_____." I thought, "IBGirl??" "What's that??" Must be some silly play on words, as in "I be a girl." I was so curious, I had to ask, and I learned that it stood for "Isola Bella Girl." The student explained that when she was growing up "alone in the mainstream," she would attend a summer camp in northwestern Connecticut, Isola Bella. After her first summer there, she could not wait for the school year to be over so she could go back and be with "kids like me," as she put it. From then on she went to Isola Bella every summer, and she became a counselor when she was old enough. Her connection to this camp was so strong that she christened herself "IBgirl."

I heard variations of this "my summer vacation" theme during many a fall semester over my years teaching at Gallaudet. Listening to these stories, I became more and more convinced that the 70+ summer camps listed on the Clerc Center Web site had to be some kind of treasure trove. In theory, therein would lie the answer to the juxtaposition so often mentioned by the individuals who contributed essays for *Alone in the Mainstream* (Oliva, 2004): "Well, academically I think it [public school] was better than a deaf school, but socially it was just the pits." Summer camps could and should take up at least some of the slack from this juxtaposition, wouldn't you think?

Thanks to generous funding from the Gallaudet Research Institute (GRI), I was able to visit nine summer camps/programs and three weekend programs over several summers. Three programs were in the eastern United States, six were in the Midwest, and three were further west.

Directors' Survey and Research Goals

From the comments I heard from my returning-from-summer-vacation students, I developed a sense that there were differences between summer camps—students would say that some programs were more like "any old camp" or a "regular camp." While describing their summer work experiences, they might also say it was a "mainstream camp" or a "Deaf camp," with the word "Deaf" signed with emphasis to indicate that the camp provided a "culturally Deaf" experience. Although I had yet to attend or observe any camp, I did have this little precursor that I might intuitively grasp what my students were referring to or inferring from once I saw these programs in action.

My goal was to learn if these camps could counteract and alleviate the social isolation stemming from spending weeks, months, years "alone in the mainstream." With this goal came a kind of corollary that for this counteraction and alleviation to happen, the camps would need to be welcoming to youngsters not fluent in ASL. If the potential campers were in mainstream settings without an interpreter, chances were they would know little if any ASL. If they were mainstreamed *with* an interpreter, they would likely have learned to sign from *watching* the interpreter, and this would mean that their sign skills could be limited—they would have *some* sign skills but not be fluent in ASL.

My first step was to conduct a survey via email, to representatives from about 75 camps on a list maintained by the Clerc Center—the most comprehensive list available—and 29 responded. Of those who responded most thoroughly, the directors were either deaf themselves, or closely allied with deaf-focused organizations. The camps run by service organizations and non-deaf-focused nonprofits by and large did not respond. Many, if not most, of these are "camps within camps," meaning that a parent camp serving all disabilities devotes a week or two to deaf campers.

Only five of the respondents indicated that they were doing any specific or direct marketing to mainstream schools. Most of their marketing efforts were directed toward traditional residential schools for the deaf, and toward the well-known deaf-focused community service organizations in their own and nearby states. Their comments included statements like "We get a few [mainstreamed kids] but not enough—they are afraid to meet other deaf/ hard of hearing kids." In addition, several commented about not having access to mainstreamed children: "How can we let them know about our camp?"

The survey asked if the directors thought a periodic nationwide meeting of Deaf camp directors would be helpful, and the response was overwhelmingly yes, although the directors expressed concern about whether most could afford to attend—both money-wise and time-wise. This is significant because without such periodic meetings, camp directors would have little opportunity to discuss concerns with others facing similar concerns.

Because deafness is such a low-incidence disability, professionals and volunteers who work with deaf children need a forum to discuss common issues so that solutions can be formulated and implemented.

As for topics the directors thought should be discussed at such a hypothetical nationwide meeting, their responses reflected both generic camp concerns (rainy day activities, outdoor activities, theme-based programming) and concerns specific to deaf camps. In the latter category were concerns such as perceived lack of experience with debriefing processes in deaf campers, and how to attract more campers from mainstream schools.

Overall, the survey results gave just a glimpse of the camps, but they helped build my network for me. From the survey, I was able to move on to see which directors would welcome me to come and actually observe their camp in action.

My next step was to submit a proposal to the Gallaudet Research Institute in order to get funding to actually visit these camps so I could get a sense for how welcoming they would be to deaf and hard of hearing children and youth from general education settings. My research questions were ambitious. They were aimed at information that would help to identify characteristics that would enable a summer (or weekend) program to be welcoming toward and enriching for "solitaire" deaf and hard of hearing middle- and high-school students.

Over summers during 2004–2008 (with a few additional observations in 2010), I spent a few days at nine well-known and lesser-known summer camps all over the United States. My decisions regarding which to observe were based, for the most part, on preliminary interactions with the directors of these programs—those whose directors welcomed me and thought the study was worth their participation. Two directors offered me on-site accommodations; when I visited the others, I stayed at nearby motels.

These forays—and to me they were indeed adventures—into a phenomenon that few other "outsiders" have seen collectively left me with one primary impression that I wish to emphasize throughout my reporting thereof: *all the programs are labors of love.* Every single program is managed by individuals who go far beyond the call of duty to make these programs happen. The weekend programs were part of the ongoing work responsibilities of the coordinators—a good and fortunate thing. But the week-long and longer programs are almost exclusively managed by volunteers, or by very minimally paid individuals.

The counselors tend to be college students, which is true in the world of camping in general. They also are very low paid, if they are paid at all. And yet, all of these individuals do this work because in their deepest hearts they know that the young deaf and hard of hearing children and youth are desperate for affinity with their like-peers. Many counselors are former campers, and thus they are very aware of this need.

Starting Out: Camp I

The first observation was at Camp I and involved 10 days of observations and interviews. My graduate assistant and I observed daily activities and interviewed each counselor as well as the director, assistant director, and two parents. I was so fortunate to have the funds for a graduate assistant, and this young woman had attended Camp I as a child and later actually founded a camp in another state.

I chose Camp I to start off the investigation for a several reasons. Most important, the director informed me that he expected two or three non-signers to be at the camp during the upcoming session. Second, the director offered, at no charge, an on-site cabin for myself and the graduate assistant—we had not only comfortable beds but also a kitchen and space for writing and interviewing. Finally, Camp I was in a location that was relatively easy for us to travel to.

Upon our arrival, however, we were dismayed to find there were *no* campers from solitary settings, and not even campers who were beginning signers. We thus had to make some adjustments to our research plan. It is not unusual for this kind of "naturalistic" research to be full of surprises; many world-renowned anthropologists had to change directions mid-stream also. This is one of the defining features of ethnographic research. (Marshall & Rossman, 1995).

I decided that an alternative way to assess how Camp I might accommodate such individuals would be to ask the administrators, counselors, and parents hypothetical questions. We asked staff members how they would conceptualize a "successful" camp experience for campers from solitary settings, and specifically if they had ideas for activities that would lend themselves to relatively comfortable interaction between signers and nonsigners/solitaires.

In general, the counselors' remarks always returned to how wonderful they thought Camp I was, and how fortunate the campers were to be having these experiences. Through the enlarged social network provided by the camp, the counselors uniformly felt that *all* campers would have a happy realization that the world of d/Deaf peers is larger than they had previously experienced. Regardless of their educational placement(s), *all* campers would have a greater chance to forge bonds with peers whom they might otherwise never meet. The counselors saw this as an important part of developing self-esteem, identity, and a sense of belonging. They almost unanimously mentioned that because deaf and hard of hearing children were being educated in environments with little exposure to positive deaf role models (either adults or peers), they had an extraordinary need for this boost to both identity and self-esteem. They also unanimously felt that a summer camp designed for hearing children could not provide the same depth of role model involvement provided by a "Deaf" camp.

In a nutshell, it was not so much a question of the kind of activities offered—this camp had waterfront activities, arts and crafts, games, hiking, and other common summer camp activities. But it also had all deaf counselors, all deaf campers, and deaf guest speakers for evening programs. It was more about the shared experiences, unique to deaf and hard of hearing-youngsters, that made this camp different from a "regular" camp.

Answering Unasked Questions

Because I was not able to hone in on my original research question(s), but had 10 days to spend at this historic program, I simply opened my mind to whatever I might see. I tried to follow the naturalistic tradition of Margaret Mead, Robert Coles, and other cross-cultural investigators. My assistant and I recorded our reflections daily.

The first thing I noticed, and I admit it took me aback because I in no way expected this, was that almost all of the Deaf parents (i.e., the parents of campers who were themselves Deaf) personally drove their children to camp rather than sending them on a plane or a school bus as did most of the hearing parents. In line for registration, milling around nearby, and out on the lakefront pier upon completing registration, they were having a grand old social time chatting it up with each other. Seeing this actually gave me a "déjà vu" back to my first few days at Gallaudet College in August of 1971, when my parents dropped me off for the first time. It reminded me of the carefree socializing in the Gallaudet "S.U.B" (student union building), where students would congregate in the upstairs lounge or the downstairs vending machine area at all hours of the day to socialize. These moments—when my parents dropped me off in 1971, when I observed the socializing in the student union in subsequent years, and now at the lakefront of this summer camp in 2005—all had special meaning, because now, knowing sign language, I could myself participate in this kind of banter, whereas in my K–12 and college years in the "hearing world" I had been unable to do so. At any rate, the Deaf parents who had brought their kids to Camp I were clearly enjoying themselves, taking advantage of the broad social network that exists within the Deaf community. How very animated, happy, in their element, these parents were. They were in a carefree setting discussing their lives with others with whom they shared a deep common bond of being Deaf and using sign, and they now had the additional bond of being parents of Deaf children.

One must remember the perspective of a deaf child from a hearing family: While growing up in that family I never was able to actively follow or actively participate in this kind of "normal" social conversation—"shooting the breeze" or "chatting it up." So when I saw this kind of "normal conversation" at Gallaudet and now was seeing again at Camp I, I would get this eerie little feeling, "oh, this is so nice," and "oh, I am so happy for them," and "oh, I wish I'd had that in my life." And by "that" I mean a whole family with whom I can communicate "in a group." Here, in 2005, at this summer camp, I was not a bystander!

As a researcher, seeing this phenomenon solidified another concept that was swimming around in my head from all those conversations with my returning-from-summer-vacation undergraduate students. Their comments and enthusiasm had me starting to think of "Deaf camps" as carriers of [Deaf] culture, as extensions of the residential schools that were downsizing and even closing: I was becoming hopeful that these camps could pick up the slack, so to speak. Not only did I feel hopeful that deaf camps could perpetuate deaf culture, but I also, and more strongly, felt hopeful that deaf camps could really offer individuals who were alone in the mainstream (like me), who had "no other place to go," a way to find others who shared their experience. Deaf culture is evolving, and it will continue to evolve, along with technology and other factors. But children of today and tomorrow will continue to have this need for "a place of their own" within which they can discover their shared experiences and identities, and expand and enrich their social networks and social capital.

Here are a few excerpts from my very first journal entries at Camp I:

> Last night during the "orientation" I was aware again of what a "DEAF" environment this is. I think a child with even beginning sign skills would feel out of place unless there were several like him here. So far I have noticed that a few kids use more English signs, and that makes me wonder if they are following (understanding) all the "fast ASL" that the counselors are using. The counselors seem almost uniformly "fast ASL" users.

> Another fascinating thing is how the Camp employs, in addition to counselors, "volunteers" for various other tasks (cooking, cleaning, etc.). All of these people are Deaf. . . . Some seem to have "regular appointed jobs" and others seem to have sort of self-appointed roles. It's like a family with a traditional uncle who fixes things, an aunt who makes great apple pie, and a family historian!

I spent 10 days learning about the culture and activities offered in a "traditional" Deaf camp. Because I had never been to a sleep-away camp even for hearing kids, this was a valuable glimpse into the phenomenon in general. My graduate assistant, however, was a former camper and staff member of this particular camp. Some researchers might suggest this would have created too much bias, but I don't think so. She had not been back to Camp I in more than 5 years, during which time she founded and managed a camp herself on the opposite side of the country and also started graduate school. This distance and her ensuing maturity allowed her to provide keen personal insights relevant to my original research questions, which I will share.

This young woman was mainstreamed all of her K–12 years. For K–6 in the 1980s she was in a self-contained classroom for deaf students. There were five or six other deaf students in her class, and she regrets that for all those K–6 years she was the only female student. After trying a distant middle school with a deaf program for 7th grade, her parents suggested she try the local middle school, the same one her sister was attending. She thought it would be great to ride a "normal school bus" (her words) and be closer to home. She reports that she became close to both her interpreters and her note taker—she often ate lunch with them instead of with her peers. In her words that follow, we get a precursor of what we heard in our interviews with and surveys from other deaf and hard of hearing individuals of her generation and the subsequent one:

> I made few friends in high school. All of conversations were superficial and I was known as the "deaf girl" in school. I was invited to a few parties, but still got left out. I was involved with sports—swimming, volleyball, softball, and skiing throughout high school. That helped me [make some friends and keep busy].
>
> The first summer I came to [Camp I], I was homesick for a few days. . . . I wasn't a fluent ASL signer, but at end of the camp, I didn't want to go home. I finally felt like I had friends with whom I could have more than just superficial conversations. I made many close friends at [Camp I] and stayed in touch with them through the year—we promised each other that we would come back to Camp I. During the school year, my parents allowed me to fly to and visit them for spring break or a weekend.
>
> The older I got, the more upset I would get about leaving camp, so I tried to convince my parents to let me go to [nearby Deaf school], but they didn't think that would be best for me. While we have been here this week, I shared this with [the assistant director and her assistant]. Guess what? They felt the exact same way when they came here. [One of them] was able to convince his mother to let them go to [a specific Deaf school]. He went to [that Deaf school] for the last two years in high school. I would not be surprised if many others have same stories.

Different Camps for Different Purposes

Once the visit to Camp I was wrapped up, I began to seek other programs to observe. I knew from the director's survey which programs were open to observers; using this information and various program dates listed on camp Web sites, I began to plot my visits for the following summer. I was very curious to see how these programs and the staff would compare with those of Camp I.

Of all the programs I was able to visit (and a few I could not because of time/funding constraints), all except for two of the administrators who enthusiastically welcomed me were Deaf. They saw the value of the research and went out of their way to make my visits as easy and comfortable as possible. I found the programs to be different from each other in several ways: where they got their funding, the proportion of deaf and hard of hearing staff to hearing staff, the program emphasis, the kind of participant attracted (in terms of language use, area of residence, socioeconomic status), and the degree to which the camps offered educational activities focused on deaf-related issues (identity, self-esteem, access, resources).

I had conceived of this research in 2005 because I thought summer camps held promise for enriching the lives of solitary and/or nonsigning deaf and hard of hearing children by enlarging their world of peers like themselves. Once I realized at Camp I that I might not find such children at many of the publicly known camps, I intuitively shifted my focus to be less direct. I modified my research design and submitted this to the GRI. Thankfully, they funded my work again, and I was able to proceed. With this second grant, I developed some specific questions for the administrators (the director, assistant director, the program coordinator—whom I spoke with varied from program to program). Here is a sampling of the questions:

How would you describe a successful camp experience for your campers?

Are there any constraints that prevent you from offering the programs/activities you feel the campers need?

What about children and youth who have no or very little contact with other deaf/hard of hearing children—do you do anything special to meet their unique needs?

Preparing this manuscript in 2012 from interviews and observations that took place in 2007–2010, it seems that the best information I can convey to parents and other concerned parties would be a sense of "different camps for different purposes." I found myself grouping them in my mind, and this grouping to me is a logical way to categorize them—the categories expound the strengths of each. Most likely, a deaf or hard of hearing child would benefit from having experiences with all three over the course of the K–12 years.

Traditional

I observed and interviewed at three "traditional" Deaf camps, including Camp I. Most camps in this category were founded decades ago by Deaf individuals and are by and large still run by Deaf individuals. The camps (and the founders) are well known within the Deaf community. These are excellent programs for children/youth who are comfortable with ASL. They provide ample opportunity for deaf and hard of hearing children to meet and learn from numerous other deaf and hard of hearing children and adults. These are the camps with the largest number of deaf and hard of hearing children and adults, generally 40–60 campers. In addition, they tend to have significant numbers of higher achieving deaf and hard of hearing children and youth—that is a plus also. Although they manifest a strong Deaf culture and signing milieu, these camps varied in the amount of emphasis placed on educational elements, such as lectures and goal-oriented group activities geared toward enriching social capital as well as generating personal and community bonds.

Grant-Driven

The second category of programs I came to call "grant-driven" or "activity-grounded/funder-directed" camps and programs. From the director's survey, Web site reviews, and the stories from my returning-from-summer-vacation students, we can safely surmise that most summer camps fall in this category. Individuals learn of a grant opportunity for anything from teaching art or music to providing safety information (drugs, sex, etc.) to teenagers to educating about some specific career focus. They apply for funding, and presto, they have a summer camp. Often these run for several years, some for decades. By and large, the Deaf camps in this category were founded by nonprofit service organizations or agencies. Most are managed by hearing individuals, although they do try in varying degrees to hire deaf and hard of hearing counselors and other staff. In some cases, the founder was a relative of a DHH individual.

I include in this category the numerous camps sponsored by service organizations such as Lions and Sertoma and by churches or religious denominations. The Lions and Sertoma (and similar organizations) tend to offer a week or two of programming for deaf and hard of hearing youth within a full summer of week-long programs for children with varying disabilities/disadvantages. Some of the faith-based camps are specifically and only for deaf and hard of hearing children.

I observed four camps in this category. All four were funded for a specific kind of program, and all were run by deaf and hard of hearing service organizations. Camp II received grant funding from various social service entities. One of the granting agencies stipulated that the funds be earmarked for ubiquitous teen issues—alcohol, smoking, and relationships. Another was focused on "access": how to use an interpreter, how to advocate for one's rights as a deaf person, and so forth. Thus, the campers (who were actually called "students") spent the greater part of the day listening to lectures in a traditional classroom—the camp's funding sources directly determined their programs, with various speakers and media addressing topics related to these grants. Late afternoons and evenings were filled with fun activities that took advantage of the amenities at the host site.

The staff members at Camp II were all individuals who had been associated with the camp during the previous several years. Assisting two senior staff members were several young counselors-in-training who had been through this program in prior years. Many of them had also attended a more traditional (fun-and-games) summer camp run by the same agency for younger children. And so, for more than half the people in attendance, both staff and campers, this was also "old home week." This was a bit reminiscent of the "Deaf-parents-homecoming" phenomenon at Camp I. A difference was the location (standing on college campus concrete rather than lakeside sand) and also the language in use. At Camp I, the language was more "natural ASL." At Camp II the language was more English-like, obviously due to the fact that virtually all of the deaf participants were from mainstream programs and/or had hearing parents.

Regardless of these differences, regardless of the time spent in the classroom learning about sex, drugs, and access, it was clear that for these campers, this was yet another gold mine of opportunity. They could make new friends, see the friends they knew from last summer, and learn something valuable at the same time. Especially for the campers from the mainstream, here was an opportunity to hear about and discuss important adolescent issues while in direct communication with both teachers and peers, rather than through an interpreter or transcriber.

Accordingly, and not very surprisingly, in spite of considerable time the campers spent in the classroom learning about the designated subject matter, the staff members who responded to my survey all honed in on goals unrelated to any of these grant-dictated topics—mention of the classroom content was secondary and minimal:

> I hope the kids make life-long friends. It is about finding themselves, finding out about their hearing loss, and finding out that they are NOT ALONE.
>
> I want them to [go back home] feeling great about themselves . . . and feel safe and comfortable with my staff, and bond with them so that they have an adult that they can communicate with and who [understands what they are going through in their mainstream schools].
>
> I hope that [Camp II] will offer self-identity, leadership, friendships, and opportunities that the students may not be exposed to [elsewhere].

In all of the camps in this category, the programs were dictated by where the funds came from rather than by a vision from a Deaf adult about what deaf and hard of hearing campers need. Nevertheless, the use of Deaf counselors enabled the campers to have more access to communication and especially with an adult who had "been there" with regard to mainstreaming. Virtually all the Deaf staff I interviewed at these four camps (approximately 15 individuals) commented either that the camp experience was something they missed growing up, or that they wanted the campers to have the same positive experiences they had had attending camps with other deaf children.

One of these programs was very similar to Camp II in that the activity focus was education concerning important adolescent issues. The other two, however, were focused on what we might call educational-recreational activities. The Deaf staff members I interviewed very much believe in the value of these pursuits as directly building self-esteem or otherwise providing something the campers were probably not getting in their mainstream setting.

Deaf kids need art more than hearing kids?? Yes, indeed, I feel they do, because that is the only way they can "express" themselves, their innermost feelings. I have seen a lot of kids enjoying themselves much more when there is a "Deaf" artist! I feel they do better with a Deaf Artist/art teacher than a hearing art teacher. A Deaf art teacher goes into depth and explains clearly and directly. IF the child goes to a hearing art class, they miss out a lot because they can't watch the hearing teacher or interpreter at the same time that they need to look at the art and also what classmates might be painting or drawing. I myself missed out a lot in school, and oftentimes I would have to ask the student next to me what we were supposed to be doing.

Although these programs must focus on the grant-driven content, their directors do find ways to emphasize program elements that encourage the children to explore their own experiences from their everyday lives. So rather than present a lecture about Deaf culture or about growing up deaf, the instructor or facilitator will weave questions or topics in this area into the main (grant-funded) activities and/or into the debriefing or discussions about the activity. I found this a very powerful feature of these programs. It would behoove all summer and weekend programs for deaf and hard of hearing children to have this element at least to a rudimentary degree if the program is new and the founders/managers want to explore what is comfortable for the children (and their parents).

At least some of the time, instructors at these programs put the campers into small groups where they could learn from their diversity—this is another very positive and growth-enhancing element.

We tend to attract all kind of kids—ASL-fluent kids, kids with CIs, oral kids, solitaires, etc. Since the staff members are both hearing and Deaf (some with CIs, some more SEE-signing than others, etc.), we are able to make each activity accessible to all. We provide voice interpreting for those who need that. We do, however, emphasize the Deaf/ASL element of Camp II and encourage oral kids to learn how to sign. It is truly amazing to see some kids learn some signs and become more confident in their interaction with other kids. We emphasize team-building and openness when interacting with the campers. In the end, they often overcome any initial frustration and become friends with one another.

Two of the funder-directed programs attract youngsters primarily from a particular region, either statewide or from a larger metropolitan area. The other attracts campers from all over the United States. When campers come from a more limited area, they may already have significant familiarity with each other; this may be good for some campers, not so good for others. No one camp can meet all the needs of a single child. To maximize experience with both program activities and with similar and diverse peers, families should plan to send their child to more than one program over the course of at least the high school and preferably the middle school years as well.

Grant-driven camps do attract solitaires. One of these programs, however, does attract a significant number of mainstreamed deaf and hard of hearing children. (Some counselors commented that they would like to attract more to their camps but feel frustrated by parents' and other adults' lack of understanding that a child who is not fluent in sign could benefit from attending their program.)

> We receive a lot of those types of children. [Our state] has a lot of rural areas and so we get [10 or more students] each summer that come from an isolated background. For those children, our camp has a huge impact as we're often the only place they can be immersed in a [clear communication] environment, the only place they meet other deaf adults/role models and the only place they can communicate with friends easily. . . . We spend a lot of time making sure everything/everyone is communication accessible. . . . During my welcome speech the first night of each session, I make sure to let them know that I do not care if they are signing or oral children, and that I view them as children, period. I encourage them to communicate with each other through any means possible and tell them that we will model the appropriate behavior that we expect from them.

I want to reiterate that the managers and counselors I interviewed said little about the actual program/activity focus—for example, they did not talk about providing the children with information about drugs, about the specific sport in question, or whatever the subject matter was. Rather, they talked about the overall impact on the campers from being in the presence of other deaf and hard of hearing children *and* adults. These counselors understand that this bringing together of the children, *that* is the main purpose of the Camp II, and it is to that goal that they are dedicated. And even if they only reach the parents or teachers of a handful of solitaires, they feel that their programs *do* serve such children well.

> From the day they arrived to the day they left, I saw tremendous changes in each child. . . . The very first day they were very scared, shy, quiet. Toward the middle of the week they have become very open and more social and toward the end they have became much more open and not want to leave! I [see it and also] I hear this from teachers how much those workshops have impacted the kids! They all look forward to coming back. They are so much happier and want more and more workshops! [Later in the year] I go and visit the schools; I become a magnet to them; they all come up to me asking when [can they come to the Camp II again]?? Believe me, they were like [a caterpillar in] a cocoon and turned into a butterfly at the end! For those who return to the next program, these kids help new kids to become comfortable. I just know this because I have seen those transitions every year.

Unique and Modern, But Sadly Defunct

I observed at two programs in this third category. They were founded around 2000 and ran for eight to 10 years. Both have shut down for various reasons. The bottom line is always money: If they had had more funds, they could have done more recruiting of both campers and staff. Both were founded by a duo of one Deaf and one hearing person. I am giving them plenty of ink because they represent both heroic efforts by the founders and a "new breed" of summer programs. I believe we will see more programs like this. As time goes by, more and more adults—parents, interpreters, Deaf adults—will become impassioned by the great need and step up to the plate.

The first of these was a day camp run by a hard of hearing woman and her mother. They held it on their very spacious family property, and ran a week-long program each summer for 10 years. Although the camp was set in a rural area, the founders managed to network with state officials, school officials, rehabilitation officials, and neighbors/friends to bring in children within a good-size radius. The children they served had few other options.

But alas, over the years it became harder to reach the children because they were increasingly being educated as solitaires in their neighborhood schools as opposed to in larger mainstream programs. The pool of youngsters came to increasingly include those who were oral and whose parents did not see value in their being with other deaf and hard of hearing children. In addition, more and more of these children were being required to attend summer school for academic deficits. Numbers declined, and the Deaf founder decided to put her efforts elsewhere. She now teaches ASL in numerous venues around that rural area.

The second of these unusual programs was essentially a program within a preexisting summer camp for hearing children. The founders liked this camp's philosophy and program content so much that they were inspired to bring in eight to 12 deaf adolescents for six to seven consecutive summers. The camp itself was unique in that approximately 50% of the staff members were international, and each counselor was expected to teach an activity throughout the program. Each day was full of classes in just about anything you could think of, and campers were encouraged to attend any activity they wished. An important point: ASL classes and ASL-performing arts activities were part of the offering, and the hearing campers (and the deaf campers) could choose these activities.

The founders were motivated by their own relationship, which had evolved over a few years and which started when they both were staff members at this camp, teaching ASL to the (hearing) campers. This statement by the hearing partner is quite telling:

> We learned so much from our cross-cultural friendship and wanted to share that experience and all that we learned with others. The divide between deaf and hearing people presents a very interesting cultural niche that asks both groups of people to recognize the uniqueness of the other and the similarities they share. Also I personally was so astonished by the richness and depth of Deaf culture, something I had absolutely no contact with before meeting [my Deaf friend]. . . . For these two groups of people to truly see each other [without prejudice] means starting with children. The challenge of allowing friendships to build, learning to happen, and fun to be shared takes patience, time, the ability to allow kids to [go at their own pace].

These two young women got the program going pretty much single-handedly. In subsequent years, they were joined by others they had trained and instilled with their vision. The 10–12 deaf campers were recruited from the nearby geographic area, and interpreting students were also recruited from the same area. There were scholarships for the deaf campers, and the interpreting students were all volunteers—the directors were able to recruit enough volunteers so that the deaf campers could each attend whichever activity session they wanted, all day long.

During my observation, I could see this vision that they had. Below is a quote from the Deaf partner, and it helps us to see that vision more clearly:

> I grew up wishing for a different [kind of] education and a different kind of interaction with the people around me. As a deaf child I felt a lack of emotional sensitivity in [hearing] surroundings. The hearing world felt totally foreign and closed to me. This hugely impacted the choices I made and I felt very unsure how to successfully present myself as a deaf person to the world. I didn't want my deafness to define my life, but I didn't know how not to let it define my life. I didn't feel any situation was available to me where I could meet people on an emotional level on a daily basis, without putting up a front. [This camp] offered this kind of potential.

Both young women explained that because the camp was focused on cross-cultural sharing anyway, having ASL and Deaf culture as part of the offerings, and campers "from that country" in the environment, it all seemed like a natural extension. The hearing partner had been amazed to learn about Deaf people and their language and their culture through what became a close friendship. The Deaf partner was thrilled to see the kind of "environment" where her deafness would not define her, where she would not have to be "tough" or always on her guard. They each wanted these experiences, almost like the flip sides of a coin, to be available to others and they valiantly made it happen to the best of their ability. They started to carve their dream into this woodwork, so to speak.

During the few days I observed at this camp, I was able to interview five of the Deaf staff members who were working there that summer. Three felt that the camp was not really serving the deaf campers' needs, whereas the others felt it was helping them "learn to interact with hearing people." The comments from the first group are worth sharing and provide food for thought:

> Some deaf campers are counting the days till they can go home. One camper told me, "I was mainstreamed for 10 years and here I am at this camp, being mainstreamed again! I am tired of interpreters! I want to be with other deaf kids!" I do like the kind of activities that [the camp] offers, but I don't like the philosophy of a [strict] "inclusive environment" for deaf campers. This program benefits the hearing campers more than the Deaf campers because they get to learn a new language, if they want to. The Deaf campers are stuck with usually so-so interpreters.

The word from all of these counselors was that many deaf and hard of hearing college students and recent grads would prefer to work in an environment where everyone can sign. One of these deaf and hard of hearing staff members was in a coordinating position—she was responsible for everything related to ASL, from the daily classes to several performances in special events. She thought the idea of teaching ASL in this program was great, but she felt that the deaf and hard of hearing campers also needed time to be with each other. She commented (and I noticed) that at meal times the deaf campers always sat among themselves, with the possible exception of one camper who was an excellent athlete and seemed to make hearing friends from that. She also relayed to me that she had actually suggested that the deaf and hard of hearing campers have more activities where they could be together, but the hearing director was philosophically opposed to this. She was, however, ultimately allowed to have some activities for the deaf and hard of hearing campers only during campfire time because those times were so music-oriented and also in the dark.

Unfortunately, this innovative program ran for less than 10 years. The founders were just out of college and itching for other horizons. So over the seven to eight years that the program ran, it was consecutively under the wing of those who had trained under the original founders or subsequent coordinators. All the while, these young pioneers had to recruit campers, find donor and grant funds to pay the deaf and hard of hearing campers' tuition, recruit the volunteer interpreters (eight to 12 of these), and continually educate the camp owners (i.e., the hearing owners of the overall camp) and train the rest of the hearing staff members.

Yet, this story of a short-lived uniquely conceptualized program is not without lessons. First, how the vision was conceived—the partnership between two creative and forward-thinking individuals, one hearing and one deaf, seems to be without precedent. Second, the biggest barriers the partners experienced were related to the hearing staff's understanding of the deaf campers' needs and the challenge of finding young interpreters (who would fit into the camp culture) who also had enough skill to provide adequate interpretation and maturity. Third, clearly the hearing camp owners never really took the program to heart, because once the supply of creative, motivated, Deaf-culture-savvy young staff members began to disintegrate, they made little if any effort to keep the program going. In other words, they really did not have whole-hearted support "from top management" despite their herculean efforts. Too bad. They had a great vision. We have an idea of what worked and what did not work—and a vision that would probably appeal to and be enriching for those "alone in the mainstream."

Weekend Programs: Bring Them On!

During my investigation of summer programs and camps, I learned of a then-new program held at a retreat center in Central Texas that was designed specifically to bring together mainstreamed high school students. It was cosponsored by one of the major camp supporters, Communication Services of the Deaf (CSD, based in South Dakota), and the Educational Resource Center on Deafness (ERCOD), a state agency in Texas. Actually, learning of this program is what prompted my grant applications—my first idea was to interview the participants and their parents several years after they had participated in this program. Intuitively I knew this would be a good way to learn of the program's impact, when the participants and the parents had 2–4 years' hindsight.

Unfortunately, some individuals holding the purse strings said "They won't remember!" Not being deaf themselves, apparently their reference was their own teen years; they couldn't know the strong feelings experienced when a deaf or hard of hearing teen meets other deaf and hard of hearing teens for the first time. Of necessity I changed my research focus a bit, but I was able to include observation at three weekend programs within the overall summer camp project that was eventually and very generously funded (more than once) by the GRI.

The Discovery Retreat, which began in 2005, is a weekend full of activities focused on an academically oriented theme that changes every year— recent themes include robotics, video game development for iPhones and other platforms, health care careers, and videography. They generally attract about 30 students—the retreat site necessitates limits on the number of boys and girls, and some applicants must be turned away. If not for this stipulation, enrollment would probably be closer to 40 or 50. The event now takes place twice a year and always includes nationally known deaf and hard of hearing experts involved in those fields. Having the participants learn from deaf and hard of hearing role models is an important element of the program.

Typically, two thirds of the participants have varying degrees of sign language skill and the others are oral. The staff always includes individuals with varying communication styles/preferences, and they provide captioning and both oral and sign interpreting as needed. Different sponsors provide funding each year, often related to the theme. In addition, Gallaudet University and the National Technical Institute of the Deaf (NTID/RIT) have provided sponsorship annually. The program is thereby offered free of charge to all children. (In fact, all the weekend programs I observed and/or learned about charged no or very low fees.)

David Coco, Deaf himself and a cochlear implant user, has been the coordinating force behind the Discovery Retreat. In an update via email he commented:

> Several recent Discovery Retreats have had unexpected and surprising outcomes. One example is robotics. Before our retreat that focused on robotics, Texas School for the Deaf (TSD) students had no experience with robotics. Now, three years later, TSD offers a class on robotics and TSD students re-

cently won first place in a regional robotics competition. Discovery Retreat sparked an interest in students and staff alike, and provided a platform for pursuing this interest. (D. Coco, personal communication, March 25, 2013)

I was able to observe the Discovery Retreat twice and have already recommended that several individuals wanting to start weekend programs go and observe for themselves. It is worth seeing not only the program elements, but also how the youngsters' ways of interacting with each other evolve in just 48 hours, how the captioning and interpreting interface with the activities, and the overall tone of the program. To learn now that the subject matter has even spawned offshoots in the teens' academic programs is a considerable bonus. Observers will see that the program is provided in an environment geared to the unique needs of deaf and hard of hearing high school students. No one is a "bystander." In a conversation with Coco, during one of my observations, he commented, "The theme is important—so the kids learn something valuable, but the most important thing is to bring them together so that they can meet other kids like them; and so often meeting other deaf and hard of hearing kids at the Discovery Retreat is a first for them. They never want to leave!"

I also visited a program in Wisconsin. The Wisconsin Educational Services Program—Deaf and Hard of Hearing Outreach has been sponsoring the Teen Getaway Weekend (for high school–age students) and Teen Getaway Weekend Jr. (for middle school–age students) in alternating years since 2007. Each weekend program is determined by a committee of mostly deaf and hard of hearing adults who work in varying professional capacities around the state. Watching youngsters engage in activities specially designed by adults who really "get it" about their lives was amazing. The participants would be placed in groups to work on a project such as a team flag, team slogan, or team skit—all tasks requiring ample communication—and the counselor/volunteers would guide the kids to include all team members, regardless of communication or language skill. (I was able to turn this observation into a class project for one of the classes I taught for recreation majors at Gallaudet. Six undergraduates raised money to fly themselves, along with me, to Wisconsin to work as volunteers at a Teen Getaway Weekend Jr. It was a truly unforgettable experience for them, as they got a glimpse of helping youngsters "climb their ladder," as one of the summer campers in retrospect shares later in this chapter.)

Daniel Houlihan, who has been coordinating these Getaway Weekends since 2007, wrote in an email update:

> Our camper attendance has been steady with an average number of 45 annually since 2007. The number of nonsigning campers has been increasing annually and now we have almost equal numbers. We have been able to recruit DHH role models to participate in the TGWs—they provide valuable feedback for our continuous improvements. Wisconsin School for the Deaf has been great for sharing staff resources and we have good collaboration with other statewide and nationwide organizations for funding/sponsoring interpreting, transportation, and other professional services.
>
> (D. Houlihan, personal communication, March 26, 2013)

Houlihan also shared that the program continues to include workshops on topics the participants might otherwise never experience, in a setting designed with their unique needs in mind. For example, program staff provided a workshop focused on teaching participants about the differences between educational interpreters and community interpreters (i.e., interpreters for adults). They also provide opportunities for the youngsters to talk about common issues they all face in school and at home, and particularly how being deaf impacts these.

In addition to observing these two weekend programs, both of which continue to be sponsored by outreach programs that have grown out of the state Deaf schools and therefore are managed by adults who have themselves experienced the dearth of social capital that goes hand in hand with the mainstream experience, I also observed a weekend program established by a cochlear implant surgeon, David Kelsall, of the Colorado Neurological Institute. His astute assistant Judith Stucky has managed the CNI Cochlear Kids Camp for 12 years as of this writing. This program takes place at the YMCA of the Rockies, which is situated on the edge of Rocky Mountain National Park in Estes Park, Colorado. It is a family program and is run twice a year, once with families with younger children and once with families with older children. This division is not strict, however, and families attend when they can.

I observed this program in action on two occasions, and had an oppor-tunity both times to talk with Stucky about the goals and philosophy of the program. It is a carefully designed, wonderful program for families with children with cochlear implants, regardless of whether the family commu-nicates using spoken language, sign language, or both, although it tends to attract more families using spoken language. It is staffed almost exclusively by volunteers, and every effort is made to welcome everyone. It provides educational workshops for the parents while the children are engaged in various fun/educational activities. Stucky explained an example of an in-novative aspect offered at some camp sessions:

> We divide the teens into those with CIs and those who are teenaged hearing sibs. We split our lecture hall in half with a wall down the middle. We set up 8–10 round tables in each half. We assign 2 to 3 CI teens to sit at each table in the "CI" half; we do the same on the other side of the wall with hearing sibs. Then we invite parents to sit at any table (other than where their own kids are). We do a sort of "speed meeting" where parents stay at that table for 12–15 minutes and they can ask the teens any questions they'd like about what their experiences or perceptions are, etc. The only 2 rules are that no parent can report back to a particular teen's family about what was said and parents have to LISTEN . . . they can't criticize, correct or preach to the teens. In this setting, the teens are the experts and the rest of us need to truly listen to what they have to say. After 12–15 minutes, a bell rings and parents rotate on to another table. In total, parents sit at 3–4 tables in a given session. They are encouraged to spend about ½ their time in the teen side and the other ½ in the sib side. (J. Stucky, personal communication, March 20, 2013)

This is such a unique idea, and we imagine that works very well. We hope the folks at CNI can find a way to sensitively educate parents and others about the issues the teens have talked about in this setting, although we understand the need to provide a very safe space for the teens and com-mend them for doing so.

Because regional weekend programming is a major part of our recom-mendations, we highlight one more program that we learned of after Gina had finished making her rounds, so to speak. The staff at the Maine Edu-cation Center for Deaf and Hard of Hearing Children (MECDHH) has developed a unique program called "Kids Like Me." MECDHH provides an after-school program in various regions, rotating around the state; the K–5 groups meet for 2 hours once a week for 8 weeks at a time. The Web site gives a clear idea of the kind of activities provided: "games, journaling, role playing, art projects, problem solving, small group discussions and assistive technology demonstrations are designed to build assertive listening and communication skills, self-esteem, leadership, personal awareness and a strong, positive identity as a deaf or hard of hearing individual." For middle and high school students, MECDHH provides three "Kids Like Me" weekends annually. These include one overnight, and they are hosted in various locations. Students often attend more than one; in fact, they are encouraged to attend regularly. Here is what the MECDHH provides to the Maine teens and tweens:

> Our program provides a stimulating context for building friendships and self-advocacy skills, expressing thoughts and feelings, and sharing cooperative learning experiences. Activities may include: games, canoeing, kayaking, hiking, camping out, orienteering and rock climbing and other activities in the great outdoors. (http://www.mecdhh.org/statewide-educational-services /public-school-outreach/kids-like-me/)

Camp and Weekend Experiences in Retrospect

Gina's study of summer camps eventually included observations (1–9 days long) at 10 camp programs and five weekend programs; she observed two of the weekend programs twice. She interviewed all the directors of the camps and the assistant directors of half of these. She also interviewed the founders of several of these programs, and approximately 80% of the counselors employed during the summers she did the observations. She also collected paper-and-pencil surveys from approximately 30 directors (out of over 70 camps) and interviewed approximately 20 college students looking back on their experiences as campers. (Some of these numbers are approximations because even though the "official study" ended in 2009, Gina continued to informally observe and interview people beyond this time frame.)

We wrap up this chapter with the voices, once again, of the 18–34-year-old cohort, the same age group we focus on in Chapters 2–4. Listen to what they say about summer camps, starting with comments about attending a "hearing camp."

> I attended a hearing camp for one month. The first day I was excited. [My oral school] suggested I go there to practice my mainstreaming and communication skills to prepare for my first year in a mainstream school after I [would] graduate next year [from the oral school]. There were over 50 to 60 hearing students all talking and playing. I [tried really hard] to think positive, thinking "I will have the opportunity to interact during activities such as horseback riding and etc." But communication was a problem, especially during nighttime activities by the campfire. I was always lost during campfire stories. I always had to find someone who is easy to understand verbally and depended on that person to interpret for me. It was always brief/summarized not descriptive. One sentence to explain the whole story. I [pretended to be] fine accepting this, but inside I was frustrated and furious. I [was forced to] "think positive and survive." I hated this feeling of "survival" because [the oral school] wanted us to survive in a hearing world and not be involved in the deaf world.

Most of the campers looking back expressed regret that they learned about deaf summer camp opportunities so late in their young lives. In some cases they were in their last summer of their high school years. They speculated about how their lives might have been different if they had had the opportunity to attend more programs during more summers. This excerpt is from a young man who was not fluent in ASL at the time he attended this summer program, a program geared more for oral youngsters:

> I listened to [the other campers'] stories. [I learned that] some had already experienced other deaf camps. I became jealous, wishing I had those experiences to socialize with my peers [especially using ASL] when I was younger. I thought, "Why didn't I learn about deaf experiences earlier and now when will I ever have the opportunity?" I could have been a lot more involved in the deaf community earlier in life. Maybe I could have had more impact on my region. I am from [state] and many deaf youth from [this state] do not go to college, or do not get good jobs and suffer many struggles compared to other states. If I had become involved earlier like at ages 13, 14, or 15, I could have [passed on what I had learned] and could have made a difference for them. Help them climb their ladder too.

Wow. This is awesome. A young adult is saying that if he had known more about Deaf camps at a younger age, he would have passed this information to other deaf and hard of hearing children in his school program. We love that statement, "Help them climb their ladder too."

The remarks below are from an individual who also talks first about a summer program for oral students and how much she loved it. Then she talks about "aging out" of that program and how her obviously resourceful mother found another program for her, this one with campers who use sign language. The way she talks about her transition with this program is thought-provoking.

There was nothing more refreshing than being with others like myself, and my world changed from that first deaf summer camp experience at [the oral camp]. I was finally in a place where frustrations and being different were nonexistent. I hated when camp ended, because it meant going back to the world where I was not equal. I wanted to take my camp friends home with me. Summer memories and writing letters to my camp friends were the important connection that kept me afloat through the school year, and I went back to [the oral camp] again the following summer, staying for a longer session and making even more friends. The concept of summer camps and having deaf friends became my new salvation. My life changed for the better as I had a new focus on who I was as a deaf individual and how I fit in to the world.

Once I outgrew [the oral camp], my mother learned about [another camp]. A friend from [the same oral camp] signed up with me and we looked forward with much anticipation. What we did not realize prior to arriving at [this camp] was that it was a signing camp. Because I had no knowledge whatsoever about signing and the Deaf culture, on that first day I literally begged my mom to take me back home. To my surprise, my mother advised me to stay and try to learn some sign language. My friend and I cried at the dinner table that first night because we were surrounded by people who were speaking with their hands, an unknown visual language to us. The initial experience was akin to being mainstreamed but only worse because we could not communicate with others who were just as deaf as we were. This quickly changed the next day as everyone welcomed us with a new way of communicating with [each other]. Another transition, and my life was never the same. Sign language became a new language for me, hence a wonderful way to communicate. A new identity was born, and beautiful memories were created. I gained a new sense of confidence and developed stronger physically and mentally.

Clearly, even youngsters raised orally long for association with friends "like me." The following comments are from an individual who called his summer camp "a stepping-stone" into a world where he no longer felt alone and realized there are plenty of others who share his experience. He had previously attended a regular summer camp where he had used a sign language interpreter on a daily basis. His words drive home the idea that even youngsters who have cochlear implants and may function with some success in some K–12 situations can greatly benefit from the social capital they gain at these programs.

> When I attended the [name of program], it really opened my eyes and "woke me up." I wanted to attend this program to see what it would look like to have full communication access. I did not expect or realize the diversity among deaf people. Some were oral, some used cued speech, and some even used ASL. I felt uneasy at first trying to communicate with everyone with no interpreter. We all were focused on each other instead of having to watch an interpreter, and it was like a paradigm shift. It made me think "Gee! I could contribute a lot more to the world!" If it wasn't for [this program], I would not have become involved with the deaf community [and all the other opportunities this led to]. It gave me friendships that I would always cherish and that will always support me. Even if I make mistakes, I will always have their support.

Parents, Please Send Your Child to Camps and Weekend Programs!

Perhaps the most important lesson from Gina's research into summer and weekend programs was that the best element(s) of each of these camp/weekend programs could or should be emulated to improve or develop programs that include more and more of these strong points. A single program will not be able to be "all things to all people." However, the great variety of programs available means parents can send their deaf and hard of hearing children to at least one program every summer from middle school on, and to weekend programs during the school year. (If no weekend program exists in a certain geographical area, parents may consider setting one up, which is relatively easy, compared to a summer program.) Attending summer and weekend programs enable the deaf or hard of hearing child's sense of self to grow most efficiently. Each experience with these programs will add to the child's knowledge and sense of safety with the myriad of options for her social capital/social support in her soon-to-come adulthood.

The considerable variation in the kind of program offered means that deaf and hard of hearing children have a wide range of opportunities, both in the kind of activity they can be involved with and in the variety of peers they can meet (from all areas of the country). The volunteers or almost-volunteers who manage and staff these programs recognize that deaf and hard of hearing children today seriously need these programs, especially as an increasingly greater majority are mainstreamed. We would like readers to note the considerable creativity and planning skills that go into pulling off something like a summer camp or a weekend program. We are in awe of all and we hope we can relay some of this awe herein. We hope parents and other readers will be inspired to enroll their deaf or hard of hearing child to a program *every* summer and to a variety of other programs during the year, and/or even be inspired to start a new program. There is always room for more. A deaf or hard of hearing child can't get too much social immersion with others "like me."

8

Scholars, Parents, Advocates, and Allies: Working for Change

"The future belongs to those who believe in the beauty of their dreams."

(attributed to Eleanor Roosevelt)

ALL THE members of our focus groups were passionate in their wishes to share their stories so that current and future deaf and hard of hearing children will have significantly better K–12 experiences. More than half of them are pursuing degrees or working in areas where they can have influence on current and future children. Today there are numerous educators, sociologists, psychologists, linguists, neuroscientists, and so forth, who were once children subject to the system—"experiments," if you will. We ourselves were once those kids. We and our participants therefore have unique insight, and we can possibly spare parents, teachers, and others invested in deaf and hard of hearing children some heartache.

In Chapter 7 we spoke of the advocacy work of deaf and hard of hearing adults, including scholars, parents, advocates, or some combination thereof. In this chapter we share a multitude of unique and valuable contributions to research, advocacy, and program development being made as we type these words, by deaf and hard of hearing professionals, parents, and advocates (and our hearing allies) not only in the United

States but around the world. In so doing, we hope to make a thoroughly convincing argument for strategic, formalized, and ongoing involvement of deaf and hard of hearing professionals in EHDI, NCIEC, ClassroomInterpreting.org, state education agencies, and, above all, in the federal government agencies that fund those entities.

In Chapter 5 we expressed the hope we see in the annual EHDI conference. This conference, along with its organizer the National Center for Hearing Assessment and Management (NCHAM) illustrates a very important recognition by those in power that deaf and hard of hearing children and their families have unique needs and thus require unique resources.

Remember, however, that there currently is no system or conference that brings together teachers of the deaf and K–12 interpreters from the various regions and states. We see this as a serious problem, as it reduces their power and ability to influence change and represents a situation of very limited support for development within their professions. These teachers and interpreters are as isolated as the students they work with, and this is an issue of concern.

The changes needed to the current system of educating deaf and hard of hearing children must be guided by the advice, research, and advocacy of d/Deaf and hard of hearing adults who themselves experienced general education classrooms during their formative years. Here we recommend action of different types and provide examples of endeavors that have and will make important contributions toward turning the tide for the current and next generations of deaf and hard of hearing children.

Publish in Medical Journals

The first work we showcase involves nine scholars, all Deaf except one, all associated with esteemed universities, working together to impact the people who parents first hear from regarding their child's hearing loss: medical professionals. The scholars are affiliated with the universities of California, Washington, Utah, Rochester, and Hamburg; Swarthmore College; Rochester Institute of Technology; and Gallaudet University, and they represent a variety of fields including pediatric medicine, linguistics, cross-cultural studies, and psychology. Their work hones in on the concerns felt and relayed by the Deaf scholars and parents who have been attending EHDI regarding early language deprivation and its long-term impact.

These scholars have published articles aimed at reaching medical and related professionals. Their work has appeared in the *Journal of Clinical Ethics,* the *Journal of Medical Speech-Language Pathology,* the *Harm Reduction Journal,* and in an edited collection, *Cochlear Implant Research Updates* (Umat & Tange, 2012). In the articles, the authors echo what the Deaf professionals involved in EHDI have been saying, making their points with strong justification and appropriate authority from their broad base of disciplines and knowledge. Publishing articles in these journals is a professional milestone for the authors and represents an even bigger milestone for the Deaf community. The articles are a shining example of Deaf scholars doing whatever they can to impact the lives of the current and future generations of deaf and hard of hearing children. We summarize the main contributions of this recent work below.

The *Harm Reduction Journal* is "written for and by physicians, nurses, attorneys, clergy, ethicists, and others whose decisions directly affect patients. More than 70% of the articles published are authored or coauthored by physicians" (www.harmreductionjournal.com). In "Language Acquisition for Deaf Children: Reducing the Harms of Zero Tolerance to the Use of Alternative Approaches," Humphries et al. (2012b) chastise the medical and audiological professions for advocating the "speech-only approach" with deaf infants and toddlers:

> Because of lack of training and lack of coordination among professionals, there is a great deal of misinformation about the use of speech and sign language with deaf children who undergo cochlear implantation. Specifically, many medical professionals do not fully understand the ramifications of promoting speech-exclusive approaches and denying sign language exposure to a deaf child before and after implantation. (p. 3)

The authors go on to explain the simple and well-known fact that because of brain plasticity in the first few years of life, infants and toddlers must be exposed to a *full language,* day in and day out, in order to naturally develop language. Hearing infants and toddlers are constantly exposed to spoken language—the "ubiquitous conversation" and "Pac-man phenomenon" that we mentioned in Chapter 2. Hearing infants are generally surrounded by people talking, be it family members or on the television, radio, and so forth, and they thus acquire language effortlessly. Deaf children born into families that use a full sign language acquire language in this same effortless manner. However, when deaf children are born into hearing families, physicians and audiologically oriented professionals frequently advise the parents to focus on spoken language only. They advise the parents to "wait" until the child is old enough to be surgically implanted and then to focus on exposing the child to spoken language. Those who advise this, the authors maintain, are albeit unintentionally *doing harm*. These medical and related professionals—mistaken but universally regarded "experts" that they are—are unintentionally relegating deaf and hard of hearing infants and toddlers to *linguistic deprivation*.

> Linguistic deprivation carries with it a spectrum of problems. . . . Cognitive activities that rely on a firm first language foundation such as mathematics . . . and the organization of memory are then disordered or disrupted. Linguistic deprivation also diminishes one's educational and career possibilities . . . one's professional opportunities are highly circumscribed. Additionally, linguistic deprivation leads to psychosocial problems due to the isolation and frustration one experiences from diminished linguistic and cognitive capability . . . Clearly, linguistic deprivation constitutes a multi-faceted harm to the individual. (p. 6)

The authors further delineate the actions that lead to harmful linguistic deprivation for possibly a majority of deaf children. More often than not, the medical professionals tell parents they need to choose spoken language *or* signed language. Humphries et al. (2012a) label this action a "failure to inform." The professionals to whom parents are referred when they first learn their baby is deaf frequently do not understand the gravity of linguistic deprivation. Many of these professionals are unfamiliar with the long-standing documentation about how deafness in infancy in families that do not use sign language frequently leads to difficulties with both expressive and receptive language (including reading and writing). Further, many of these professionals do not understand the fullness and richness of sign language, nor do they realize that in families in which even just one parent is fluent in sign language, children deaf from infancy *do* develop full language and *are* able to read and write in the native spoken language, often far better than children born into families in which no one can sign. This lack of knowledge on the part of medical and related personnel translates into a lack of information conveyed to vulnerable families who have just learned that their infant is deaf or hard of hearing. The families subsequently most frequently choose to have their child implanted and not to use signs at all, when really it can only help to use both. Research is increasingly pointing to the benefits of bilingualism, and the professionals who are in contact with families during the deaf or hard of hearing child's infancy need to be up on the latest and be conveying this information to the families, along with the information about implants.

A chapter in *Cochlear Implant Research Updates* (Umat & Tange, 2012) by the same group of professionals (Humphries et al., 2012a), includes a description of the wide range of functions children are able to obtain from implants as well as a stern proclamation that the research is far from comprehensive and provides minimal if any basis for the wholesale promotion of the devices as a cure-all for deafness. The wide range of benefits obtained and not obtained by children is telling. The success children have with implants is so variable. Parents and/or physicians considering cochlear implants for their children or patients must be aware of this variability, such as:

- Cannot distinguish speech sounds from environmental sounds, and cannot distinguish between environmental sounds.
- Can distinguish among environmental sounds (such as distinguishing between a knock on a door and a fire alarm) . . . but have minimal advantage in speech, such as being able to distinguish the number of syllables in a speech stream but not being able to distinguish words.
- Can converse with family members and close friends, using speech-reading and context in addition to the auditory information that CIs provide.

• Can converse with strangers, but must use speech-reading and context in addition to auditory information. (pp. 196–197)

In all of their articles, this knowledgeable and astute group of authors offers a remedy to this state of affairs, and that is for physicians, audiologists, and others to learn about, recommend, encourage, and support families of newborn deaf children to adopt a bilingual, bimodal approach. In other words, expose the children to sign language, and expose them to spoken language—do both. Realize that American Sign Language is a full-fledged language, taught for foreign language credit at many colleges and high schools. Know also that ASL does not mean verbal language comes to a stop. The authors close with yet a third article (Humphries et al., in press), to be published by the *Journal of Medical Speech-Language Pathology*, with a summation of a remedy:

> Raising a deaf child with CI and exclusively spoken language risks delay in language and associated cognitive development as well as academic and psychosocial difficulties. The degree of risk varies depending on multiple factors that are not easily amendable or predicted, including the child's socio-economic status. Raising a deaf child with CI and spoken language along with sign language capitalizes on bimodal-bilingual language development that encompasses the multiple variables and factors we have discussed in this paper. Using a bimodal-bilingualism approach for children with CI is the safest method to ensure that those children, regardless of socioeconomic status or any other factors, are provided with the best opportunity for maximal language development, and, hence, the optimal chance for good cognitive development, academic success, and psychosocial well-being.   (p. 28)

Here are nine scholars echoing the perspective of thousands of Deaf individuals and their hearing allies, backed by research, saying that cochlear implants are not reason enough to rejoice in the idea that deafness can be "cured" or eradicated. Further, these scholars are saying that deaf children deserve a language-rich daily environment and that the push for speech-only does them harm. We urge you to find these articles (and we are sure many more will be published in the coming years) and read them for yourself.

One point we want to make clear, echoing the work of these scholars: Medical professionals and parents must have in the forefront of their minds that if there is no sign language in use with a deaf infant prior to receiving the implant, the infant will be in a state of language deprivation. When the device is implanted at 12 months or thereabouts, the infant is then subjected to intensive training to learn what the sounds mean—infants do not automatically begin to pick up language the minute the implant is turned on. Learning what the sounds mean is a long and arduous process. Language deprivation does not stop automatically, but rather may taper off slowly, meaning that more years of language lag will accumulate ill effects.

Ask Our Own Deaf Children How Things Are Coming Along for Them

Mark and Melanie Drolsbaugh are Deaf parents of three children. Darren is 13 and late deafened (meaning he was born hearing, and lost his hearing later in childhood, thus his spoken language is clear, like that of a hearing child). Brandon (10) and Lacey (7) are both hearing. All the children attend the neighborhood school, and Darren is the only deaf child in that school. As Darren has gotten older, fodder for Mark's engaging and informative entries on his blog Deaf Culture Online (deaf-culture-online.com) has come from watching his older boy deal with "alone in the mainstream" issues. Mark's stories reveal some of the day-to-day issues involved in raising a deaf or hard of hearing child, as a Deaf parent, and illustrate the individual and family level advocacy work that takes place.

In particular, Mark has written about Darren's summer camp experiences. Because Darren loves baseball and is a talented athlete, his parents "decided to reward this kid's passion for baseball by signing him up for an exclusive, professional baseball camp. Two weeks of bona fide instruction, drills, and games under the tutelage of the very best in the business." Sure enough, Darren learned much about baseball at this camp. But it seems that he (and his parents) learned some other things as well.

Mark explained that Darren was texting him every day. He thought this was because of how much he was enjoying the camp. However, a few weeks after Darren returned home, the family received their copy of his group picture.

I'm standing there, looking at Darren's team picture—I notice all of the kids have beaming smiles on their faces. Except for Darren. He looked like he just came out of a dentist's office. He had a mostly emotionless expression, looked a little sad.

Time to talk to the kid.

"Darren, come here for a minute. What did you think of baseball camp?"

"It was good." (Shrugs)

"No, really. Tell me what you really thought about it. Fun? Boring? Awesome?"

Darren shrugged again. "Look," I said, bringing the picture to his attention. "This kid looks happy. That kid looks excited."

"All right," I continued. "Let's look at you. How are you feeling in that picture? It's okay, you can tell me."

"Sad."

"That's okay. It's good to be honest about how you're feeling. What made you feel sad that day?"

"I don't really know any of those kids."

"Hard to understand them?"

"Yes. It didn't feel good. I liked the games but didn't know the kids. I love baseball. I love pitching. Just not there."

The following year, after this sad summer experience, the Drolsbaughs decided to send Darren to three different camps that had special programs for Deaf children to see how he would respond. Mark makes the point in subsequent blog entries that Darren did not text him every day from these camps. In fact, Mark never heard from Darren unless Mark initiated the contact.

The kid had the best time of his life. Camping, canoeing, visiting a water park, storytelling, swimming, and numerous other activities. He flat-out loved his camp counselors and raved about them on the ride home. He got along great with his peers. The only thing he was disappointed in was the fact that the camp was only one week, not two.

"You want to go back next year?" I asked.

"Yes! For two weeks!" was the enthusiastic reply. This coming from the same kid who shrugged *"Eh, it was okay"* after an exclusive baseball camp with hearing kids a year ago.

We are not telling this "camp story" to reiterate what we have already said in the chapter about summer camps. Our point here is more about the parents' understanding and acceptance of Darren's experiences. The point is that because of their own experiences, they were and are better able to advocate for their son and come to certain—we believe accurate—conclusions as well. Darren's enthusiasm about the Deaf camp got his father thinking about Darren's school experiences.

> Of course Mel and I have noticed that Darren's interaction with his hearing friends is at its best during recreational activities such as baseball, football, or bike riding. During indoor parties or casual gatherings, he becomes quiet and often isn't able to keep up with the conversation. Video games might break the awkward moments of silence but that's pretty much it.
>
> *Time to pick the kid's brains again.*
>
> "Say, Darren, would you like to go to a deaf school someday?"
>
> "No. I'd miss all my friends."
>
> Now for the stumper:
>
> "That's true. Hey, but what about [the Deaf Camp]? You said you wanted to go again?"
>
> His eyes light up and he gives an emphatic "Yes!"
>
> "All right," I continued. "Now what if you could go to school with all your deaf friends from [the Deaf Camp]?"
>
> This time, it hits him. He looks at me. No words come out. The silence is deafening. It was a clear paradigm shift, a reality check. Then he musters,
>
> "They have schools like [that Deaf Camp]?"
>
> (http://www.deaf-culture-online.com/)

It is a rare hearing parent who could help his or her deaf or hard of hearing child envision possible futures apart from the same old "alone in the mainstream" lifestyle, help the child see a way out of "nudging and asking," help the child see a way out of the "bystander role."

One day while we were working on this manuscript, after we had decided to use this excerpt from Mark's blog, Mark sent an email to Gina, continuing to share about Darren.

> Dear Gina,
>
> Last Friday, Darren finally snapped. He threw a fit like no other and cussed a blue streak. This was two minutes before his school bus arrived so Mel

had to hurry him out the door where he promptly tossed his backpack a good 30 feet.

I was already on my way to work when this happened. Mel paged me and said she had second thoughts about him going to school in such a distressed emotional state. So I did a U-turn and picked him up at school. We spent the day just hanging out and the things he said were amazing. None of it would surprise you.

What gets to me is that none of Darren's teachers have any idea what he's going through. If I tell them, they'll be shocked (he asked me not to say anything—I cited a vague "family emergency" as the reason I picked him up). He's on the honor roll and they gush about his work ethic, personality, and sense of humor.

At the same time, his interpreter was with him when I picked him up and even though I said nothing, the look on her face clearly indicated she knew what was going on. Again, this is obviously no surprise to you.

Everything Darren said that day rang 100-percent true. He said, "I'm tired of being a stalker and want to be a leader." I asked him to clarify *stalker* and he said he follows a group of kids around in the cafeteria and eats lunch with them, but he's left out of their conversation.

(M. Drolsbaugh, personal communication, June 29, 2012)

And so here we see the concept of solitaires "separated by miles and years." This happened in 2012 to a 13-year-old. His teacher thought "he is doing just fine," just like the deaf and hard of hearing adults in Gina's 2004 study reported: This syndrome is universal, and timeless, apparently. The interpreters know what's really going on. And the 13-year-old knows he is a "bystander," but since even adults don't know what to call this phenomenon, he has appointed the word *stalker* to approximate what he is feeling. *Stalker* is in some ways rather appropriate.

Define the Unique Experiences of Deaf and Hard of Hearing People

Darren coopted an existing word to describe a feeling he couldn't define otherwise. As Deaf people and their allies have labored to tell their stories, direct research into areas they intuitively know will shed light on the language issues faced by deaf children, and work for social change to benefit these children, they have struggled to give names to phenomena they uniquely perceive. Mindy Hopper's and our own identification of "ubiquitous conversation" and the "Pac-Man phenomenon," as well as Oliva's 2004 participants agreeing to give themselves the label "solitaires" are good examples.

The term *audism,* however, is perhaps the best example—a neologism that has found its way into the esteemed *American Heritage Dictionary (AHD),* through the efforts of Deaf professionals and their allies. In May of 2012, a member of the Deaf Academics Listserv, a group of almost 300 scholars from 20 countries sharing their scholarly works and ideas online, informed the members that the *AHD* had posted a definition of audism on its Web site. In a nutshell, everyone agreed it was a poor, inaccurate definition. Debate ensued. Some wanted the definition to have more of this, some more of that. On and on it went for a week or so. Then, one of the members, John Lee Clark, a deaf-blind poet and blogger (www .johnleeclark.com) took it upon himself to email one of the dictionary editors.

Dear Editors:

When I learned that you had added an entry for the word "audism" in your esteemed dictionary, I was thrilled. [The term] was coined in 1975 by Tom L. Humphries to name the prevalent attitude and assumption that hearing people are superior to deaf people. The word became a wellspring of dialogue about the discrimination against deaf cultures and languages. Since . . . Harlan Lane's extended discussion on institutional audism in a book called *The Mask of Benevolence: Disabling the Deaf Community* (1992), there has been a steady stream of writing, artwork, and film on the subject. And here, at long last, was validation from a powerful source of authority!

Then I read the definition. "Discrimination or prejudice against people based on the fact that their ability to hear is impaired or absent."

The term *hearing-impaired* is a favorite of hearing journalists and bureaucrats who mistakenly believe they are being politically correct when they use it instead of *deaf.* Deaf organizations the world over have denounced the usage. . . . The whole history of audist [beliefs] about deaf people and deafness is contained in this single word, *absent.* The most relentless and harmful statement is that the absence of hearing or speech equals the absence of intelligence. . . . Deafness [has been depicted as] a state of nothingness, of silence. [That the word] *absent,* with its long history of destruction, should be used here to describe deaf people is truly appalling.

So that's what you have given us: An audist definition of audism. Do you realize that it is like defining racism as "discrimination against people whose skin is defective or discolored"?

(J. L. Clark, personal communication, September 1, 2012)

As a result of John's unsolicited letter, an *AHD* editor worked with him and several other esteemed individuals, including Tom Humphries, who coined the term originally, and Dirksen Bauman, professor in the Gallaudet University Department of Deaf Studies—who along with his Deaf graduate students produced the film *Audism Unveiled.* The *AHD* replaced its definition with the following:

1. The belief that people with hearing are superior to those who are deaf or hard of hearing.
2. Discrimination or prejudice against people who are deaf or hard of hearing. (http://ahdictionary.com/word/search.html?q=audism)

Fight Audism: Global Solidarity, Local Struggle

One of our focus group participants declared, "We were the first global citizens!" How right he was! Recall also that a Gallaudet freshman, upon reading *Alone in the Mainstream* in 2004, said how nice it was to know that there were other "solitaires" in the world even though they are separated by "miles and years." Indeed, the push for mainstreaming is worldwide, and the issues thus, are worldwide.

The next story touches on at least three issues germane to this entire volume. The storyteller is Cindy Officer, a Deaf mother of two hearing children and one deaf child. We share her experience here as a stark example of audism. Officer has published a commentary about this incident on the *Deaf Studies Digital Journal* (Officer, 2010). Our summary below includes direct quotes either transcribed from that commentary or obtained through emails and personal conversations with Officer between June 29, 2012, and April 22, 2013. The situation reflects upon mainstreaming in general, audist behavior by persons of authority, and interpretation issues.

At the time this situation unfolded, Officer's deaf child was a student in a county system that has a 95% college acceptance rate among its graduates. The parents of the students in this school are generally affluent and well educated. At the time of this story, the county had three elementary programs for deaf and hard of hearing children in three different schools, in three different geographical locations within this county: One was an oral program, one was a cued speech program, and one was a sign language program. The county was considering putting all three programs in a single school building, and representatives announced that they would hold focus groups for interested parties to provide feedback on this idea.

Officer reported that approximately 15–20 deaf or hard of hearing adults showed up for this event. Many were parents or grandparents of deaf and hard of hearing children currently attending one of these three elementary school programs. Also in attendance were former students (graduates) of the county's DHH program (including their middle- and high-school programs), and several Deaf professionals with children in other area counties and/or with professional expertise in education. When they first arrived at the assembly, an administrator addressed the crowd explaining that there would be four focus groups in four specified rooms, but that they needed the deaf and hard of hearing stakeholders to be in a specific two of these four rooms due to the limited number of interpreters on hand.

The deaf or hard of hearing adults complied. The room that Officer entered had eight Deaf participants and five hearing participants, plus the hearing facilitator and her hearing note taker/assistant. The facilitator instructed the group to respond to two questions in turn, starting at one end of the table and proceeding one by one around the table. The questions were "What is important to consider in DHH programs?" and "What specific recommendations do you have for the redesign related to instruction, social interaction, resources, and services for the deaf and hard of hearing students in the program?"

Cindy shared with us:

> The discussion began seamlessly with the first four hearing participants voicing their comments . . . the note taker wrote speakers' comments on the flip

chart and taped them to the wall. When it came to the first deaf speaker, the process lurched and stalled. Her comments were not recorded. The next person, a hearing mother of a deaf child, spoke and the smooth process of speaking-transcribing picked up again. After her, the five next deaf stakeholders articulated their suggestions but very little of what they said made it to the flip chart. Comments by deaf participants ended up on the wall vague and often contrary to the speaker's intent. Most were simply not recorded on the flip chart at all.

Oh dear. It's the voice interpretation problem rearing its ugly head. Recall from the chapters on educational interpreting that this is one of the hardest parts of an interpreter's job. Many skilled interpreters fall short at interpreting and conveying an articulate message from the signer, even if the signer is fully articulate in sign communication. Officer knew something was not right and decided to do her best to set things right:

> I began to write down on my own notepad what the other deaf and hard of hearing participants had said. When my turn came, I used my own voice and first I reiterated what the other deaf participants had said. I made it clear that I noticed their remarks were not recorded accurately and I thought they should be so I wanted to repeat what they had said.
>
> As I spoke the note taker did start to write on the flip chart but I noticed she was not accurately recording what I was saying. A few times I paused to check in with the deaf participant to make sure I had accurately captured their comments. As I did this, the facilitator's irritation started to become obvious. My innards tightened and nausea swept over me. . . . It sickened me to have to regurgitate the comments of my peers but I couldn't stand for them to be omitted.

Officer conveyed to the facilitator and the other focus group participants what the other deaf and hard of hearing parents had said—that they wanted the school to be sure that the children's deaf or hard of hearing identity is honored and nurtured. They wanted the school to encourage a "positive world view" of deaf and hard of hearing individuals and to avoid actions that promote audism. They also wanted to see the school system hire more deaf and hard of hearing adults, and to not be looking for places to cut such important role models or interpreters for budgetary reasons.

As she was conveying this list of recommendations that had come from the deaf and hard of hearing adults in the focus group, which had been omitted from the flip chart recording, the facilitator did something so very unprofessional:

> As I read through this list of missing/omitted comments, the facilitator grew increasingly frustrated with me. With a strong scowl on her face, she said, "We are running out of time. Put that away! PUT. THAT. A-WAY!"

Wow. As Officer described how the facilitator spoke to her, you almost have to see it. The facilitator used her pointed finger to emphasize each word: PUT (finger jab) THAT (another finger jab) AWAY!! (more finger jabs). Can you imagine? A facilitator of a school-initiated focus group yelled at one of the participants. And this happened when she, the facilitator, and her note taker were so clearly and obviously at fault. But wait, it gets worse:

> This same facilitator, within minutes of silencing me, began the next round and freely allowed the first two hearing participants an authoritative mono-logue perpetuating the misconception that "deaf children with such young brains would be sorely overwhelmed and confused by so many modalities and so many languages." Soon, other hearing people began agreeing and voting on one another's comments [and the note taker was keeping a tally on the flip chart]. . . .The deaf participants tried to interject but the two interpreters could not voice for eight. Soon deaf participants fell silent. Again using my voice, I interrupted, "Is this a vote? Why the tally marks?" The facilitator responded very curtly, "This is not a vote." The commotion ended and turn-taking resumed. But the tally marks on the flip chart remained.

We are not sure if you, the reader, after reading everything else we have written here, can fathom the grotesqueness of this, the sheer mind-boggling horribleness, the unfairness, the stigma, the prejudice. This focus group facilitator, an official in a wealthy urban school district, was showing clear signs of audism. We could chalk this up as merely unprofessional behavior. But suppose this had been a Caucasian facilitator talking to a minority focus group member, such as an African American or Latino participant while discussing the fate of the minority children? Surely there would have been an uproar. Maybe the facilitator would even have been fired or demoted or surely severely reprimanded. With audism, people don't quite realize that it is there. But the deaf and hard of hearing children *feel* it, and Deaf professionals are very aware and can articulate about it, as this scholar did.

Strengthen Families for Success, One Family at a Time

We have relayed the hope we feel with the steady involvement of Deaf professionals in the national EHDI arena—making presentations at the annual conference and sharing their expertise with individuals who work with families during their child's infancy and preschool years. Additional Deaf professional involvement is happening at the state level through different programs that promote the idea that Deaf mentors or Deaf role models can provide critical support and should be included in every family's individual family service plan (IFSP), which is mandated by IDEA. Deaf mentors/role models are trained professionals or paraprofessionals who go into the home and/or provide small classes to family members, covering areas such as what it means to be deaf or hard of hearing, information about local/regional gatherings of other families with deaf and hard of hearing children, sign language resources, and so forth. The main goal, whether articulated or not, is to help the family envision the child as an adult. Often the Deaf mentor is the first deaf or hard of hearing adult family members have ever met, and the relationship helps immensely to reduce fears about their child's potential future. This is very much in line with the concept of "horizontal identity" that Solomon (2012) explains in his bestselling *Far From the Tree*: Parents of any child who is different from them need to learn about that identity, and a deaf or hard of hearing child is a prime example of this.

The impetus for Deaf mentors/role models has come from Deaf professionals, because of input from numerous knowledgeable Deaf adults over the last few decades. We spoke in Chapter 5 of Kelby Brick's advocacy work. Beth S. Benedict, a professor in Gallaudet University's Department of Communication Studies, has been involved in EHDI for the last 10 years. Because of Benedict's involvement with EHDI, not only did she co-develop (and is co-director of) the Deaf and Hard of Hearing Infants, Toddlers and their Families: Collaboration and Leadership Interdisciplinary Graduate Certificate offered by Gallaudet, but she also serves on the Joint

Commission on Infant Hearing (JCIH). JCIH includes representatives from the American Association of Pediatrics, the American Academy of Audiologists, the Alexander Graham Bell Association, the Council on Education of the Deaf, and several others. Due to Benedict's efforts, along with those of other Deaf professionals, the *JCIH Year 2007 Position Statement: Principles and Guidelines for Early Hearing Detection and Intervention* includes the following:

> The deaf and hard-of-hearing community includes members with direct experience with signed language, spoken language, hearing-aid and cochlear implant use, and other communication strategies and both audio and visual technologies. Optimally, adults who are deaf or hard-of-hearing should play an integral part in the EHDI program. Both adults and children in the deaf and hard-of-hearing community can enrich the family's experience by serving as mentors and role models. Such mentors have experience in negotiating their way in a hearing world, raising infants or children who are deaf or hard of hearing, and providing families with a full range of information about communication options, assistive technology, and resources that are available in the community.   (http://www.jcih.org/posstatemts.htm)

Benedict's involvement with mentoring actually began with her own deaf parents. When she was a child, her parents were approached by a woman who happened to live in their neighborhood and who had learned that the child she recently adopted was deaf. Lee Katz, the mother of this adopted girl, was henceforth "adopted" by the Sonnenstrahl family, and the daughter became one of Benedict's playmates. Katz learned so much from the Sonnenstrahls and other deaf families that she went on to found the American Society for Deaf Children (ASDC) in 1967. This was the first organization founded by and for parents of deaf and hard of hearing children. Katz led this organization until her untimely death in 1974, but Benedict remains involved today on the ASDC board and as past president (B. Benedict, personal communication, March 2013).

Lee Katz's daughter, Lizabeth, relayed a heartwarming story that goes to the heart of the role Deaf mentors can play for hearing families:

> A few Deaf families, particularly the Sonnenstrahls and the Paddens, welcomed me warmly into their homes and served as fabulous role models.

They introduced my parents and me to the world of deafness. The Padden's daughter Carol was a frequent playmate. These two families were like an extended family for my own family—I learned as much about being deaf as I would have learned from being in a residential school learning from deaf residential advisors, but [it was] more meaningful because it was in a home setting and learning family values in a Deaf culture. My parents realized that I (and they) needed this close association with Deaf families. It would be ideal if all hearing families with a deaf baby/child could have this close association. The results would be a tremendous and positive effect on those families. I feel really fortunate to have had those experiences and am thankful for it.   (L. Katz, personal communication, June 19, 2013)

Beth Benedict and others in the United States have diligently been working on the concept of Deaf mentors/role models for several decades. Other countries, including Italy, Austria, and Dubai (United Arab Emirates), have invited Benedict and her colleagues to present about EHDI and related issues. The global nature of this movement is further illustrated by groundbreaking research on the topic that was conducted in the United Kingdom. Rogers and Young (2011) of the University of Manchester conducted a study of Deaf role models, convening focus groups in England, Wales, and Ireland. Nineteen Deaf role models ranging in age from the mid-20s to mid-50s were involved. These subjects had various hearing abilities and varying language use (British Sign Language, English, both). They reported that the families they worked with benefitted from meeting a Deaf adult because such invariably gave them a more positive idea of their child's potential—some families, even in this century, were surprised that a Deaf adult could achieve professional status and actually get a driver's license (!). And, a great majority of the time, the Deaf role model was the first deaf or hard of hearing adult the family and the child met.

Several U.S. states have Deaf role model programs. New Mexico, Maine, Maryland, and Minnesota were the four we were able to learn most about, although unofficial counts tell us that such programs exist in 10–20 states. Officials in those states stand ready to assist anyone who wishes to establish such a program; these states have been successful at getting federal and/or state dollars to pay for these services.

While talking with various professionals about Deaf mentor/role model programs, we also learned more about another program that we would be remiss to not mention: Hands & Voices (handsandvoices.org). Hands & Voices was founded in the mid-1990s by a group of parents in Colorado and now boosts a national/international office. On staff is Karen Putz, Deaf herself and the mother of three deaf or hard of hearing children, who provides both headquarter-based and chapter support for ensuring the inclusion of deaf and hard of hearing adults in Hands & Voices work. And she has been advocating for deaf and hard of hearing children for quite some years through her blog A Deaf Mom Shares Her World (Karenputz.com).

Hands & Voices supports official chapters in 33 states, with eight additional states in the process of becoming official (J. DesGeorges, personal communication, March 7, 2013, April 26, 2013), and a prolific slate of conferences, presentations by board members, and so forth. "Guide by Your Side" is one of their most successful programs; there are currently 19 of these in various states and Canada. The program description mentions that state chapters, although established following official Hands & Voices principles, are encouraged to include

> not only Parent Guides, but trained Deaf or Hard of Hearing (DHH) Guides to families with newly identified babies, young children, or to seasoned parents with teenagers who are deaf or hard of hearing. Exposure to DHH adults can provide families and DHH children/youths with invaluable perspectives that come from personal experience. Emphasis on matching adults with families and kids of like-communication modality is commonly practiced, but not necessarily required.
> (http://www.handsandvoices.org/gbys/faq_guidPrinciple.htm)

At the National Association of Deaf (NAD), Tawny Holmes, yet another Deaf professional with the needs of deaf and hard of hearing children in her heart, serves as an appointed board member focusing on education. As of this writing Holmes is finishing law school and has obtained a legal fellowship with Bingham McCutchen, one of the top 100 law firms in the country. The main focus of her fellowship will be providing training to parents across the country on their rights in the Least Restrictive Environment–Individual Education Program process. Her workshops will instruct parents both about the unique educational needs of deaf and hard of hearing children and how parents can use parts of the law and research to knowledgeably and successfully work with school personnel to ensure that their child's needs are met.

Our vision is this: that Hands & Voices, the NAD, and ASDC will collaborate on such advocacy. Hands & Voices has state chapters and excellent access to parents within the states. ASDC has over 3,000 members nationally who can further assist with outreach. And the NAD has Holmes with her fellowship to provide this all-important training. For the three organizations to join forces on this would have the most awesome impact on families and thereby the children—the best of all possible support. That's what we all want.

We hope that these diverse examples of the work of scholars, parents, and advocates, along with what we have said in our other chapters, give irrefutable evidence that deaf and hard of hearing adults, who understand the experiences of deaf and hard of hearing children and youth like no one else can, should be seen as critical partners in all efforts for the life enhancement of these children. All professionals working with families of children who are deaf or hard of hearing—physicians, nurses, early intervention specialists, audiologists, speech-language pathologists, teachers, interpreters—can and should convey and reinforce to parents the importance of reading about and consulting with deaf and hard of hearing adults. The professionals should convey a positive view of deaf and hard of hearing adults and the contributions they make—such comments will go a long way to reducing insidious audism.

Forty-plus years of research studies and publications illustrate our collective intelligence, critical thinking, and dedication to the cause of deaf and hard of hearing children. For the children of today and tomorrow to have the best possible futures, there must be a place at the table for people like us and colleagues like those introduced to you in this chapter. We call for the ongoing, sustained, and highly valued privilege of working with and for the families of deaf and hard of hearing children and youth.

9

Turning the Tide:
Making Life Better

"As other researchers in the deaf education world have observed, placement decisions, unfortunately, have little to do with learning."

(Ramsey, 1997, pp. 115–116)

I T I S so clear to us what needs to be done. We are not saying it will be easy, but we think it is clear. In this final chapter we offer broad recommendations for systemic change and specific recommendations for changes for families and schools that will impact positively on the lives of deaf and hard of hearing children and youth. Our focus, as it has been throughout this book, is on making life better for those who are alone in general education settings.

Broad Systemic Recommendations

Many individuals (of various professional backgrounds, workplaces, and persuasions) are involved in supporting deaf and hard of hearing children and their families. These individuals often are only aware of their own narrow professional niches, and associate mostly with others from the same professional niche. What would it be like if individuals whose common goal was to improve education and lives for deaf and hard of hearing children and their families actually talked and worked together on a more regular basis? What would it be like if instead of looking for differences in approaches, we looked for commonalities?

For the maximum well-being of deaf and hard of hearing children, there must be a gigantic increase in the connectivity of all entities. This collaboration can be undertaken at the state level or federal level, or it can be initiated by an organization. The National Summit on Deaf Education has begun this work, and it needs to be continued. Those with usually minimal knowledge of issues affecting deaf and hard of hearing children, such as federal and state policy makers, public school administrators, special education directors, and those involved in the general audiology-speech professions must partner with those who have specialized training. They must partner with administrators of schools and programs for deaf and hard of hearing children, with faculty and graduates of Deaf Education/Deaf Studies/ Educational Interpreting programs, and with advocacy organizations such as the National Organization of the Deaf (NAD), A. G. Bell, Hands & Voices, and the American Society for Deaf Children (ASDC). People who typically do not talk to each other about their common concerns for deaf and hard of hearing children must start doing so in a significant way to reduce the fragmentation that pervades the system. One of their first efforts can be to take a hard look at the current situation of deaf and hard of hearing children who are widely dispersed throughout the general education system, and identify the activities or functions needed to support them. From these identified needed supports we envision the development of a new profession, the "Educational Specialist–DHH." The creation of this new profession is our second system-wide recommendation.

Gallaudet University, Rochester Institute of Technology, and other universities with existing programs can and should participate in this effort to define, envision, and build this profession. The goal is to give all deaf and hard of hearing children (including those who are the only deaf or hard of hearing student in their schools) a professional within the school system who knows about education, language development, and social development of deaf and hard of hearing children and whose primary role is to follow these children throughout their school careers. There are many possible roles for this new professional, but we feel a large role must be advocacy, needed for academics, for extracurricular and incidental learning, and for the IEP process. This new profession will include knowledge of issues and skills to support learning (particularly language acquisition issues), interpreting (not how to interpret, but principles and evaluation thereof), assistive technology, social skills, culture, social capital, and educational law. Skills at working with parents, coordinating events, connecting deaf and hard of hearing students with each other, and being aware of community support and resources should all be a part of their responsibilities, as well as advocating for students and the teachers and interpreters who support them.

Right now, in public schools all over the country, there are too many professionals providing deaf and hard of hearing children with 15 minutes of service here, 15 minutes of service there, and often none of them knows much about the whole picture. Services are much too fragmented and, as a result, children are falling through the cracks. Children deserve ongoing support from an individual who has been schooled in all the issues they face. Creating such a profession will result in improved education for *all* deaf and hard of hearing children, not just those who were fortunate enough to have been born into educated, middle-class families whose parents may have the time and the skills to go into the schools and perform many of the functions just described.

We know that others are working on the idea of collaboration and coordinated efforts to better meet the needs of deaf and hard of hearing children. We are inspired by this work. We encourage readers to join existing efforts in existing organizations, and to keep collaboration and openness high on their agendas.

Our third broad recommendation is specific to the United States Department of Education. States must be required to gather and report on achievement data by disability group. Stakeholders must know how deaf and hard of hearing students are doing academically, apart from and compared to other groups of children. The IDEA indicators that states are required to respond to should be focused more on literacy goals, whole child goals, and the results of education in general rather than on mere facts concerning the number of students who have IEPs who are in regular education classes or the number of these students who are graduating. These latter data suggest that successful educational placement is about placing all deaf and hard of hearing children in general education classrooms (e.g., the location of the schooling is the goal), and our book and many other books, journal articles, Web sites, and organizations attest against this goal. We need to collect data on educational achievement for deaf and hard of hearing children in general education settings. We need to know if the current system is resulting in well educated, healthy, happy deaf and hard of hearing children. The data as they are currently collected do not give us this information.

We need to bring back the focus to the Individual Education Program— we need to provide educational settings that meet children's individual needs. And we need to go back to the original intention of the law, which by focusing on the IEP, necessitates the availability of a continuum of educational placements.

The federal government must ensure that there will be some school environments that provide full access to communication and conversation for deaf and hard of hearing children both inside and outside of the classroom. This translates into ensuring the survival of some specified number of state schools for the deaf and large mainstream programs. We propose that the remaining schools for the deaf be given full support by the federal government to become viable 21st-century schools. They would become essentially regional boarding schools and their entire environment would provide all-around access to incidental learning as well as to direct communication in the classroom. As they would be under the federal government, rather than state governments, they could be called Regional Deaf and Hard of Hearing Education Centers: federally supported centers that serve children in specified geographic areas including multiple states. This would take some creative management with the federal government a player, but as a result no undue or unfair financial burden would fall on individual school districts. The result could be a continuum of educational choices without the current financial costs to individual school districts.

Is this a pipe dream? Perhaps, but this is what is needed in order to truly meet the educational and social needs of deaf and hard of hearing students.

We invite all to join us in our dreaming, because the current system is truly not working. Change starts with the courage to think and act differently.

Recommendations for Families and Service Providers of Infants, Toddlers, and Preschool Children

We talked in both Chapters 5 and 7 about the existing system for supporting early intervention. We applaud the National Center for Hearing Assessment and Management and all individuals involved in providing information and services to families with young deaf and hard of hearing children, and we offer two important recommendations to make these services stronger and remedy a still-prevalent gap in language acquisition for infants and toddlers.

First, it behooves all involved in early intervention to educate themselves regarding the research coming out of the Visual Language and Visual Learning (VL2) Labs—the work of Laura-Ann Petitto and her colleagues. It is time to accept that deaf and hard of hearing children will do better, in general and in specific areas, if they are exposed to both spoken and signed language from birth. Related to this recommendation, there remains a need for learning materials (DVDs, Web materials, etc.) that Deaf mentors and/or trained early intervention specialists can use to help parents maximize their infants' visual attentiveness, visual learning, and visual language from the day they are brought home from the hospital. Such materials need to be built into a curriculum specifically designed for use by hearing parents with their infants, toddlers, and preschool children. This curriculum should assume that the family will also be building their child's skills in spoken language and auditory listening skills and clearly model for the parents how to use both visual and auditory languages in the home and related environs.

Naturally, suggesting that parents and other family members learn and use sign language with their deaf and hard of hearing infants and toddlers has huge ramifications for them. Still, families do difficult things all the time for their children. We strongly believe they can do this too. We hope they will take every opportunity to educate themselves about issues regarding visual language development. We hope they stop believing ignorant "experts" who say sign will interfere with speech development. This is decidedly not true, and, in fact, as we go to press, research is emerging that shows the opposite (Hassanzadeh, 2012). Hassanzadeh compared seven implanted children of deaf parents who used ASL in the home with seven matched children of hearing parents who did not and found that children of deaf parents performed significantly better on speech perception, speech performance, and language development. EHDI professionals must have access to and pay attention to such research and thereby encourage families to use both spoken and signed languages in the home for at least the first several years. When their child reaches age 5 or 6, parents will have a better idea of what really works. And, by employing both languages, not only do the parents ensure the best possible language development, but they also open both the child and themselves to social opportunities with other families and children—deaf, hard of hearing, and hearing.

Second, we would like to see EHDI conference planners make a concerted effort to provide early intervention professionals with information about the K–12 years. Families need a clear picture of the opportunities, potential, and pitfalls that will be on the horizon as the child grows. While the very early years are of crucial importance to building a strong path to success, information about the K–12 years would provide transition into successful school years as well.

EDHI professionals and parents of the very youngest deaf and hard of hearing children are a highly motivated group and a relatively organized group. There is a place for them to come together to discuss recommendations such as the ones we are making. There is a system in place where they can meet one another and discuss national agendas and needs. There is research money available as well. But those in the K–12 educational system have no such system in which to meet and discuss broad issues of concern regarding education of DHH students. The recommendations in the next section are for thousands upon thousands of public schools, millions of general education administrators and teachers, and millions of hearing peers. Reaching them is daunting. But press on we must.

Recommendations for the K–12 System

In making the following recommendations, we recognize that there will be differences in specifics related to grade level—specifics of implementing these recommendations for third graders will be different than those for high school students. We trust that parents and school personnel can and will be creative in putting our recommendations into action appropriately.

Include Deaf and Hard of Hearing Children as Part of Overall School Diversity

The current push toward multiculturalism in educational settings should be extended to include deaf and hard of hearing students. Society at large, and schools in particular, should define *diversity* broadly (the broadness concept is, in fact, part of the true definition of the word), so that children with differing abilities are seen as a part of the rich diversity within the world. Administrators, teachers, and peers who view deaf and hard of hearing children through this lens would be more likely to welcome such children into their schools. This openness should translate into greater acceptance of visual learning as well as of technology designed to make the general education setting truly inclusive for these children.

One excellent suggestion from Hopper (2012) is the idea of electronic "text translators" situated in places where incidental learning is likely to take place—hallways, the cafeteria, the gymnasium, and so forth. Voice recognition software would pick up conversation taking place in specified vicinities. This technology would allow deaf and hard of hearing children to read the transcripts whenever they want, presumably making it easier for them to participate in conversation. Everyone has access to the ubiquitous conversations in a school hallway or lunchroom except the deaf or hard of hearing child. Providing access to incidental learning in this manner may be eyebrow-raising as it is so unusual, but we hope at least people are able to recognize the importance of it. The worse response would be to dismiss it as not needed or not educationally important. Incidental learning from the conversations happening all around us, as we have said repeatedly in this book, is vitally important for many reasons. We hope some schools will be bold enough to experiment with this.

We would also like to see schoolwide practices that reinforce the idea that deaf and hard of hearing children deserve direct communication. Recall the story about the cooking class in Chapter 6. We see no reason why the student's classmates could not have enough visual communication skills to include a deaf or hard of hearing classmate in a cooking lab—or a biology lab, or anywhere that group work is required. Student groups could be rewarded for their equitable involvement of the whole team rather than for the speed at which they reach the end product. Teachers should allow enough time so that student groups that include a deaf or hard of hearing child are not penalized for their inclusion efforts, which may very well take additional time. Teachers too should make direct communication with the deaf or hard of hearing student a priority.

Viewing deaf and hard of hearing students as part of the multiculturalism in a school would also provide impetus and sustained support for ASL classes or clubs and for special events that feature deaf and hard of hearing adults from the community. At the high school level, schools can support ASL for foreign language credit. Activities such as these send a message to deaf and hard of hearing students that they are valued and that people don't see their hearing loss as "their problem." Deaf and hard of hearing students in such schools will feel less alone, marginal, or isolated when there are constant reminders that people are interested in them enough to learn more about them and others like them.

Finally, it may go without saying that deaf and hard of hearing children, like all children who are seen as different, are at risk for bullying. School bullying policies and practices should bear this in mind and all school personnel should be aware of this additional risk.

Make IEP Processes Empowering and Focused on the Whole Child

Our study participants remember experiencing IEP meetings as critical and punitive. For example, they recall being challenged with, "Why aren't you using your FM system?" IEP meetings should be the result of ongoing collaboration between the students and the professionals who are working with them. An adult who is well versed in the whole student needs of deaf and hard of hearing children should work closely with each student, so that the IEP can address academic, extracurricular, and incidental learning, and social-emotional needs. Earlier in this chapter we recommended the development of a new profession, the Educational Specialist–DHH, with individuals highly trained to serve in this capacity for all the deaf and hard of hearing children within their jurisdictions. The involvement of these professionals in the IEP process would better ensure that all children's various needs are met.

Following are a few more specific recommendations for making the IEP process more positive and helpful:

• Educate students and parents yearly about the purpose of the IEP. Circumstances change for the child and the family, and a refresher will be of benefit to all.
• Give the student a leadership role in the development and monitoring of his/her IEP.
• Invite sports coaches or other extracurricular leaders to IEP meetings. These adults often have different and important perspectives on the deaf or hard of hearing student.
• Schedule IEP meetings with an interpreter other than a student's regular classroom interpreter(s)—this interpreter should not attend IEP meetings. If information from the classroom interpreter is needed (and the regular interpreter does often have an important perspective to share), this should be obtained in advance by the coordinating professional.

Properly Educate and Evaluate Classroom Interpreters, Itinerant Teachers, and Counselors

From both our informants and the leaders in the field of educational interpreting with whom we spoke, we learned that schools are not able to appropriately evaluate the interpreters working with deaf and hard of hearing students. Often the persons most aware of this are the interpreters themselves, and it would behoove them to share their feelings and to insist that they receive both annual evaluation by skilled interpreters and support for professional development opportunities. It is unfortunate that this responsibility must first fall on the interpreters themselves, but this is simply a matter of fact. Beyond this, however, public school administrators at every level should push for policies that ensure that deaf and hard of hearing students have optimal access to classroom information. The administrator responsible for deaf and hard of hearing students must be educated about issues in K–12 interpreting, including the varying needs of children at different grade levels, and especially about issues of evaluation—such as the fact that only a highly skilled sign language interpreter trained in evaluation can evaluate another interpreter. Finally, a budget sufficient to hire and retain top quality interpreters must be assured.

Resource room issues loomed large in the memories of our participants. They remember rigid policies surrounding required attendance and rigidity in the structure of the activities themselves. Additionally, there was wide variation in what occurred inside the resource room in different schools. Our participants recalled feeling resentful about being required to attend resource rooms because of the "real" classes they subsequently missed. They were able to tolerate this requirement when they saw real academic help being provided. When no help was given, this required attendance created anger and boredom.

We wondered why our participants said little about their "TODs" (teachers of the deaf), and we can only surmise that because they were all high achievers, they saw these teachers rarely if at all. Instead, they were simply required to spend time in these resource rooms. At any rate, resource rooms are one issue that can and should be addressed by the new Educational Specialist–DHH.

School counselors need multicultural competence and knowledge of specialized services and resources within the Deaf community. Our respondents said overwhelmingly that their counselors did not have helpful information, such as regarding students' eligibility for financial support for college through state vocational rehabilitation agencies. This lack of information actually resulted in delays in college attendance. Our informants advised that school counselors be educated about colleges such as NTID, Gallaudet University, and CSUN and also about those all-important summer and weekend programs, and be aware of students' needs for social capital with other deaf and hard of hearing children and adults. Finally, they wanted school counselors to really understand their needs. They didn't want to have to give their counselors "Deafness 101" and "Deafness 102" before the counselor could be of any assistance. They also did not want their classroom interpreter in the rare personal counseling sessions they had.

Give General Education Teachers a Crash Course

Individual classroom teachers often make the difference between a school year that is positive and enriching and one that is negative, boring, or even hurtful. Teachers who go into the experience of teaching a deaf or hard of hearing student with curiosity and enthusiasm will create better experiences not only for this student, but for each and every child in the classroom. Teachers can include subject-matter sign language in situations in which a signing deaf or hard of hearing child is in their class; given basic skills, all students and teachers will be able to converse directly on some level with the deaf and hard of hearing student, and some classmates may be inspired to become fluent. This will reinforces the value and message of diversity: All of us in this classroom are a family and we help each other and make sure to include all members.

Ensure Deaf and Hard of Hearing Children's Access to Extracurricular Activities (Including Incidental Learning)

Perhaps the biggest challenge for schools is to make extracurricular activities of all kinds welcoming to deaf and hard of hearing children. Coaches and other adult leaders should insist that the deaf or hard of hearing child and his teammates *share* responsibility for communication, recognizing that direct communication is the only means by which the child can be truly included. There are some resources for activity-specific signs, and if none can be found it is easy enough to call in a local deaf or hard of hearing adult or mentor—or the new professional, the Educational Specialist–DHH. A team or club (the softball team, drama club, marching band, etc.) including a deaf or hard of hearing member should be a diversity-related issue, and an opportunity for all to learn together what it means to be inclusive. To include a deaf or hard of hearing student who does not sign, teammates can look at text or other ways to communicate. Or they may simply decide that yes, some basic signs will be good for the entire group.

Enhance Deaf and Hard of Hearing–Focused Summer, Weekend, and After-School Programs

It is vitally important that all deaf and hard of hearing children have connections with other deaf and hard of hearing students and their families. A critical mass of age-mates is ideal, but our participants told us resoundingly that finding even one other "like-me" person made a world of difference. This is true for students who have cochlear implants and who know no sign as well as for those who do sign. If parents and the EHDI coordinators make sure this happens in the 0–5 years, by the time they reach elementary school, the children will already intuitively understand how they benefit from knowing others "like me." We strongly recommend that attendance at summer and weekend programs be part of the child's IEP. Parents and other advocates should push for this. Given the absence of incidental learning that takes place in the general education setting, summer and weekend programs are not a luxury, but a necessity. The child is being short-changed in the school day, and these programs can provide a partial but significant remedy. Our participants attested strongly to this need.

Parents and professionals should undertake an assessment of weekend and summer programs available within driving distance to them. Existing programs should be evaluated for what they provide and how they provide it so that the most benefit can be obtained. If more programs or different programs are needed, establish these. For older children, parents should be encouraged to plan for their child to attend existing larger camps for deaf and hard of hearing children (e.g., Camp Mark Seven, Youth Leadership Camp, Aspen Camp, etc.).

We would also like to see online forums for deaf and hard of hearing age-mates; "VP pal" programs, modeled on penpal programs, which would connect deaf and hard of hearing children to each other using videophone formats; and programs for parents and families—both for information and for social support. These are good formats for introducing deaf and hard of hearing adults to hearing parents. If early interventionists initiate such programs, continuing them for school-aged children should be relatively easy.

We advocate against segregating students by language and communication modality—that is, nonsigning students should not be separated from signing students. Separation based on communication modality is detrimental to the students' unencumbered search of others "like me." Deaf and hard of hearing children are defined by so much more than how they primarily express themselves. They need each other; creating a critical mass of deaf and hard of hearing students is challenging enough without figuring in the often-limiting ways they are different from each other.

Recommendations for Research: Focus on Incidental Learning

At the present time the great majority of research dollars are spent on audition, speech, and to a lesser extent, language acquisition in general (e.g., not focused only on speech). We are aware of research dollars going into visual language and visual learning and hope this will grow. We would like to make a case for research into social capital, identity, and self-esteem issues. We want to mention again Mindy Hopper's groundbreaking study on incidental learning that we highlighted in Chapter 2—the first study to actually, concretely, demonstrate the incidental learning that is missed by a deaf or hard of hearing child in a general education setting. Incidental learning is intimately connected with friendships, social capital, identity, and self-esteem issues. Other groundbreaking work is being done in the area of pragmatic language—language used in social interactions—particularly by Christine Yoshinaga-Itano and her colleagues. The work of these scholars suggests that pragmatic language grows from incidental learning (Goberis et al., 2012), and we are certain that researchers will see the promise of more study on incidental learning. Such study should be undertaken all over the country in various settings, and it should especially include students who use amplification, at various grade levels, because so many people assume these students are doing just fine and this is not always true. We need to know how much (or little) deaf and hard of hearing students are picking up in those hallways, school buses, locker rooms, and cafeterias.

We recognize that our recommendations are a tall order. But we know there are many who will agree with them, and who are already working on them in some form or another. Our greatest wish is that those reading our book will be inspired to do more, say more, and pay more. Build bridges. Make life better. Our children deserve no less.

References

Alice Cogswell Act of 2013. http://www.ceasd.org/child-first/alice
-cogswell

Antia, S., Jones, P., Luckner, J., Kreimeyer, K., & Reed, S. (2011).
Social outcomes of students who are deaf and hard of hearing in
general education classrooms. *Exceptional Children, 77,* 489–504.

Antia, S., Jones, P., Reed, S., & Kreimeyer, K. (2009). Academic
status and progress of deaf and hard of hearing students in general
education courses. *Journal of Deaf Studies and Deaf Education,
14,* 293–311.

Bailey, J. (2010). *Letter from RID Government Affairs to Alana Miller,
General Accountability Office, October 1, 2010.* Retrieved from
www.rid.org/content/index.cfm/AID/225

Bahan, B., Bauman, H-D. L., Darnall, L., Montenegro, F., & Stein-
berg, E. J. (2008). *Audism unveiled* [DVD]. San Diego, CA:
DawnSign Press.

Bat-Chava, Y. (2000). Diversity of deaf identities. *American Annals
of the Deaf, 145,* 420–428.

Borg, W. R., & Gall, M. D. (1989). *Educational research.* White
Plains, NY: Longman.

Brown, S., & Schick B. (2011). Interpreting for children: Some important differences. *RID VIEWS,* Fall.

Clark, J. L. (2012, May 26). *An open letter to American Heritage Dictionary.* Retrieved from http://www.johnleeclark.com/?p=52

Clifford, J. (2008). *The instructional episodes of itinerant teachers of
students who are deaf or hard of hearing* (Unpublished doctoral
dissertation). Gallaudet University, Washington, DC.

Cohen, G. L., & Steel, Claude M. (2002). A barrier of mistrust: How
negative stereotypes affect cross-race mentoring. In J. Aronson
(Ed.), *Improving academic achievement: Impact of psychological
factors in education* (pp. 305–331). Boston, MA: Academic Press.

Cokely, D., & Winston, E. (2010). *Interpreter practitioner needs assessment trends analysis. Final report submitted on behalf of the National Consortium of Interpreter Education Centers.* Retrieved from http://www.interpretereducation.org /wpcontent/uploads/2011/06/FinalPracTrendsAnalysisMay2010.pdf

Drolsbaugh, M. (2013). *Madness in the mainstream.* Spring House, PA: Handwave Publications.

Erford, B. T. (2007). *Transforming the school counseling profession.* Upper Saddle River, NJ: Pearson Education.

Eriks-Brophy, A., Durieux-Smith, A., Olds, J., Kitzpatric, E., Duquette, C., & Whittingham, J. (2006). Facilitators and barriers to the inclusion of orally educated children and youth with hearing loss in schools promoting partnerships to support inclusion. *The Volta Review, 106,* 53–88.

Erikson, E. (1968). *Identity: Youth and crisis.* New York, NY: W. W. Norton.

Foster, S., & Cue, K. (2011). Roles and responsibilities of itinerant specialist teachers of deaf and hard of hearing students. *American Annals of the Deaf, 153,* 435–449.

Gallaudet Research Institute. (2011). *Regional and national summary report of data from the 2009–2010 annual survey of deaf and hard of hearing children and youth.* Washington, DC: Gallaudet University.

Gannon, J. (2012). *Deaf heritage: A narrative history of deaf America.* Washington, DC: Gallaudet University Press.

Glickman, N. (1996). The development of culturally deaf identities. In N. Glickman & M. Harvey (Eds.), *Culturally affirmative psychotherapy with deaf persons* (pp. 115–153). Mahwah, NJ: Lawrence Erlbaum.

Goberis, D., Beams, D., Dalpes, M. Abrisch, A., Baca, R., & Yoshinaga-Itano, C. (2012). The missing link in language development of deaf and hard of hearing children: Pragmatic language development. *Seminars in Speech and Language, 33,* 297–309.

Habermas, T., & Bluck, S. (2000). Getting a life: The emergence of the life story in adolescence. *Psychological Bulletin, 126,* 748–769.

Hassanzadeh, S. (2012). Outcomes of cochlear implantation in deaf children of deaf parents: Comparative study. *The Journal of Laryngology & Otology. 126,* 989–994. doi: http://dx.doi.org/10.1017/S0022215112001909

Hopper, M. (2011). *Positioned as bystanders: Deaf students' experiences and perceptions of informal learning phenomena* (Unpublished doctoral dissertation). University of Rochester, NY.

Horejes, T. (2012). *Social constructions of deafness: Examining deaf languacultures in education.* Washington, DC: Gallaudet University Press.

Hott, L., & Garrey, L. (2007). *Through deaf eyes* [DVD]. Washington, DC: WETA and Florentine Films/Hott Productions, Inc.

Humphries, T., Kushalnagar, P., Mathur, G., Napoli, D. J., Padden, C., Rathmann, C., & Smith, S. R. (2012a). Cochlear implants and the right to language: Ethical considerations, the ideal situation, and practical measures toward reaching the ideal. In C. Umat & R. A. Tange (Eds.), *Cochlear implant research updates*. Retrieved from http://www.intechopen.com/books/cochlear-implant-research-updates /the-right-to-language-ethical-considerations-ideal-situation-and-practical -measures-toward-reaching-the-ideal. doi:10.5772/35558

Humphries, T., Kushalnagar, P., Mathur, G., Napoli, D. J., Padden, C., Rathmann, C., & Smith, S. R. (2012b). Language acquisition for deaf children: Reducing the harms of zero tolerance to the use of alternative approaches. *Harm Reduction Journal, 9*(16), 16–24. doi:10.1186/1477-7517-9-16

Humphries, T., Kushalnagar, P., Mathur, G., Napoli, D. J., Padden, C., Rathmann, C., & Smith, S. R. (in press). Bilingualism: A pearl to overcome certain perils of cochlear implants. *Journal of Medical Speech-Language Pathology.*

Jambor, E., & Elliott, M. (2005). Self-esteem and coping strategies among deaf students. *Journal of Deaf Studies and Deaf Education, 10*, 63–81.

Joint Commission on Infant Hearing. (2007). *JCIH Year 2007 Position Statement: Principles and Guidelines for Early Hearing Detection and Intervention*. Retrieved from http://www.jcih.org/posstatemts.htm

Kleiber, D. (1999). *Leisure experience and human development: A dialectical interpretation*. New York, NY: Basic Books.

Kovelman, I., Shalinsky, M., White, K., Schmitt, S., Berens, M., Paymer, N., & Petitto. L. (2009). Dual language use in sign-speech bimodal bilinguals: fNIRS brain-imaging evidence. *Brain & Language, 109*, 112–123. doi:10.1016 /j.bandl.2008.09.008

Kushalnagar, P., Mathur, G., Moreland, C., Napoli, D. J., Osterling, W., Padden, C., & Rathmann, C. (2010). Infants and children with hearing loss need early language access. *The Journal of Clinical Ethics, 21*, 143–154.

Ladd, P. (2003). *Understanding deaf culture: In search of deafhood*. Bristol, UK: Multilingual Matters.

Lane, H., Hoffmeister, R., & Bahan, B. (1996). *A journey into the deaf world*. San Diego, CA: DawnSign Press.

Langer, E. (2007). *Classroom discourse and interpreted education: What is conveyed to deaf elementary school students?* (Unpublished doctoral dissertation). University of Colorado, Boulder.

Leigh, I. W. (2009). *A lens on deaf identities*. New York, NY: Oxford University Press.

Lytle, L. R. (1987). *Identity formation and developmental antecedents of deaf college women* (Unpublished doctoral dissertation). The Catholic University of America, Washington, DC.

Marschark, M. (2007). *Raising and educating a deaf child: A comprehensive guide to the choices, controversies, and decisions faced by parents and educators* (2nd ed.). New York, NY: Oxford University Press.

Marshall, C., & Rossman, G. B. (1999). *Designing qualitative research* (3rd ed.). Thousand Oaks, CA: Sage.

Maxwell-McCaw, D. (2001). *Acculturation and psychological well-being in deaf and hard of hearing people* (Unpublished doctoral dissertation). The George Washington University, Washington, DC.

McAdams, D. P., Josselson, R., & Lieblich, A. (2006). *Identity and story: Creating self in narrative.* Washington, DC: American Psychological Association.

Mertens, D. M. (1998). *Research methods in education and psychology: Integrating diversity with quantitative and qualitative approaches.* Thousand Oaks, CA: Sage.

Mitchell, V. J., Moening, J. H., & Panter, B. R. (2009). Student-led IEP meetings: Developing student leaders. *JADARA* (Conference issue), 230–240.

Mitchener, J., Nussbaum, D. B., & Scott, S. (2012). *The implications of bimodal bilingual approaches for children with cochlear implants* (Research Brief No. 6). Washington, DC: Visual Language and Visual Learning Science of Learning Center.

Moores, D. (2008). Inclusion, itinerant teachers, and the pull-out model. *American Annals of the Deaf, 153,* 273–274.

Morere, D. (2011). *Reading research and deaf children* (Research Brief No. 4). Washington, DC: Visual Language and Visual Learning Science of Learning Center.

Musselman, C., Mootilal, A., & MacKay, S. (1996). The social adjustment of deaf adolescents in segregated, partially integrated, and mainstreamed settings. *Journal of Deaf Studies and Deaf Education, 1,* 52 – 63.

National Association of School Psychologists. (2012). *Students who are deaf or hard of hearing and their families* [Position statement]. Bethesda, MD: Author.

National Center for Hearing Assessment and Management. (2013). *About us.* Retrieved from http://www.infanthearing.org/about/

National Deaf Education Project. (2005). *The national agenda: Moving forward on achieving educational equality for deaf and hard of hearing students.* Retrieved from http://ndepnow.org/agenda/agenda.htm

Nicodemus, B. (2009). *Prosodic markers and utterance boundaries in American Sign Language interpretation.* Washington, DC: Gallaudet University Press.

Officer, C. (2010). Commentary: A sound disappearance. *Deaf Studies Digital Journal, 2.* Retrieved from http://dsdj.gallaudet.edu/index.php?issue=3&section_id=3&entry_id=107

Oliva, G. (2004). *Alone in the mainstream: A deaf woman remembers public school.* Washington, DC: Gallaudet University Press.

Oliva, G. (2012). Sign language interpreters in mainstream classrooms: Heart-broken and gagged. *StreetLeverage.* Retrieved from http://www.streetleverage .com/2012/02/sign-language-interpreters-in-mainstream-classrooms -heartbroken-and-gagged/

Peck, C. A., & Furman, C. (1992). Qualitative research in special education: An evaluative review. In R. Gaylord-Ross (Ed.), *Issues and research in special education* (pp. 1–42). New York, NY: Teachers College Press.

Peterson, R., & Monikowski, C. (2011). Perceptions of efficacy of K–12 interpreters. In K. M. Christensen, *Ethical considerations in educating children who are deaf or hard of hearing* (pp. 129–153). Washington, DC: Gallaudet University Press.

Petitto, L. A. (2013, April). *How the human child discovers language: New insights from the neural foundations of language, the bilingual brain, and the visual phonological mind.* Presentation at the Early Hearing Detection and Intervention Conference, Glendale, AZ.

Petitto, L. A., Katerelos, M., Levy, B. G., Gauna, K., Tetreault, K., & Ferraro, V. (2001). Bilingual signed and spoken language acquisition from birth: Implications for the mechanisms underlying early bilingual language acquisition. *Journal of Child Language, 28,* 453–496.

Petitto, L. A., & Kovelman, I. (2003). The bilingual paradox: How signing-speaking bilingual children help us resolve bilingual issues and teach us about the brain mechanisms underlying all language acquisition. *Learning Languages, 8*(3), 5–18.

Preisler, G., Tvingstedt, A. L., & Ahlstrom, M. (2005). Interviews with deaf children about their experiences using cochlear implants. *American Annals of the Deaf, 150,* 260–267.

Putnam, R. (2000). *Bowling alone: The collapse and revival of American community.* New York, NY: Simon & Schuster.

Ramsey, C. (1997). *Deaf children in public schools: Placement, context, and consequence.* Washington DC: Gallaudet University Press.

Registry of Interpreters for the Deaf. (2010). *The educational interpreter's niche in RID from the practitioner's perspective: Survey results submitted by the Educational Interpreter Committee.* Retrieved from http://www.rid.org/UserFiles/File/pdfs /About_RID/For_Educational_Interpreters/Edterp_Survey_Results.pdf

Rogers, K., & Young, A. (2011). Being a deaf role model: Deaf people's experience of working with families and deaf young people. *Deafness & Education International, 13,* 2–16.

Russell, D., & McLeod, J. (2009). Educational interpreting: Multiple perspectives of our work. In J. Mole (Ed.), *International perspectives on educational interpreting* (pp. 128–144). Brassington, UK: Direct Learned Services Ltd.

Russell, D., & Winston, E. (2013). *TAPing into the interpreting process: Using participant reports to inform interpreter education.* Manuscript in preparation.

Schick, B. (2007). *EIPA guidelines of professional conduct for educational interpreters.* Retrieved from http://www.classroominterpreting.org/eipa/guidelines/index.asp

Schick, B. (2008). A model for learning in an interpreted education. In M. Marschark & P. Hauser (Eds.), *Deaf cognition: Foundations and outcomes* (pp. 351–386). New York, NY: Oxford University Press.

Schick, B., Williams, K., & Kupermintz, H. (2006). Look who's being left behind: Educational interpreters and access to education for deaf and hard of hearing students. *Journal of Deaf Studies and Deaf Education, 11,* 3–20.

Schweitzer, C. (2011, April). *Effective itinerant services for students who are deaf or hard of hearing: The Wisconsin process education.* Presentation at the National Summit on Deaf Education (Webcast).

Seal, B. C., Nussbaum, D. B., Belzner, K.A., Scott, S., & Waddy-Smith, B. (2011). Consonant and sign phoneme acquisition in signing children following cochlear implantation. *Cochlear Implants International, 12,* 34–43.

Skelton, T., & Valentine, G. (2003). "It feels like being Deaf is normal": An exploration into the complexities of defining D/deafness and young D/deaf people's identities. *Canadian Geographer, 47,* 451–466.

Solomon, A. (2012). *Far from the tree: Parents, children, and the search for identity.* New York, NY: Scribner.

Stanfield, J. H., II. (1994). Ethnic modeling in qualitative research. In N. K. Denzin & Y. S. Lincoln (Eds.). *Handbook of qualitative research* (pp. 175–188). Thousand Oaks, CA: Sage.

Stanton-Salazar, R. (1997). A social capital framework for understanding the socialization of racial-minority children and youth. *Harvard Educational Review, 67,* 1–40.

Stanton-Salazar, R. (2001). *Manufacturing hope and despair: The school and kin support networks of U.S.-Mexican youth.* New York, NY: Teachers College Press.

Stewart, D. W., & Shamdasani, P. (1990). *Focus groups: Theory and practice.* Newbury Park, CA: Sage.

Tatum, B. (1997). *Why are all the black kids sitting together in the cafeteria?* New York, NY: Basic Books.

Traxler, C. B. (2000). Measuring up to performance standards in reading and mathematics: Achievement of selected deaf and hard of hearing students in the national norming of the 9th edition Stanford Achievement Test. *Journal of Deaf Studies and Deaf Education, 5,* 337–348.

Umat, C., & Tange, R. A. (Eds.). (2012). Cochlear implant research updates [In Tech Open Access version]. doi:10.5772/1160

U.S. Department of Education. Individuals with Disabilities Education Act. [20 U.S.C. 1416(a)(3)(A)].

U.S. Department of Health and Human Services. (2010). Early Hearing Detection and Intervention Act of 2010.

U.S. Government Accountability Office. (2011). *Deaf and hard of hearing children: Federal support for developing language and literacy* (GAO 11-357) [Report to Congressional Requesters]. Washington, DC: Author.

Van Cleve, J. (1993). *Deaf history unveiled: Interpretations from the new scholarship.* Washington, DC: Gallaudet University Press.

Van Cleve, J., & Crouch, B. (1989). *A place of their own: Creating the deaf community in America.* Washington, DC: Gallaudet University Press.

Weinberg, N., & Sterritt, M. (1986). Disability and identity: A study of identity patterns in adolescents with hearing impairments. *Rehabilitation Psychology, 31,* 95–102.

Weiss, H. B., Bouffard, S. M., Bridgiall, B. L., & Gordon, E. W. (2009). *Reframing family involvement in education: Supporting families to support educational equity* (Equity Matters Research Review No. 5). New York, NY: The Campaign for Educational Equity.

Wilkens, C. P., & Hehir, T. (2008). Deaf education and bridging social capital: A theoretical approach. *American Annals of the Deaf, 153,* 275–284.

Winslade, J. M., & Monk, G. D. (2007). *Narrative counseling in schools* (2nd ed.). Thousand Oaks, CA: Corwin Press.

Witter-Merithew, A., & Nicodemus, B. (2012). Toward the intentional development of interpreter specialization: An examination of two case studies. *Journal of Interpretation, 20,* 55–76.

Index